Prayer: A Personal Relationship with God shakes up our conventional thinking about prayer, describing it as a personal relationship and lived experience with God. Sr. Mary Bride Njoku, OSB, acknowledges that prayer is a complex reality and a mystery of faith. She delves into the deep recesses of this mystery in a soul-searching manner, gently and systematically uncovering its hidden riches in praying the Scriptures (*lectio divina*), contemplation, the Liturgy of the Hours, and the celebration of the Eucharist. As Sr. Mary Bride reflects on prayer in its various forms and historical development, she proves herself a connoisseur of liturgical worship.

Prayer is elegant in style, captivating in content, profound in its theology, and exciting in its originality. The logic of its arguments is compelling and its language lucid and intelligible. Every chapter communicates new insights and reflects astonishing wisdom. It receives my high recommendation to all priests, religious and lay faithful, who desire to deepen their relationship and union with God in prayer.

+Lucius Iwejuru Ugorji
Bishop of Umuahia

This new book, *Prayer: A Personal Relationship with God*, is a welcome introduction to a better understanding of Christian prayer and its practise. Sr. Mary Bride relies primarily on the proven tradition of the Church in the meditative reading of Holy Scripture (*lectio divina*), contemplation, and the Liturgy of the Hours of the Church within the rhythm of the day as sources of encounter with God.

The peak of her presentation is the interpretation of the Eucharist as a re-presentation of the mystery of salvation through Jesus Christ. *Prayer* will appeal not only to the religious and to priests, but is addressed to all Christians who long to deepen their interior life through prayer. Every chapter is pleasant to read and spiced with helpful examples and clear guidance.

Prof. Dr. Pius Engelbert, OSB
Abbot emeritus of Gerleve, Germany

PRAYER

A Personal Relationship with God

MARY BRIDE NJOKU

LEONINE PUBLISHERS
PHOENIX, ARIZONA, USA

NIHIL OBSTAT
    Very Rev. Fr. Dr. George Maduakolam Okorie SMMM,
    Superior General & the President of the Conference of Major
    Superiors of Nigeria (Men)

IMPRIMATUR
    ✠ Lucius Iwejuru Ugorji, DD
    Bishop of Umuahia

The Scripture citations used in this work are mainly taken from the *Christian Community Bible: Catholic Pastoral Edition*, Revised 60th edition, copyright © 2014, by Claretian.

Published by Leonine Publishers LLC
Phoenix, Arizona
USA

ISBN-13: 978-1-942190-53-0

Library of Congress Control Number: 2019939431

10 9 8 7 6 5 4 3 2 1

Visit us online at www.leoninepublishers.com
For more information: info@leoninepublishers.com

Dedicated to

our Mother Foundress,
Rev. Mother Mary Charles Anyanwu, OSB,

the Nuns of Paschal Abbey Nike, and

filiations

Contents

PART ONE

Jesus' Life as the Foundation for the Christian Life of Prayer

PART TWO

The Expression and Nourishment of this Relationship through the Four Forms of Prayer

Chapter Five: Liturgy of the Hours: A Sharing in the Prayer of Christ 175

Abbreviations

Documents of the Second Vatican Council

DV   Dogmatic Constitution on Divine Revelation *Dei Verbum*, 1965.

SC   Constitution on the Sacred Liturgy *Sacrosanctum Concilium*, 1963.

Documents of the Popes

DD   Apostolic Letter on Keeping the Lord's Day Holy, *Dies Domini*, Saint John Paul II, 1998.

EE   Encyclical Letter on the Eucharist in Its Relationship to the Church, *Ecclesia de Eucharistia*, Saint John Paul II, 2003.

EG   Apostolic Exhortation *Evangelii Gaudium*, Francis, 2013.

MD   Encyclical Letter on the Sacred Liturgy, *Mediator Dei*, Pius XII, 1947.

VD   Apostolic Exhortation *Verbum Domini*, Benedict XVI, 2010.

SC   Apostolic Exhortation *Sacramentum Caritatis*, Benedict XVI, 2007.

Documents of the Holy See

C   Canon or canons of *Codex Iuris Canonici*, 1983.

GDC   *General Directory for Catechesis*, 1971.

GILH   "General Instruction of the Liturgy of the Hours," Congregation for Divine Worship, 1971.

Others

ABD   *American Biblical Dictionary*
CCC   *Catechism of the Catholic Church*
CTM   *Currents in Theology and Mission*
LH   *Liturgia Horarum*
PL   *Patrologia Latina*
RB   *Regula Benedicti*

Foreword

Over the years, spiritual writers have come to describe prayer as "seeking God," "union with God," "raising our heart and mind to God," and the like. In this work, *Prayer: A Personal Relationship with God*, Sr. Mary Bride Njoku, a Benedictine nun of the Paschal Abbey Nike, shakes up our conventional thinking about prayer. She describes it as a personal relationship and lived experience with God and underscores that the power of prayer is always a result of having fallen in love with God. This fact is rooted in the primordial human longing for the transcendent. The passionate yearning for a God to adore and implore emanates as a response to a loving invitation from God Himself. Responding to this invitation of love, as the author asserts, "one loses oneself in the unfathomable, plunges oneself into the inexhaustible, in order to find peace in the incorruptible." The author perceives prayer as a complex and deep reality—a paradox and mystery of faith—and delves into the deep recesses of this mystery in a soul-soaring manner, gently and systematically uncovering its hidden riches.

Her description of prayer as a personal relationship is rooted in the Holy Scriptures. In the Bible, "prayer" is always used to refer to our entire relationship with God and indeed our spiritual life in general. For instance, in responding to the request of the Apostles to teach them how to pray, Jesus Christ taught them to address God as "Our Father" (Lk 11:1-13) and thus presents prayer as a loving relationship between a heavenly Father and His children. While backing up her view on prayer as a personal relationship with God, Sr. Bride draws from a stimulating mix of Holy Scripture, the writings of renowned spiritual authors, and her personal insights.

The author challenges certain assumptions and common views about prayer. To a large extent, her work is a silent rebuttal of a view of worship that puts a dichotomy between prayer and moral life. The relationship with God in prayer is kept alive through a lively faith, a constant meditation of His word, a regular reception of the Sacraments, and a filial obedience to His Commandments. One leaves much to be desired if one strives to pray but turns one's back on God and His Commandments. It is little wonder that Christ repudiates the hypocrisy of the Pharisees, who recite long prayers and despoil the property of widows. For religiosity without morality is sham.

A crucial section of this study is the first part of the work, which is centred on Jesus' life as the basis for the Christian life of prayer. It is a rigorous exposition of Christ's relationship of love with His Father, expressed in a constant communion with Him in prayer, both privately and publicly. Thus, it provides the foundation for the second part of the work, which deals with *Lectio Divina* (praying the Scriptures), contemplation, the Liturgy of the Hours, and the Holy Eucharist. In this section of her work, the author argues that one of the principal means of fostering and deepening the relationship with Jesus is through reading, reflecting on and internalizing the Scriptures through *Lectio Divina*, contemplation, the Liturgy of the Hours, and the celebration of the Holy Eucharist. She strongly opined that the relationship of a Christian with Christ is formed, deepened, and sustained within the

Church by these forms of prayer, which are firmly rooted in the Bible.

The author's treatment of the Adoration as a prolonged praying of the Eucharist is particularly noteworthy. The Eucharist is a Sacrament of faith. It is a Memorial—the representation of the Sacrifice of Calvary,—a Banquet, and the Real Presence of Christ. If by Real Presence, we mean that the glorified Christ is truly present, body, blood, soul, and divinity under the appearance of bread and wine, then He is to be adored in His divine majesty and infinite goodness. Adoration is thus an essential and integral part of the Eucharist. At Mass, the Adoration of Christ commences at the Consecration. It is prolonged and intensified outside Mass in the Adoration of the Blessed Sacrament. In this regard, Saint Augustine reminds us that "no one eats that flesh without first adoring it; we should sin were we not to adore it." Similarly, the Fathers of the Second Vatican Council maintain that "only in adoration can a profound and genuine reception mature (*Sacrosanctum Concilium*, 66). Adoration is also a prolongation of the communion with Christ in the Eucharist.

While Sr. Bride laboriously examines Christ's life of constant communion with the Father in the first part of this work and as she extensively reflects on our relationship and union with God in the four forms of prayer treated in the second part of her work, she proves herself a connoisseur of worship in its various forms and historical development. The work is elegant in style, captivating in content, profound in its theology, and exciting in its originality. The logic of its arguments is compelling and its language lucid and intelligible. Every chapter in it communicates new insights and reflects astonishing wisdom.

This work is an outstanding book on prayer. I highly commend its author for graciously offering us this painstaking, well-researched and well-written work. It is like good wine. It is to be sipped to be relished in its luscious richness. I do not hesitate to recommend it to priests, religious, and lay faithful, who earnestly desire to deepen and sustain their relationship and union with God in prayer.

✠Lucius Iwejuru Ugorji

Bishop of Umuahia

Introduction

The key to journey into prayer is love—God is Love—and the underlying theme is the relationship with God in Christ. Nevertheless, we must first of all understand what the Scripture means when it proclaims that God is Love.

God Is Love

We have used and abused the word "love" that it seems to have lost a great deal of its meaning. Like every word in the Bible, however, it must be read in the light of the Spirit. We have to situate it properly where it belongs, namely, in the very centre of Christian experience. Love, then, is a realm, the realm of things divine, because Love is God.

What the Gospel wants us to realize is not so much that God is *Love* as that Love is God. This means that we should quit expecting love to tell us what God is, instead let God tell us what love is. Once that is done, the reality is obvious; we arrive upon the costliest thing that has ever been said about God: something grim enough and relentless enough to be at home anywhere, without ever having to give up or let go, no matter what happens; something that will not let anyone think any longer simply of affection, of kindliness, or tenderness.[1] God's love is desperately bent on working out a dream and it never minds what it costs

---

[1] Cf. Paul SCHERER, "The Love that God Defines," in *Theology Today*, vol. 21, 1964, pp. 159-160.

anybody. That love cost Him "that radiant life" which the world "hated and hounded and struck in the face, nailing it on Good Friday to a cross, spread-eagled against the sky."[2]

All along, from the Garden of Eden to Bethlehem and Calvary, God had been weaving a pattern. With the dawn of Easter it became clear, to every "No" that life had been trying to say, He began with the resurrection of Love to pound the table with His "Yes." Thus, at last, even failure and death could make sense. Therefore, this incredible verdict, "God is Love," so austere and shield-less, had paid down on life's counter every little bit of what love costs, and that is why we cannot stop there. Say such a costly thing about God, and surely you have to say as costly a thing about us. One cannot just take it for granted that nothing more is expected of us now than "little deeds of kindness, little words of love." No! This love must be paid for.

It has been said that God never asks of us anything that He does not give. So He says; "A new commandment I give to you; that you love one another"—here is what He asks—then comes those terrible words; "as I have loved you"—and here is what He gives. He loves us and expects us to pass it on. He is holding out to us "His own dangerous life, both hands full." All He ever wants to know, is whether or not, we will "buy" that love on His terms, at that price— as He has loved—self-emptying love in giving one's life. To be able to pay for this love one must have a personal relationship with Him who is Love, otherwise such a price would be impossible for anyone to pay. The great lesson we learn about God in Jesus is that He only lives for giving, even at the point of death on a cross. If we live with the

---

[2] Paul SCHERER, "The Love that God Defines," pp. 159-160.

same readiness to surrender our lives to one another, we are living the very life of God and this would mean buying this Love on His terms and at that price.[3]

An Important Turning Point

With this background on the meaning of love, it is easier to understand that God does not exist in isolation but is a relational God—God in a communion of love as the Father, the Son, and the Holy Spirit. Prayer, then, is a person's entry into this Trinitarian communion of love, where the human being allows itself to be submerged by God's eternal love. There, "the truth of God's love in Christ encounters us, attracts us and delights us, enabling us to emerge from ourselves and drawing us towards our true vocation, which is love."[4] This is the very essence of the Christian experience, which is the new life in Christ, this new life being essentially a life of divine love. The power of God lies in the communion of persons—Father, Son, and Spirit—who share an intimate love overflowing into creation. When extended to us humans in the throes of injustice and suffering, the hallmark of that love is "a terrible yet tender mercy"[5] given in Jesus' life unto death. The costly love of friendship is the shape divine love takes in humanity. So love, even from the side of God, knows a

---

[3] Cf. Ladislaus BOROS, *Pain and Providence* (Baltimore: Helicon, 1966), p. 72. Cf. also Karl RAHNER, "Reflections on a Theology of Renunciation," in *Theological Investigations 3* (Baltimore: Helicon, 1967), pp. 47-57.

[4] Pope Benedict XVI, Post-Synodal Apostolic Exhortation, *Sacramentum Caritatis*, On the Eucharist as the Source and Summit of the Church's Life and Mission, n. 35.

[5] Scott O'BRIEN, "Partakers of the Divine Sacrifice; Liturgy and the Deification of the Christian Assembly," in *Liturgical Ministry* 18 (2009), p. 76.

necessary pain in surrender if life-giving union is to be born and thrive freely with and among people.

As the people of God, Christians understand themselves as pilgrims permanently on the way to the interior, the origin and the source of life, hope, and strength. Since this is a life-long journey, growth and advancement are not a once-for-all thing, nor a steady onward and upward progress toward perfection. On the contrary, it is a risky venture, a struggle, a grappling with angels which can, by the grace of God, accomplish much. In this struggle, there, at the very heart of our being, we are passionately being taken up into the totally free, totally loving, totally self-communicating, mutual love of the Father, the Son, and the Holy Spirit. This is the action of a beckoning, wooing Holy Spirit who seeks from our inmost being to lure us towards the fulfilment of our humanity against all odds. The "wooing-ness" of this Spirit of God in us, elicits desire for adoration, worship, and reverence for God. When this happens, the soul is said to have fallen in love with God. This is also what happens in human love. For we do not experience falling in love as something that we do, but as something that happens to us, that lifts us out of ourselves and transports us, however fleetingly, to a place of supreme fulfilment—a foretaste of heaven.

The power for prayer is always a result of having fallen in love with God. Before one desires to pray, something had already happened to the person—he/she had fallen in love—because the desire to pray does not come from that person, it is something that the person finds in him/herself. Just as when a person approaches another for a love relationship, something had previously happened to the person—he/she had fallen in love. The move to get connected with the other person comes as a result of that "thing" which had already transpired in him/her. Therefore, we could not be praying unless God had placed it in our hearts to pray. Obviously not every person feels this impulse, but if one believes in God and is open to His Spirit, one sees prayer as an opportunity set before him/her.

This fact is rooted in the powerful human longing for the transcendent, which Teilhard de Chardin expressed so well in *The Divine Milieu*.

> What I cry out for, like every being, with my whole life and all my earthly passion, is some- thing very different from an equal to cherish: it is a God to adore. To adore, that means to lose oneself in the unfathomable, to plunge into the inexhaustible, to find peace in the incorrupt- ible, to be absorbed in defined immensity, to offer oneself to the fire and the transparency, to annihilate oneself in proportion as one becomes deliberately conscious of oneself, and to give of one's deepest to that whose depth has no end.[6]

The passionate yearning "for a God to adore" emanates as a response to a loving invitation from God Himself. It is a longing for a relationship in which God is the initiator, constantly seeking to elicit a human response. Responding to this invitation of love, one loses oneself in the unfath- omable, plunges oneself into the inexhaustible, in order to find peace in the incorruptible. On the way to this peace, which is union with God, that person will meet the living and risen Lord. But he/she will also inevitably encounter the suffering and dying Jesus of Nazareth, the Crucified.

---

[6] Pierre TEILHARD de Chardin, *The Divine Milieu* (New York: Harper and Row, 1960), pp. 127-128.

Consequently, the whole life of a Christian is a continual process of becoming, growing, and maturing in this love relationship. It is a relationship whose quality is an on-going sacrifice, an ever-new conception, birth, and adoration of God's presence within oneself. It is also an endless new readiness to let the suffering as well as the transfigured face of Christ be imprinted on one's being. The "sacrifice" which this divine-human relationship denotes and the inevitable suffering the practice of love entails is "shot through with paradox, and that paradox, of course, is climactically located at the cross."[7]

Therefore, it is a response to God's invitation of love that the Christian wants to make visible in his/her living, praying, and celebration of the Liturgy of the Hours and of the Eucharist. There is no one single formula for expressing, showing, or responding to this love. Circumstances allow each person to pray/love in different ways—sometimes liturgically, at other times privately and some other times in awe and silence. "Successful" prayer is not something to be evaluated. Emphasising this point for the consecrated men and women, Pope Benedict XVI in his Post-Synodal Apostolic Exhortation *Sacramentum Caritatis* reminded the consecrated persons that the principal purpose of their lives is: "the contemplation of divine things and constant union with God in prayer" (c. 663 §1). Explaining this further, the pope referring to *SC* 81, pointed out that though they provide many services in the area of human formation and care for the poor, education and health care, consecrated men and women should know that the

---

[7] Bruce T. MORRILL, "Christ's Sacramental Presence in the Eucharist: A Biblical-Pneumatological Approach to the Mystery of Faith," in *American Theological Inquiry,* vol. 4, no. 2 (2011), pp. 3-25, here p. 13.

essential contribution the Church expects from them is much more in the order of *being* than of doing.

Contemplation and union with God are made visible in one's *being*. This means that prayer is essentially *being*, and who a person is must find *expression* in (the person's) life. This expression of one's being is translated into different moments in one's life: moments of joy, sorrow, adoration, celebration, thanksgiving, petition, praise, and worship. At these different moments, the soul pours forth its *being* into words to God: thanking Him, adoring, begging, petitioning Him, celebrating Him, or asking for his forgiveness. Moreover, there are different forms of prayer which provide opportunities for expressing one's *being* before God alone in private prayers and communally in the liturgical celebrations. Thus to show gratitude to God for the "costly love of friendship" which He extended to us, Christians celebrate this fact in the liturgy, thereby sharing in the very life of God revealed in the saving deed of Jesus, whose death and resurrection disclosed the depth of this love.

In line with this fact, this work will be divided into two parts: the first part will study Jesus' life as the foundation for the Christian life of prayer. This will be done in view of demonstrating how Jesus displayed a relationship of love with His Father. Hence, he was in constant communion with the Father in prayer both privately and publicly. Then the second part will be dedicated to the four forms of prayer: *Lectio Divina*, Contemplative Prayer, Liturgy of the Hours, and the Holy Mass, which are all echoes and imitation of Jesus' way of praying. It is in imitation of Jesus' diverse forms of praying that the Church developed her different forms of prayer. These Four Forms are going to be presented as means, expressions, and nourishments of our individual and communal relationship with God. The first two, *lectio divina* and contemplative prayer, are processes of growth in personal relationship with God and as such are valid instruments for progress in this human-divine bond. Contemplative prayer will be shown to be the vocation of every baptised Christian and the primary duty of all the religious both the so-called "contemplative" and the "active" religious institutes. The last two forms of prayer, the Liturgy of the Hours and the Holy Mass, are the common prayers of the Church. They are prayers said in the name of the Church whether they are recited in private or in common.

Since my reflection on prayer has not been in isolation but often in the context of praying and doing *lectio divina*, my thanks therefore are offered in the first place to God Almighty who is indeed the real Author to any part of this work that is inspiring. There has also been an enabling environment in conversations with people, retreats, advice received, directions, and encouragements. Special thanks to Most Rev. Lucius Iwejuru Ugorji, DD, Bishop of Umuahia, who in the midst of his tight schedule spared time to go through this book and endorsed it with an *Imprimatur*. A big "thank you" goes to my friend Sr. Mary Clare Amorino, OSB, the computer expert who helped in pasting the images and making some notable corrections. I am also grateful to her Superior, Mother Abbess M. Franziska Kloos, OSB, St. Walbuga's Abbey Eichstaett in Germany, who exempted her from some of her duties in the community so that she would have the time to do this. Thanks also to Rev. Prof. Dr. Pius Engelbert, OSB, Abbey of Gerleve in Germany, for reading through this work and making some suggestions. Furthermore, I thank Very Rev. Fr. Dr. George Maduakolam Okorie, Superior General of the

Congregation of the Sons of Mary Mother of Mercy, who proofread the work and was gracious to give the *Nihil Obstat*. Special thanks are also due to Rev. Fr. Dr. Anthony Alimnonu C.S.Sp. who also proofread the work. Finally, I wish to express my profound and abiding gratitude to the Mother Abbess Franziska Lukas, OSB; Sr. Monica Lewis, OSB; and all the nuns of Abtei Dinklage in Germany, where I lived as I was writing this work, for their love and hospitality. I also desire to thank and acknowledge Rev. Fr. Emeka Okite, for his help in providing me with some materials for this research.

PART ONE

Jesus' Life as the Foundation for the Christian Life of Prayer

The word "prayer" is so common in our language that it is difficult to use it meaningfully. Like the word "love" which is used to refer to so many mundane things, "prayer" is used to describe a variety of diverse experiences: distress cries to God, a formality before meals and meetings, an experience on mountaintops and desert places, and a ritual in church, to name only a few. Prayer for some is a spontaneous emotional outpouring, for others a fixed rational formula to be recited, and for few an experience which is ecstatically based. Prayer, as employed here, is a generic term to describe every aspect of our *conscious* relationship with God. Prayer represents what I mean by spiritual life—daily existence lived in relationship with God, or what I mean by piety—the daily practice of living in the presence of God through confession, adoration, petition, praise, and thanksgiving all in imitation of Jesus Christ whose life epitomised this.

Adoration is focusing one's life upon the qualities of God. It is a life of total submission to the will of God and to His majestic presence in the whole world adoring His presence everywhere which makes possible viewing every aspect of life as a miracle. Confession is conducting a self-examination of one's personal and communal life in the presence of God. It is a continuing judgment of one's actions in the light of God's will and action. Petition is bringing one's desires in line with God's desires. It is attuning one's heart, mind, and will to the heart, mind, and will of God. Praise is the continual anamnesis and narration of the mighty deeds of God. It is the celebrative awareness of God's activity in our midst. Thanksgiving is one's daily active expression of gratitude to God for His continuing actions in history. It is the conscious intention of co-operating with God in the establishment of His Kingdom.[8]

For such an understanding of prayer to prevail, we need to recover the proper place of religious experience. Numerous examples of prayer in the Bible support this understanding. Moses' experience with the burning bush led him to bring to his people a vision and message of liberation. Jesus' struggle at Gethsemane led Him to make a conscious decision to choose the foolishness of the Cross. The awareness of the presence of Christ in the breaking of bread at Emmaus led the disciples to choose a life of apostleship. Paul's experience on the road to Damascus led him to change from a persecutor to a defender of the faith. None of these experiences or their resulting actions was purely rational or intuitional. Each represents a concrete experience which through the complimentary use of the intellect led to new sorts of moral behaviour. Each also represents a new consciousness of God and praxis

---

[8] Cf. John H. WESTERHOFF III, "Learning and Prayer," in *Religious Education Vol LXX*, no. 6 (1975), pp. 605-618, here p. 610.

according to His will. In that sense each is an example of prayer.[9]

It was Jesus' exemplary life of prayer that prompted the disciples to request that He teaches them to pray (Lk 11:1-14). So He gave them guidance on the rudiments of prayer from His practical experience. Because of this, this part will give elucidation on prayer in order to further demonstrate how Jesus displayed this conscious communion with His Father.

---

[9] Cf. John H. WESTERHOFF III, "Learning and Prayer," p. 612.

Chapter One: Elucidation of Prayer

What could help us to have a clearer vision of what prayer is all about? Who could offer an adequate definition of prayer? Prayer is a mystery; sometimes we think we know what it means and at other times it eludes our understanding. Christian prayer is many things and has many facets, but undergirding them all is the longing for the restoration of the awareness of the presence of the Love that "never lets anyone out of his ken."[10] Prayer is also, as Macquarrie proposes, a "fundamental style of thinking" that is "passionate and compassionate, responsible and thankful, that is deeply rooted in our humanity and that manifests itself not only among believers but also among serious-minded people who do not profess any religious faith."[11] Because of this inexpressible nature of prayer, it must be experienced and not only taught, for when one experiences prayer one realizes that it is *essentially* a *dynamic personal relationship* with God in Jesus Christ. Religious fulfilment or rather human fulfilment is obtained in a dynamic and deepening relationship with Jesus. In his book, *A Journey into God*, Delia Smith writes:

> Prayer is a mysterious thing that has its roots in God—is a relationship in which God is the initiator, constantly seeking to elicit a human response. It is on-going relationship, and like

---

[10] Douglas V. STEERE, "Solitude and Prayer," in *Worship*, 55, no. 2 (1981), pp. 120-136, here p. 122.

[11] John MACQUARRIE, *Paths in Spirituality* (New York: Harper and Row, 1972), p. 30.

> any other, it can't be programmed or labelled
> and packaged...prayer is life, living, growing,
> developing but always in secret—like a tiny seed
> buried in the earth steadily yet imperceptibly
> thrusting itself upward to the light.[12]

It is this initiative of God that makes the relationship a divine one rather than a human one (cf. Rom 8:5-11). What is required on the part of the individual is openness to the divine direction of the Spirit. In a human relationship one can reach out to another person with all one's strength in the hope of personal encounter. However, unless a person chooses to receive and to give himself on a personal level there is no genuine encounter. The choice to receive and to give oneself characterizes the open relationship. So it is with our relationship with God in Jesus Christ. This is why Pope Francis, in his Apostolic Exhortation *Evangelii Gaudium,* invites all Christians to a "renewed personal encounter with Jesus Christ, or at least an openness to letting him encounter them; I ask all of you to do this unfailingly each day" (*EG* 3).

Prayer, then, is a lived, personal relationship with God characterized by different desires and motivations such as adoration, contrition, thanksgiving, supplication, conversion. When we pray, we simply open up to the God who is already open to us. Since Christian prayer is part of a dialogue which God has already started, it follows that it need not be an anxious stream of words, a pursuit of the right phrase, or the best formulation. Instead it is a way of responding to a love which is deeply personal, and which encounters us in concrete and personal ways. Because of

---

[12] Delia SMITH, *A Journey into God* (London: Hodder & Stongton, 1989), p. ix.

this, prayer can never be categorized. It cannot be streamlined or bottled up by personal idiosyncrasy. It is a free and open relationship with God who is a living reality. The person praying can cry out of rage from the depth of distress or shout out of joy and thanksgiving. Prayer attempts to express in words the person's deepest needs and feelings. An example of this is the prayer of Hannah in 1 Samuel 1:9-18 or the rendering of thanks to God by the psalmist in Psalm 100. It is an encounter that takes place in a free and friendly atmosphere. It is an upsurge of the Spirit of God dwelling in an individual from the depths to the surface. This becomes a living spring in the person, welling up to eternal life (Jn 4:14). It is an insatiable longing which thirsts more when it is satisfied. In prayer a person discovers that God has given him/her the right to pray, not to beg for alms but to demand that happiness which God, in the mystery of his infinite love, promised freely, asking only that he/she accepts it. Saint Paul says that if there is anything you need, ask for it with prayer and thanksgiving (Phil 4:7).

Prayer as a Relationship

The Scriptures are the record of the personal *relationship* (covenant) between God and His people. In it we see how this relationship worked itself out in the lives of God's people, and how God remained faithful to them, guiding every aspect of their history in order to draw them closer to Himself (salvation history). In the New Testament we also see how, in the person of Jesus, salvation history reaches its highest point, with the inauguration of the new covenant in Jesus' blood (Mk 14:24). Through prayer, the believer meets God as a Person, the eternal "Thou." In this encounter, the Christian does not come to petition anything from God, because he knows that God's love for humanity is granted. He approaches Him so that he himself might change. By coming into contact with Love, he realizes how far he is from it, and so feels even more deeply the need for divine grace and the benevolent love of God. So three things qualify such a personal relationship:

1. A vibrant *affinity* between two people,
2. An active, ongoing *communication* and interaction (spiritual, and/or emotional, mental, etc.) between two people,
3. A communication that is not superficial or transitory. This communication must be "deep" and leads to *companionship* (in Greek *koinonia*).

We have said that prayer is a mystery whose process establishes a bond, a personal relationship between God and the soul. This covenantal tie is characterised by the following qualities:

- It has to be first of all rooted in God.
- It must be dynamic and an on-going relationship, therefore it can never be programmed, labelled, or packaged.
- In order to be a "personal" relationship, it has to assume a one-on-one involvement. Nobody comes in to this; the other person or the Church in her teachings can contribute to your understanding of what this relationship entails, but they can never come in between you and Him. The truth of this one-on-one "personal relationship" is concisely expressed in the first two verses of Andreas Knapp's poem, entitled *Konkurrenzlose Liebe* (Unrivalled Love): "Please try not to love God through me. It is unworthy of God

to be loved through a person."[13] So prayer is a direct and personal bond that needs no springboard.

- It ought to be progressive, for it is a process and a journey of discovery.
- It calls for a constant commitment.
- Such a relationship is life, living, growing, and developing but always in secret. We have to work hard to keep it alive, vibrant, and in constant good repair just as in any human relationship.

Furthermore, a personal relationship with Jesus Christ demands that we approach Him with the same desire for union, communication, consistency, and closeness that we have in our human relationships. It demands that we accept the historical Jesus as a human and spiritual being, the Second Person of the Holy Trinity, who continues to care for humanity. In AD 452 the Council of Chalcedon with the formula "one *hypostasis*[14] in two natures" and its four negative adverbs: *inconfuse, immutabiliter, indivise, inseparabiliter*[15] (unconfused, unchangeable, indivisible, and inseparable) specifically declared that Christ is one in substance and equal with the Father in divine nature and

---

13 "Bitte versuche nicht durch mich hindurch Gott zu lieben. Es ist Gottes nicht würdig, ihn hinter einer Person zu lieben." Andreas KNAPP, *Brennender als Feuer: Geistliche Gedichte,* Mit einem Essay von Bischof Manfred Scheuer, (Echter Verlag GmbH, 2004), p. 17. The English translation is mine.

14 The word *hypostasis* (Greek ὑπόστασις) means underlying state or underlying substance, and is the fundamental reality that supports all else.

15 This *Definitio Chalcedonensis* is perhaps an excellent expression of the Christological tension, i.e., that the person of Christ is the highest and the insuperable way of the union between God and man, God and the world. Christian theology has frequently succeeded in finding a right balance between monism and dualism, divine transcendence and immanence.

one in substance and equal with us in human nature. So to know God is to know Him as a Person in Jesus Christ—in His body, blood, soul, and divinity. In this way, our faith in Jesus as Lord becomes explicit when we come to know Him in a personal way, in an experiential way: through an explicit act of faith in Him as Lord and Saviour. This act of faith is an invitation asking Jesus to come into our hearts, to take over our lives and be the Lord and Saviour of our whole being. This faith in Jesus is a continuous receptivity to Him, an accepting of the gift that He is and a submitting of our whole lives to Him that He might possess us and guide us. There is no escape from this explicit conversion which brings us to the experience of His person, His power, and His presence. In this way *the* Lord becomes *my* Lord and *my* Saviour (cf. Phil 3:8). However, there is also a need to rediscover that Jesus Christ is not just a private conviction or an abstract idea, but a real person, whose becoming part of human history is capable of renewing the life of every man and woman (cf. *Sacramentum Caritatis,* 77).

The *liaison* which prayer establishes between us and Jesus guarantees an experience. It is in the process of entering into this relationship that one "experiences" *something* through the experiencing of *Someone.* Hence Karl Rahner said that the devout Christian will either be "someone who has experienced something, or he will cease to be anything at all."[16] This experience demands faith and action. When Christ pours Himself out for us, and we accept Him in faith as our Lord and Saviour, He then dwells within us; transforming us, and sanctifying us so that we may live in Him

---

[16] Karl RAHNER, "Christian Living Formerly and Today," in *Theological Investigations Volume 7: Further Theology of the Spiritual Life* (New York: Seabury Press, 1977), p. 15.

and He in us. This occurs through the Sacraments, through prayer, and by faithful obedience to His words.

Personal Relationship with God

To say that prayer is a personal relationship with God is to say that there is within one's experience a *living God* to whom one addresses the words of one's prayers, towards whom one turns one's heart and whom one invokes. Because praying is like speaking to a friend, one does not speak to an imaginary friend beneficially. One can speak usefully only to a friend who is *real*, to *someone* with whom one can be face to face. One addresses only someone whom one can open one's heart, who is listening, before whose judgment one stands, and who will stand by one whether the person is in the right or in the wrong.

So before embarking on prayer, one should pause a bit and ask oneself a question. This question is very important for prayer to be real and true. When you think of prayer, when you pray, first ask yourself:

- Is there in my experience a *living God*, as concrete and as real as my friends, my relatives, *some-one* and not some-thing, not a power but a *real person*?

This question is necessary because, if we are members of a religious institute, it means that each one of us, to a greater or lesser extent, has had an experience, perhaps just incipient or germinal, of a real God. We must try to recapture this experience in our relationship with God because the root of the problem of prayer lies in the difficulty of conceiving God as a personal being. Moreover, we must bear in mind that the first people who spoke of God spoke of a *presence*, a reality that at a certain moment had overwhelmed them by its glory, its splendour, and its concreteness.[17]

Therefore, I am proposing that in this work love should be used to characterise a process of our relationship with God, rather than an end state. Love is a growth in relationship. A Christian/religious who supposedly has admitted the Lord Jesus into his/her life must necessarily, if the relationship is to grow, break some previously established ways and boundaries of his/her existence. This is done so that love, as a process of growth-in-relationship becomes capable of changing us, broadening our appreciation of facets of life, adding zest to living, making us more fully human. The process is neither smooth nor preordained. It can be a bewildering time fraught with perils as many saints have experienced. But the pattern of Jesus' own life is the model for such a process. This is often considered as life, death and through death, resurrection. Jesus' paradigm is normative for the religious, not only in the larger sense of a person's whole life, but also in smaller ways, for small deaths of self, enabling new resurrections. So for real growth-in-relationship (love) a death must occur. We must break, so as to grow. Just as each cocoon, if it is to yield its butterfly, must be ruthlessly torn asunder, and the longer it has stood and stiffened, the more force must be exerted to rend it.[18] So it is with the Christian and therefore religious life, the same paradoxical principle of dying to self in order to live is present.

A point that is important in following in the footsteps of Christ is that frustrations and disappointments could

---

[17] Cf. Anthony BLOOM, "The Life of Prayer," in *Theology Today*, 61 (2004), pp. 26-40, here p. 29.

[18] Cf. Richard SALES, *Journal of Theology for Southern Africa*, vol. 6-9, 1974/06, pp. 34-42, here p. 41.

be a help in understanding one's true relationship with God. When one experiences suffering, Jesus summons that person to plunge deeper into a relationship of trust in a gracious and loving God. He tells him/her to stop trying to run his/her lives and to hand over the controls to His Spirit within us. These moments of death to our misconceived presumption that we are self-sufficient can certainly be experiences of new life if they are rightly embraced and understood. Likewise, they can be moments in which we are faithful to the image of God in which we have been created, an image revealed to us in and through the life and person of Jesus.

The revelation of this image in the life of Christ is recently made perceptible in the life of an eight-year-old boy called Tyler, whose life shows the love, hope, and faith that can be found *only* through a personal relationship with Jesus Christ and the hope of eternity through a life with God. Tyler was a boy who went through one of the toughest battles some people must endure, and in it, with it, and through it, he showed an amazing inner strength that comes from God. He suffered from cancer and in the midst of the excruciating pain of cancer Tyler displayed the kind of faith that Jesus Himself describes (Mt 17:20), the faith that can move mountains. He displayed his child-like faith by writing letters to God and placing them in the mail box. Though Tyler still died in 2005 at the age of nine, yet he left a testimony through his life and his love for God. Tyler's life is also a lesson for everyone that a life lived for Christ is not free from suffering, but through it Christ makes the person an instrument of His love. The life of Tyler is to be found in the book entitled *Letters to*

God.[19] *Letters to God* brings out Tyler's faith and the love
he had for God. One who reads this book or watches the
movie will finish with a new perspective on prayer—a
perspective that is based on childlike dependence and
vivid awareness of the *"realness and personness"* of God
in Jesus Christ. This boy teaches us that God is real and
he turns to Him in every situation as he would to his best
friend. Thus, he writes simple prayers; reporting every
case to Him, asking Him to intervene in his life and in other
people's lives and problems. If a little eight-year-old boy
going through cancer can write simple prayers every day
to his best friend, God, then anyone can pray to the God
who is always near.

Jesus Christ Is the Object of Our Faith in Relationship

It is through faith obedience that the soul comes to experience Jesus as real. Moreover, the object of our faith
is not a set of rules or a prescribed ritual or even a rev-
olutionary philosophy. Whether we are religious, priests,
or laypersons, we trust in Jesus as a REAL PERSON. We
believe in, and dedicate ourselves to, the living Lord, who
came to earth, lived, taught, performed miracles, died,
rose from the grave, ascended into heaven, and offers new
life to all who seek Him. To be in a "personal" relationship
with Him assumes one-on-one involvement. We not only
communicate, we join Him in shared interaction. This
relationship is very personal and does not just happen

---

[19] Patrick and Heather DOUGHTIE, *Letters to God*, (Grand Rapids,
MI: Zonderkidz, 2010). This book was made into a movie in
2012.

without self-commitment. Unfortunately too many people maintain a mediated relationship with Jesus Christ, using the Church and religious activities as means of contact without ever experiencing the joy of first-hand connection with God. While the Church and other people can contribute to one's understanding of what it means to be a sister or brother, a priest or a Christian, nothing can replace that *personal* relationship with Christ. The Church is there to show and teach "how," but the individual must put it into practice.

This relationship is a process and therefore it is **progressive**: Relationships develop over time. Relationships grow. A decision to embrace the Son of God as Saviour does not mark the finish line of one's spiritual journey; it is only the beginning! While Jesus Christ knows each of us better than we know ourselves, getting to know Him takes time. It is a process, a journey of discovery that will sustain one throughout this lifetime and bring eternal joy in the life to come.

Moreover, there are some obligations in this human/ divine relationship and therefore it calls for **commitment**. Like all worthwhile relationships, one's relationship with Jesus Christ calls for personal investment in cultivating closeness with Him. The process of walking with Jesus involves an ongoing surrender to discover what He desires. Simply put, it is a day-by-day, moment-by-moment decision to commit all that one understands of oneself to all that is understood of Christ. Relationships, we know, have their ups and downs. One needs to work on them constantly. If faith is a personal relationship with Christ, what are some of the factors involved in such a relationship? As a spouse or a parent, they include saying, "I love you. I appreciate you. I love to be in your presence. I give myself to you totally. I am sorry I hurt you. Forgive me..." and so on. In other words, one has to work hard on a relationship to keep it alive, vibrant, growing, and in constant good repair. The same is true of the relationship with Jesus.[20]

It is on this personal relationship with Jesus that the happiness and the purposefulness of life depends. It is also on the basis of this relationship to Christ that our eternal destiny will be decided. Jesus is the door and there is no other entrance. Some questions that are worth asking are: What kind of relationship do I have with Jesus? Is it a relationship that is kept alive through faith, prayer, the sacraments, and obedience to His commandments? Or is it a relationship that has died through sin and indifference?[21]

Means of Nurturing this Relationship

One of the principal means of fostering a relationship with Jesus is through reading, reflecting on, and internalizing the Scriptures. Scripture is at the core of the Church's four fundamental forms of prayer: praying of the Scriptures (*lectio divina*), the praying of the Spirit of God in us (*contemplatio),* the praying of the Liturgy of the Hours, and the praying of the Holy Mass. The Liturgy of the Hours is a communal celebration of the Bible using the Psalms and a series of readings. The celebration of the Holy Eucharist is a memorial of the life, death, and resurrection of our Lord Jesus Christ as is narrated or transmitted to us through the Bible. Our relationship with Christ

---

[20] Cf. Anthony CONIARIS, *God and You: Person to Person, Developing a Daily Personal Relationship with Jesus,* (Edina, MN: Light and Life Publishing Company, 1995), p. 19.

[21] For more personal reflection on one's relationship with Christ read Anthony CONIARIS, *God and You: Person to Person, Developing a Daily Personal Relationship with Jesus,* pp. 27-28.

is formed within the community of the Church by these forms of prayers. It is deepened by meditative and prayerful reading of the Scriptures, otherwise known as *lectio divina*[22] and by the prayer of abandonment to the Spirit, which are wonderful ways of developing and nourishing that relationship, either communally or individually. One cannot speak of a "relationship" with a total stranger. Knowledge of Christ is gained through His recorded word in the Bible. It is also through this same source that relationship with Him is nurtured and kept alive. Saint Jerome (c. 340-420), the most famous biblical scholar in Christian history, said that "*Ignoratio Scripturarum, ignoratio Christi est*," (Ignorance of Scripture is ignorance of Christ).[23] Saint Augustine said: "*Titubabit fides, si divinarum Scripturum vacillat auctoritas*," (Faith hesitates if it doubts the authority of Sacred Scriptures).[24] In another place he said: "*In Scripturis discimus Christum, in Scripturis discimus Ecclesiam*," (In the Scripture we learn about Christ, in the Scripture we learn about the Church).[25] The truth of these statements has been evident in the lives of so many saints of the Catholic Church. Saint Thérèse of Lisieux appreciated the truth of these facts and carried a small book of Gospel extracts next to her heart. Blessed Elizabeth of the Trinity was deeply influenced by the Letters of Saint Paul, which led her to the excellent knowledge of Jesus Christ. In short, the Holy Bible is the source of all prayers and celebrations, and therefore, the primary means of fostering

---

[22] Literally means divine reading. We are going to take up this in the subsequent chapters.
[23] Commentary of Isaiah, Nn. 1.2: CCL 73, 1-3.
[24] Saint Augustine *De Doctrina Christiana I*, 37, 41, in PL 34, 35.
[25] Saint Augustine *Ep.* 105, 4, 14, in PL 33:401.

our personal relationship with Christ. Not having time for the spiritual reading of the Bible is always a bad sign.

Growing in this Relationship

Growing in relationship with God is a process like any other relationship. One needs to begin by listening and entering into dialogue with God's word. As the dialogue unfolds one will discover different ways of being in relationship with God. In ordinary relationships, there are moments of listening to the other and pondering the meaning of the other's words. There are moments of responding and dialoguing, as well as being with the other when no words need to be said. A relationship with God is also made up of many moments. These moments may come in any order. One begins by walking through each moment, taking as much time as needed. There are no "shoulds," "oughts," or "musts." One listens with the ear of one's heart, and allows the dialogue with God to unfold at its own time, and permits the Holy Spirit to take the lead. One needs to trust that God is eager to be with one and to share with one the inner peace and freedom one desires.

When talking of different moments of being with the Lord and different moments of responding to His demands, we should not bypass the wonderful role which "personal" encounter plays in the communal prayers of the Church. When prayed regularly, *lectio divina* can deepen one's relationship with God and does lead to contemplation.

Personal Encounter as Deepening of this Relationship

The mystery of individuality which is an indispensable fact of life plays a great role in our individual prayer lives. The deeper ground for this individuality is to be sought in the originality of the Divine imagination who created each and everyone new, different, and unique. Each one of us expresses and incarnates a different dimension of the divinity. Consequently says John O'Donohue:

> Each one of us prays out of a different inner world and each one of us prays to a different place in the Divine circle. This is the place we left to come here. This is the empty nest in the Divine where the secrets of our origin, experience and destiny are stored. When we pray, we pray to that space in the Divine Presence which absolutely knows us. This could be what is suggested in that moment in the New Testament when the Lord says of our return to the invisible world: "On that day you will know as you are known."[26]

For me, a magnificent example of a personal prayer is the prayer of Hannah in 1 Samuel 1:15. "Hannah replied... I was pouring out my soul before Yahweh." This is exactly what praying in private means "pouring out one's soul to/before God." Therefore the essence of the human soul is prayer. This is so because every aspiration of a person is intrinsically prayer. It is characteristic of a person, that any strong aspiration he has is expressed within his heart and also by his lips in prayer. Therefore, the mystery of the individuality confers great permission also on the individuality of prayer. Because of this, one does not need to mimic the pious prayers of others or of the saints if such prayer does not speak personally to you as an individual. One could say that the prayer of one's individual essence

---

[26] John O'DONOHUE, *Eternal Echoes: Exploring our Hunger to Belong* (London, 1998), p. 212.

is the deepest prayer. Indeed, personal prayer is meant to take one into the temple of one's individual essence. It is there that one's personal experiences opens to embrace the mystery of what one is living at that particular moment. At this point, one begins to have a glimpse of oneself and the areas where the Divine Healer needs to be earnestly invoked for healing and cleansing. Personal prayer helps to heal and return one to inner tranquillity and to restore belonging at the heart of divinity, a belonging from which no thought or act can ever absolutely be exiled.

There are many wonderful traditional and classical prayers, yet there is something unique and intimate about one's own individual prayer. Try to create your own prayer. If prayer as we have already mentioned is a personal encounter with the Lord, a relationship of love with the Divine Master, then it sounds absurd to mimic another person or to memorize a "formula" to express love, longing, and needs. One needs simply go to Him as to a friend, a father, etc., and pour out one's heart to Him. Such prayers are the most effective. One does not go to the Lord to say to Him what a saint has said centuries ago if such prayer does not fit nor suit one's personal needs and sentiments here and now.

Personal prayer is a moment when one listens to the voices of longing in one's soul, to the hungers, desires, wishes, and dreams. From this attention to one's soul, one then makes a prayer, as John O'Donohue puts it, "that is big enough for your wild soul; tender enough for your shy and awkward vulnerability; that has enough healing to gain the ointment of divine forgiveness for your wounds; enough truth and vigour to challenge your blindness and complacency; enough graciousness and vision to mirror your immortal beauty."[27] One has to write or, better, say a prayer that is worthy of the destiny to which one has been called. One needs to adopt a prayer pattern or words that are appropriate to one's essence.

How people pray is as personal and unique as how they express themselves in any conversation. Like Christ who often prayed alone, the Christian needs to make room for private conversation with God, according to one's needs and possibilities, under the movement of the Holy Spirit. A Christian community could offer no better help than encouraging and guaranteeing this.

---

[27] Ibid., p. 225.

Chapter Two: Praying in Christ-like Manner

> During his life on earth, Jesus offered up prayers and entreaty, aloud and in silent tears, to the one who had the power to save him out of death, and he submitted so humbly that his prayer was heard (Heb 5:7).

All four Gospels tell us that Jesus prayed. He prayed alone on the mountains and in the wilderness. He prayed on roads, in people's homes and in temples. He prayed alone with God and He prayed with and for others. He prayed out loud and He prayed silently, in His heart. Those prayers that we hear in the words of the Gospel often reflect or even repeat the prayers we find in Jewish Scriptures. Jesus prayed as a Jew and His prayers often resemble the Psalms. We can discern from His ministry that Jesus placed a higher priority on prayer than on religious duties and laws. Jesus' prayers assume that He is, in a way, in love with God and that He Himself is the beloved Son of the Father. His prayers also suggest that He knows Himself to be simultaneously at one with the Father and also distinct from the Father.

The purest definition of prayer according to the way Jesus lived and prayed is "communion and a deep personal relationship with God the Father." This explains why the underlying theme of His life, and particularly in the various accounts of prayer, is that of His relationship with His Father. For even though He Himself was God, it was necessary for Him in His humanity to live a wholly consecrated life of total dependence upon His Father (Jn 5:19, 30).

What is made more and more apparent through the reading of the Gospels is the intimacy of Jesus' relationship with His Father. This is especially true in John's Gospel, where we have so many references to the word "Father." In all the recorded prayers, Jesus calls God "Abba," Father.[28] By calling God Father in His prayer, Jesus introduces humanity to the mystery of His personal relationship with Him, and on this mystery His nature and mission depend. In the same way this intimacy is brought out in the prayer: "Father, the time has come. Glorify your Son, that your Son may glorify You" (Jn 17:1). If His prayer was intimate it was also personal. It is often recorded that Jesus spent time alone with God, time that was not easy to come by, but He recognised the importance of spending quality time with His Father. So Jesus lived a disciplined life; rising early and if necessary praying through the night, not out of a sense of duty but as a result of love.

Motives Behind Jesus' Prayers

There are some underground motives behind every prayer recorded in the Gospel that was said by Jesus. These motives can be classified into four categories: companionship and communion with the Father, Will of

---

[28] Here is a point to demonstrate that Jesus prayed like a typical Jew because the description of God as a "Father," is a recurring feature in Jewish prayer. The practice is attested first in Deut 32:6 and Is 63:16: "Do not let your compassion go unmoved, for you are our Father. For Abraham does not own us and Israel does not acknowledge us; you, Yahweh, yourself are our Father." For more information on the description of God as Father read, Carmine Di SANTE, *Jewish Prayer: The Origins of Christian Liturgy* (Paulist Press, 1985), pp. 20-21.

God, the needs of the Kingdom, and drawing energy and strength from prayer.

Companionship and Communion with the Father

The prayer of Jesus is essentially that of the Son with His Father. It is both creative and communitarian because it is the prayer of the community of Jesus, created and preserved in virtue of the divine response to Christ's effective intercession. Thus, for Jesus, prayer is principally, necessarily, and primarily an opportunity for companion and communion with the Father. It brought a time of fellowship, and the fellowship may have been just as intimate in silence as in speech. In prayer Jesus is closest to the Holy Spirit and to His Father (Lk 10:21-22). At such times, He leaves His disciples and remains alone in prayer. His are not only prayers of petition but also of union.[29] Although Jesus is apparently solitary in prayer, it is then that He is actually in His natural habitat, the unity of the Trinitarian God. Prayer is the most divine of His activities in the sense that it shows Him as the equal of the Father, the beloved Son.

In the Letter to the Hebrews cited at the beginning of this chapter, we read that Christ's prayers were expressed "with vehement cries and tears" (Heb 5:7). Jesus' strong emotion in prayer was because He knew the Father's love and sought to prevail upon that love in asking the Father to come to His aid. He acknowledged that love in another passage where He said, "You loved Me before the foundation of the world" (Jn 17:24). Jesus loved the Father and was loved by the Father. Therefore He confidently expected

---

[29] Cf. A. HASTINGS, *Prophet and Witness in Jerusalem* (New York, 1958), p. 88.

the Father to hear and answer His requests from a loving heart. He knew that any and every answer from the Father would always be an expression of that love. Jesus understood that everything the Father did in His life was out of a deep expression of love. So He sought always through prayer to maintain this love relationship. The Scriptures reveal that He and His Father were always in loving union and constant fellowship with each other. As Jesus often reminded His disciples, "I am in the Father, and the Father in Me" (Jn 14:10–11; see also Jn 10:30, 38; 14:20).

Jesus was intensely committed to prayer because this loving presence of the Father was His very life. He told His disciples, "I live because of the Father" (Jn 6:57) and prayer was His lifeline. This vital closeness of the Son with the Father is the foremost characteristic of Jesus' prayer life. It was a closeness that found expression in His constant time alone with the Father in prayer. Jesus allowed nothing to interfere with or distract Him from this intimate fellowship; neither His family, nor His disciples, nor His religious critics and opponents. There was too much at stake. The people around Him frequently did not understand this close relationship between the Father and the Son, just as they often failed to grasp what kind of relationship they themselves should have (Mt 15:17; 16:9; Mk 8:17; 16:14; Lk 24:25). This is one reason why Jesus so often had to find solitary places to be alone with the Father in prayer. But Jesus let nothing deter Him from maintaining His love relationship with His Father.

Prayer leads Jesus to the heart of His unique and highly personal intimacy with His Father. He lives by that relationship, and in it His soul finds rest. It is the deepest secret of His interior life. Prayer is natural to Him; it takes

Him to the innermost mystery of His life and establishes Him in truth.

The Will of God

The second reason for Christ's prayer was to determine the will of the Father in order that He might accomplish the Father's purpose in every way and therefore remain obedient. When Adam disobeyed God in the Garden of Eden, the relationship he had once enjoyed was destroyed; only continued obedience would have caused it to flourish. Jesus sought the will of His Father, that which was pleasing to God (Eph 5:8, 10), that He might fulfil that will or obey it. This was the sole intent of His ministry as is made evident in the Garden of Gethsemane (Jn 6:38). His whole life and ministry were the working out of the Father's divine plan and purpose for Him, and this He not only obtained in prayer but regulated by His constant communion with the Father. Consequently, He faced all of life's crises with the assurance that God's will would prevail.

Every situation and every request brought Jesus back to the purpose of His mission: the divine will, the work entrusted to Him. Prayer enabled Him to discover and to bless the plan of His Father which He had come to fulfil. When He asked for something, He wanted only the will of the Father and the desire to act in His service. In Gethsemane Jesus found peace in submission to the Father; and the submission was the fruit of prayer. So, we see in Saint John's Gospel (11:41), Jesus can give thanks to His Father before a miracle, for His Father will always hear Him. His will is completely conformed to that of the Father. His submission motivated His filial confidence, which was absolute. No prayer has ever expressed confidence so unconditionally, with such strength and audacity, hence

He could say: "When you ask for anything in prayer... it will be granted you" (Mk 11:24).

The Needs of the Kingdom

There were two occasions when Jesus offered prayers which might challenge the will of God. The first was when He made His entry to Jerusalem: "What shall I say: Father, save me from this hour?" (Jn 12:27). The second was in the Garden of Gethsemane: "My Father, he said, if it be possible, let this cup pass me by" (Mt 26:39). On both occasions He uttered a petition which might not be in keeping with God's will, but in the end confessed Himself ready for that will. This is solely because the needs of the Kingdom was His chief concern. The same passion for the Kingdom revealed itself in the personal petitions recorded in John 17. Everywhere in that prayer is the consciousness of the Kingdom and all its varied petitions have their definite relation to the Kingdom. On the cross it seemed that for one brief moment Jesus lost His consciousness of God, when in agony He cried, "My God, my God, why have you deserted me?" (Mt 27:46). But in the end the old conviction returned, that everything was in the hands of God, and once more peace returns to the spirit of Christ and He added, "Father, into your hands I commit my spirit" (Lk 23:46).

The prayer of Jesus committed Him, it was turned towards action, and in action it was expressed. It guided and directed all His activities, while at the same time elevating His passivity. Luke emphasises how major decisions and turning points are always preceded by arduous prayer. Jesus' public ministry began with the prayer at the Jordan and closed with the prayer on the cross (Lk 23:46). The Transfiguration, which occurs in the middle of the public ministry, was a moment of intense prayer when the glory of Jesus was revealed as at once that of the beloved Son and of the prophet to whom all must listen (Lk 9:28-36). Far from cutting Him off from men, prayer took Him to the heart of His mission (Mk 11:25; Mt 5:23-24), which was to save the world. Through prayer He saw more clearly the meaning of His coming; He was enabled to make human history His own and to fulfil the expectation of the Father.

Prayer enabled Him to understand by experience and to go through His vocation as suffering servant and also to answer the demands which His special vocation makes of Him. The prayer of Jesus was self-oblation, His self-oblation was prayer. His resurrection confirmed that the evening sacrifice had found favour with God. The Lord, the *kyrios*, was victorious and henceforward intercedes for us as our Mediator.

Drawing Energy and Strength

Jesus needed to "recharge" Himself occasionally. Humanly speaking we can say that there was a constant drain of His human energy due to constant demands for His sympathy and compassion. In order for Him to respond to the needs of those who flocked to Him, Jesus occasionally needed to separate Himself for communion with God (cf. Lk 5:16). Prayer was like coming home, the reunion of Son with the Father. Jesus' prayer was the summit and source of His service of God.

He came out of prayer ready for decisive action, such as naming the Twelve (Lk 6:12) or revealing His identity (Lk 9:18). He recognised the frailty of His humanity and therefore confronted all the major events of His life in prayer. Both the beginning and the end of His ministry were met in prayer. The culmination, upon the cross, was perhaps only accomplished by the battle in prayer, while He was in the Garden of Gethsemane. Before Jesus chose the future leaders of the Church He prayed all night; He was seen to pray at His transfiguration and the raising of Lazarus. Similarly, He prayed during and after the feeding of the five thousand—a time when He would have been physically and spiritually weak and susceptible to attacks from Satan.

The Prayers of Jesus

The recorded prayers of Jesus are few in number but of great importance. In the four Gospels, four types of prayers of Jesus are recorded. They are:

- *Gratiarum actio* (prayers of thanksgiving):[30] In Matthew 11:25-26 and Luke 10:21, the first of this

---

[30] This is another typical example of Jesus having prayed as a Jew. *Gratiarum actio*, in Hebrew *Berakah* (thanksgiving), was and is the primary form of prayer in Jewish liturgy and spirituality. Carmine Di Sante in his book entitled *Jewish Prayer: The Origins of Christian Liturgy* (Paulist Press, 1985), p. 17, noted that the prayer of thanksgiving was the chief Jewish prayer "because it determines the meaning and context of all prayer, as well as the dynamic movement and horizon of all liturgy and all the feasts. The *berakah* consists in an attitude-and-formula of wonder, praise, thanksgiving and acknowledgments of the unmerited divine benevolence that provides for God's children and gladdens them with the fruits of the earth and every kind of blessing." Di Sante also observed standard *berakah* words were formulated so that every Jewish prayer began and ended with them. Among the best known *berakah*, he said, is to be found in Mt 11:25-27; Lk 10:21-22, where Jesus thanks the Father for having chosen "babes" as the recipients of His revelation.

Pointing to the fact that some *berakah* in the New Testament are implicit and others explicit, Di Sante gave example of the "institution of the Eucharist" as an implicit *berakah*. In the institution of the Eucharist there are two thanksgivings, one kind is recorded. Here Jesus is confronted by a mystery of spiritual truth being revealed to those people whom we imagine lacked qualification and He gave thanks for the mysterious arrangements of an all-wise Providence of God the Father. This is an attitude of mind that is well worth our cultivating towards most of the mysteries of this life. To Jesus, even mystery affords an opportunity for giving thanks. His thanksgiving is prompted by joy at seeing His messianic mission begin to be realised according to the disposition and favour of the Father. The second recorded prayer of thanksgiving is in John 11:41-42. Jesus is about to restore Lazarus from the dead and, feeling that big issues are involved, He offers prayer. But, contrary to our expectation, it is a prayer of thanksgiving, not of petition. It is a prayer dictated by a triumphant faith, the faith that attempts big things and expects to see them done. Since this work is for the glory of God, why not be assured of it and give thanks in advance. If such a faith were ours, it might conceivably alter the nature of many of our prayers. A mystery and a venture of faith prompted Christ to give thanksgiving in prayer.

---

over the bread and the other over the chalice, but as Di Sante pointed out we do not know what form the thanksgiving took. We only know that Jesus took the bread, blessed and broke it. The very words of the blessings are not known to us. Another place Jesus uses *berakah* is in Mk 6:41 "...He looked up to heaven, and blessed and broke the loaves..." Again in Mk 8:6-7. Other references to blessings are in Mk 10:16, where Jesus takes the children in his arms and "blesses them." For more information on Jesus' uses of the Jewish thanksgiving standardized set formulas, read Di Sante, pp. 16-18.

- *Obsecratio* (petition): Here we have Christ's prayers for His disciples. There are three such prayers recorded in the Gospels. The first is for Peter who will soon have to endure a severe trial. Jesus sees it coming and He prays for His disciple that he may surmount the trial. There is no desire expressed that Peter may be delivered from the necessity of enduring the test. The prayer only desires that strength be given him for it (Lk 22:32). The second prayer is in John 14:16-17. What Jesus is thinking of is the need of the disciples in their future service. His prayer has for its chief end the supplying of those needs. Their courage and confidence will spring from their reliance on the prayer of the Lord. Thus the Master does not divorce His mission from that of His disciples.

  The other petitions for the disciples are all found in John 17. There, Jesus prays that His followers may be kept from the world's evil and sanctified through the word of truth. He prays that all who believe may be one, that the world may believe and that at last those who believe may be with Him to behold His glory. Behind all these petitions for the disciples lies a passion for the Kingdom of God. The needs of the disciples are related to the needs of the Kingdom: "That the world may believe" and "That they may behold my glory." Jesus also prayed for others. Children were brought to Him that He might pray for them and bless them (Mt 19:13), a deaf and mute man was healed through His prayer (Mk 7:31-37), and so on.

- *Postulatio* (intercession): He made a prayerful intercession for His enemies (Lk 24:34). When He was dying on the cross, He even thought of the needs of those who were putting Him to death. He prayed that they might be forgiven. It is Christian prayer at its best. It is again related to the Kingdom of God.

- *Supplicatio* (supplication): This is evident in the prayer at Gethsemane (Lk 22:39-46). This text shows Jesus offering prayer for Himself regarding the event that will soon follow. This is the first time that Jesus has said a prayer of supplication for Himself.[31]

  There was one prayer which Jesus refused to offer when He was taken prisoner. He could have prayed for legions of angels. But the prayer was never offered. Jesus refused to pray for a life of personal ease, void of suffering. Again it was the Kingdom of God that mattered. Even personal desires must be subjected to it. The first duty is to know the will of God.

The Paradoxes in Prayer

In Matthew 6:6, Jesus recommended that when we pray, we go into our room and close the door to pray to our Father in secret. Yet He himself was homeless and had nowhere to lay His head, and therefore had no private place for prayer. Then what did He do and what did He mean by praying in secret?

1. He found a variety of hideaways where He was alone with His Father.
   - The Garden of Gethsemane was one of them (Lk 22:41-44).

---

[31] Cf. S. John ROTH, "Jesus the Prayer," in *Currents in Theology and Mission (CTM)*, 33 (2006), pp. 488-500.

- The hills and meadows were also places to which Jesus used to retreat (see Mt 14:22-23; Lk 6:12).
- He often withdrew to lonely places (Mk 1:35; Lk 5:16).
- We are also told that He sometimes rose before dawn to converse with His Father (Mk 1:35; Lk 6:12).

2. Jesus prayed everywhere even in public.
- Jesus offered many prayers of thanksgiving and praise (Mt 11:25-27).
- Jesus taught His disciples how to pray (Mt 6:9-13).
- Jesus prayed for Simon Peter (Lk 22:32).
- Jesus prayed for His murderers (Lk 23:34).
- Jesus prayed at the tomb of Lazarus (Jn 11:41-42).
- Jesus prayed foretelling His death and subsequent glorification (Jn 12:24-28).
- The priestly prayer of Jesus (Jn 17:1-26).
- Saint Paul in Hebrews 5:7 said that during His life on earth, Jesus offered up prayers and entreaty *aloud* and *in silent tears*, to the One who had the power to save Him from death, and He submitted so humbly that His prayer was heard.

With the above evidences of the different places that Jesus prayed, there is a paradox in praying in secret (Mt 6:6), which means having a reserved area for prayer and praying always (Eph 6:8, Phil 4:6, 1 Thes 5:17), meaning praying anytime and anywhere. Jesus solved this enigma in and with the example of His personal prayer life. He communes with His Father anywhere and everywhere. His prayer place was portable and His method varied because

He encountered His Father in His heart. Heart is the Bible's word for the innermost recesses of our being. This is the place where all real relationships are nourished and deepened. Normally in our daily activities of walking and working we often find ourselves unconsciously thinking about, or even talking to absent loved ones (i.e., planning what we will say to them when we next meet, write, or even speak on the telephone). In the same way, we have to cultivate an inner sanctuary which will enable us to enjoy constant intimacy with God anywhere and anytime. We should make Him our constant companion and be aware of His continuous presence.

One beautiful thing about private prayer is that we do not need a preamble before we can pray. As a Christian, your heart should be ready always to whisper a prayer. You can pray now, where you are and from whatever state of mind you are in. Many of our prayer preparations only manage to distract and distance us from the Divine Presence. You need not get prepared before you can let the Lord know how you feel about something, what are your worries and aspirations. Prayers are even more effective when they are said at that instant when your mind is going through a difficult situation because at such moments prayers are more sincere and profound. Prayer is so vital and transforming that the crucial thing is to pray now. We should learn to always be in the presence of God, every second, everywhere. Once this becomes a reality in our lives, we shall then be turning to Him at every instant because we then see Him as an explicit companion that warns, challenges, and shelters us.

Jesus Our Model in Prayer

While there are many wonderful examples of prayer and passages on prayer throughout the Scriptures, we know of no better model and demonstration of a prayer life for a Christian than the life of our Lord Jesus Christ. Consecrated life today does not need simply "more prayer" but it needs specifically the kind of praying exemplified in the life of Christ. Discipleship requires that union with God which Jesus manifested in His prayer, and this must be learned from Jesus Himself (Lk 11:1). Through our baptism, and deepened by our religious consecration, the Father, through His Holy Spirit has been working to conform us "to the image of his Son" (Rom 8:29 and Gal 2:20), and this conformation and therefore transformation will pre-eminently involve and affect our prayer life.

Jesus Himself displays how important prayer is by offering His prayer life as a model. With Him as the ultimate example for righteous living, how much more should believers strive to emulate Him. He takes it a step further, though, not only does He live the example of prayer, He teaches His followers both how to pray (the Lord's Prayer) and in what manner to pray (persistently). Thus for Him prayer is not a technique for achieving some objective or goal, it is man relating every aspect of his life to God.

Jesus' prayer life was the key to both His life and ministry. Throughout the Gospels, it's clear that prayer is one of the most marked characteristics of His life. At each major juncture, at every key decision point, we find Him in prayer. It was true in the very beginning. At the time of His baptism, it was "while He prayed" that "heaven was opened" and the Holy Spirit came down upon Him like a dove while the Father audibly assured Him, "You are my beloved Son; in You I am well pleased" (Lk 3:21–22). It was true as well at the end, as Jesus continued praying on the cross (Mt 27:46; Lk 23:34, 46). Every part of our Lord's life was centred and guided by His continuing communication with the Father. The clear emphasis is that the Son of God actively and consistently prayed! And He did so with various kinds of prayer and supplication (strong entreaty and pleading) to His Father.

It was Jesus' exemplary life of prayer that prompted the disciples' request for teaching on prayer (Lk 11:1-14) and so from His practical experience Jesus gave them guidance on the rudiments of prayer, hence the Our Father. Finally, although Jesus gave little teaching on the content of prayers, He sanctioned prayer for the strength to overcome the ills of the world (Lk 21:36 and 22:46) and also for workers to bring God's purposes to fruition (Mt 9:38).

If Jesus was convinced that His life and ministry depended upon His prayer life with the Father, we as well must set our hearts to maintain uninterrupted time in prayer with our Lord. This is the key not only to our ministry but to our very life as religious and as Christians. The Christian or religious community is one of prayer, carrying on the constant prayer of Jesus according to His command "stay awake, praying at all times for the strength to survive all that is going to happen, and to stand with confidence before the Son of Man" (Lk 21:36).

The consecrated person and indeed every Christian in imitation of Christ, should be living each day in continual fellowship with the Son and with the Father, through the Holy Spirit. One should be able to say through one's prayer life, "I am in Him, and He is in me." In the different apostolates which one ministers, one should pursue a closer relationship with God through prayer and strive daily to keep the Father's love in the forefront of one's thoughts and experience. When we pray, we must remember that God loves us, has plans for us. Just as Jesus did, we must find regular times of solitary prayer to receive the Father's direction for our lives.

There should be no dichotomy between our scheduled hours of prayer and our personal life of prayer. In the same way, to make any real distinction between the life of Jesus and the specific references to His prayers is to misunderstand the nature of the true human life. Jesus' whole life was one of communion with the Father so that He not only enjoyed fellowship with His Father, but He also discovered the daily purposes of the Father for His ministry in order to walk in obedience. Therefore, rather than being an imitation of the personal prayer life of Jesus, it becomes an imitation of Jesus' personal life of prayer, for His whole ministry was an outworking of His relationship with the Father.

The Spirit of Our Prayers

According to the teachings of Jesus, the Kingdom should be the aim of our requests in prayer. We cannot avoid being personal in prayer, but this also should in some way be related to the Kingdom and its needs. Thus detached desires and purely selfish motives are not necessary because your heavenly Father knows your needs. "If earthly parents know how to give good gifts to their children, how much more shall your heavenly Father give the Holy Spirit to those who ask Him" (Lk 11:13). Individual desires may not be for the advancement of the Kingdom, nor for our own good, and must end as the Master has taught us: "Not my will but Thine be done." To make the

Kingdom the standard is to allow sufficient latitude in prayer.

Jesus has a lot to say about the spirit of our prayers. His teaching in this respect can be grouped with a fair degree of success and without doing violence to His teaching.

Sincerity

There is a place for honesty when we are alone with the Father (Mk 12:40), so we should approach God in humility with an awareness of who He is (Lk 18:10ff). If any prayer is to be sincere, there must be a sincere life behind it. When Jesus denounced the Pharisees for making long prayers and devouring widows' houses, He was condemning insincerity in prayer. These men loved to pray at street corners and in synagogues, to be seen by others. Jesus would have His disciples pray in secret. When He cleansed the temple, He declared that you cannot run a "house of prayer" and a "den of robbers" at the same time. If you pray for forgiveness, you must also forgive. The insincerity of the Pharisee and the humility of the publican are the two possible attitudes, and we know which merited the approval of the Master. The rich man's prayer in hell was unanswered because he had failed to use opportunities that had been given. All these lead us to understand that the underlying motive of a life creates the value of the prayer. Only if the living is sincere can the prayer be sincere. Therefore the inner ethic of prayer is just as severe as any that was ever enunciated and lived by Christ Jesus Himself.

Persistence

The ministry of prayer is a strenuous one. The way in which Jesus united prayer and fasting indicates that. Your prayer, like your fasting, must cost you something. It must involve sacrifice. Prayer is not the easy thing some of us imagine. In the life of Jesus, prayer was the work, and ministry was the price. For Jesus prayer was the battle. The evidence of this is the fact that it was during prayer that He sweat great drops of blood (Heb 5:7).

Prayer will prevail because of its importunity. The parables of the importunate friend and the unjust judge, emphasize that men ought always to pray and not to faint. The Kingdom of Heaven suffers violence and the violent take it by force (Mt 11:12). Prayer is neither vain repetition nor much speaking. It is the expenditure of your life's blood. It creates a passion in life and demands from us, in service and sacrifice, the very utmost we have to give. Prayer is hard work and yet, instinctive as is our dependence upon God, no duty is more earnestly impressed upon us in Scripture than the duty of continual communion with God. The main reason for this unceasing insistence is the arduousness of prayer. In its nature it is a laborious undertaking, and in our endeavour to maintain the spirit of prayer we are called to wrestle against principalities and powers of darkness (Eph 6:12).

Faith

Faith certainly does not mean that our little personal desires will be answered as we think they ought to be. Divorce some passages from their context or separate them from the whole of the teaching of Jesus, and they will seem to indicate that we can pray for anything. Such passages as John 14:13; 15:7; 16:23 and 16:26, have all conditional phrases. Everything we desire may not be for God's glory, nor the product of our abiding in Christ and may not always be asked in Christ's name. Mark 11:23-24, with its parallel in Matthew 21:20-22, is a very difficult passage. But from what we already know of Jesus and His teaching, we cannot understand that passage to mean that every little whim will be satisfied by a supernatural visitation that will remove mountains. It is but an illustration, an encouragement to have faith in prayer as Christ taught His disciples to pray. Petitions would only be answered if delivered in faith (Mk 11:24) and therefore flowing from a knowledge of the Father and His faithfulness. All that Christ has to say about ordinary desires is that "your Father knows you have need of them." The injunction is to seek first the Kingdom and the other things are added. Faith in Christian prayer is a belief in the goodness of God and the final triumph of the cause of righteousness. It is when our faith is of that quality that we ask and receive. The mission of Jesus is accomplished in a spirit of filial dependence on God, which is expressed in prayer. His precepts on prayer imply that we must pray to the Father because He is good and will give us the Holy Spirit, the fullness of His gifts (Lk 11:9-30) and the source of Christian joy (Lk 10:21). The gracious acceptance of the Father's gifts characterizes the openness to God expressed by prayer; this includes the acceptance of the Father's will, the cause of Christian joy, which caused Jesus to rejoice in prayer (Lk 10:20-21). Prayer, as Christ taught it, expresses the loving recognition of God as source of our peace and joy.

Jesus' Prayer Life: Vital and Existential

We must try to summarize the points we have made so as to give clarification to our argument. From our study of the life of Jesus, we have discovered that the frequency with which He prayed revealed the value He attached to prayer as communion with the Father. Prayer conceived in this way makes it an essential part of the human soul. Relationship with God the Father, however, is bound to be an element of all true prayer. The end which Jesus always had in view when He presented petitions was the doing of the Father's will and the coming of the Kingdom. His teaching on the subject matter of the Lord's Prayer[32] is that the validity of individual requests depends upon their relation to the needs of the Kingdom. He also made us to understand that the essential characteristics of true prayer are sincerity, persistence, and faith. Prayer first involves relationship and communion with God, and only afterwards petition. With the teaching of Jesus before us, we can be emphatic about this; petition is for the Kingdom of God, and only for personal desires as these affect the Kingdom.

We are therefore called to relive the life of communion and deep relationship with God the Father, which Jesus exemplifies and which can be concisely presented in three moments: *contemplatio, communio,* and *compassio.*

- **Contemplatio**: Contemplation is the way Jesus lived His total surrender to the Father's will, hence the relationship of loving obedience that He enjoys with the Father—a life lived in the immediacy of the Father's will (Jn 5:19, 12:49-50). Contemplative prayer, then, is what made Christ to enjoy a constant companionship of the Father. In His very words:

---

[32] This prayer is also called the Disciples' Prayer by some scholars, since it was believed that that ought to be its rightful name and not the Lord's Prayer. The Lord's Prayer to His Father was given in the Gospel of Saint John 17. The disciples had been with Jesus, and He was praying and when He finished, they said to Him, "Lord, teach us how to pray," and Jesus taught them the Disciples' Prayer, sometimes also called the "Our Father."

"I am in the Father, and the Father in Me." This is perfect union. The personal prayer of Jesus continues the revelation of the Father at His baptism and transfiguration. It is the answer of the Son to the voice of the Father. Both share in the same mystery and the same work of salvation. The only possible conclusion you can reach, when you have studied the recorded prayers of Jesus, is that Christ prayed chiefly for the doing of the Father's will. He prayed that it might be done in and through Himself and His disciples. It is the highest level to which prayer can rise—contemplation. When the prayers of Jesus passed from praise to petition, they ended on this note, "Thy will be done."

Jesus' prayer life teaches and communicates that wholeness is holy balance and integration. He taught this, not only in words, but by example. Particularly in Luke's Gospel we see Him frequently stopping His fast pace of life, His preaching, healing and travelling, by withdrawing to quiet places to pray alone or with a few of His disciples (Lk 6:12, 9:18, 22:39). If there was not a harmony between what He taught and what He did, His teaching would lack authority. Christian identity depends directly on this authority, and contemplative life is the harmony of life as exemplified in the life of Jesus.

- *Communio*: In and through prayer, Jesus lives the life of communion to the full. Although apparently He is solitary in prayer, it is then that He is actually in communion with the First Person of the Trinity in the unity of the Spirit. At other times the heavenly prophets of God joined Him in prayer (Mt 17:3). He also showed oneness to the suffering humanity as He ministers to them.

The Gospel of John makes it especially clear that for Jesus, there was always an "Other," a Thou, whom He was in relation with. In fact, we can assume that inwardly, He was in continuous contact with the Father as Beloved Other and with the presence of people and creation as "other." Thus, Jesus' prayer life sprang from His unity with the First Person of the Trinity, the Divine Mystery, and from simply "being one with" (*koinonia*) the Father in a contemplative unity, but it also blossomed forth from a continuous, inward giving and receiving in relation to the otherness of God, people, and creation.

- *Compassio:* If one is to sum up the whole character of Jesus in reference to humanity, it might be gathered into this one sentence: "He was moved with compassion." This very sentence is the driving motive for almost all His prayers for His disciples, for children who were brought to Him, for all the less privileged, and for humanity at large. When we read the Gospels, we notice that Jesus is always touched by the desperate situation of the sorrowful, the sick, the possessed, and the dead. The Bible for example does not say that Jesus wept when He heard that His friend, Lazarus, had died. But when He arrived at the tomb, seeing Mary and others weeping, "He groaned in the spirit and was troubled and wept" (Jn 11:33, 35). The sorrow of others touched His sensitive heart. Whether it was the grieving, the blind, the lame, the lepers, the prostitutes, or just plain sinners, Jesus felt their pain, prayed, and did what He could to help—observe the sequence: *He **felt** their pain, He*

prayed, *and He* **acted**. The climax of such a prayer was His prayer for His enemies (Lk 24:34). As He was dying on the cross, He even had compassion for those who were putting Him to death and He prayed that they might be forgiven.

Therefore, as sons and daughters in the Son, as sharers in the secrets of the Father's life through the revelation of the Son (Lk 10:22), we have received "a spirit of adoption through which we cry out 'Abba!' 'Father!'" (Rm 8:15). It is from this exclamation that the Christian's prayer life begins. The Christian is less than faithful to Jesus' example if he/she fails to pray much and to pray regularly. He/she is called to have a daily regimen of prayer of fixed times and even places, if possible, and at the same time to seize opportunities in the events of his/her life and in moments of quiet to commune with God the Father. This personal prayer life must be for him/her as it was for his/her Master, a source and a highest expression of his/her service to God. About the whole personal prayer life of Jesus, Irwin Ross Beiler succinctly wrote: "More compelling than anything Jesus taught about prayer by precept was what he taught by his prayer practice. He depended upon it in the great soul-moving experiences of his life...Whether he needed courage, strength, or fellowship with the Father, prayer was his reliance, his very mood."[33]

Thus Christian prayer, whether personal or collective, cannot be separated from the faith which commits the whole person. There is no break in continuity between prayer and life, contemplation and action, liturgical celebration and Christian living, because faith does not affect

---

[33] Irwin Ross BEILER, *Studies in the Life of Jesus* (New York: Abingdon-Cokesbury Press, 1936), p. 181.

a special and transient moment of life but is a life renewed by the Spirit. Faith is of its nature an activating influence and it contains the grace to act.

We do not find in the prayer of Jesus any conflict between His contemplative and His active life, between His relationship with God whom He called Father and men whom He came to save, between His communion with the Father and His ministry of compassion. Both take Him to the heart of the Father's work; the unity of His life and ministry activity is to be found here. Christ's prayer accompanies His entire ministry and His whole ministry takes place in union and in the presence of God.

The mission to humanity cannot be separated from the service of God; both are the ebb and flow of one grace, received and participated in. The Christian therefore is always in a liturgical situation. He makes his/her self-offering in his/her daily life. He/she offers him/herself, says Saint Paul, "as a living sacrifice, consecrated to God and worthy of his acceptance. That is your spiritual worship" (Rm 12:1). Whatever the Christian's situation, whether he/she is married or celibate, in time of persecution or of peace, his/her whole life must express the Amen of his/her faith. Action and prayer, service of humanity and service of God, are but two manifestations of the one charity of God which inflames the hearts of his children. Prayer and Christian living are both answers to the grace which has been received.

The Essence of Prayer: Personal Relationship with Jesus

It should be clear by now that through teaching, activity, and prayer, Jesus opens a window for others to witness

His unique relationship with His Father. It is important therefore to appreciate His "Abba" Father bond (Mk
14:36). As a man, Jesus prays and as Son, He shares in
the sociality of His Father. During Jesus' experience in the
baptism and transfiguration, or in times of prayer, what is
communicated to Him is not simply the message or ministry but *status* and *relationship*. The major focus in His life
and ministry is not based solely on the message of what He
says or does, but *who He is in relationship with the Father*.
His mission proceeds from His relational experience with
the Father. He lives in an ever-so-close relationship with
the Father and that is prayer proper.

In Jesus' prayer of thanksgiving (Mt 11:25-30), we
note that He possesses an unshared Sonship. He spoke to
the Father in prayer and then shared with His disciples
about the unique depth and intimacy He enjoys with the
Father. Jesus not only claims to know God the Father, but to
know Him in a way that no one else does (Mt 11:27). The
knowledge of the Father which Jesus claims to have is not
a possession of theological information, but a profound
experience that involves mind, heart, and will. Knowledge
of God means sharing fellowship with God. Since Jesus is
the unique Son, who alone stands in an unmediated relationship with the Father, He is able to extend a mediated
relationship of God as Father to others. Jesus makes the
Father real for us. Therefore the mediated knowledge of
the Father has nothing to do with abstract theology or
propositional learning about the nature or attributes of
God. It means an experience of the fully personal and mediated relationship between the Father and humankind. In a
sense, it means possessing an experiential knowledge of
Jesus who is God in flesh.

Moreover, through numerous encounters, Jesus articulates that the new life He embodies and offers begins with an attachment and relationship to His person, to be followed by growth in relationship to Him for our future lives and direction. To cultivate this personal relationship with Jesus does not necessarily mean spending one's whole time in the chapel praying and praising God. This is to be learned from Jesus' relationship with the Father, hence Jesus' relationality is expressed in His teaching and practical interest in others.

Jesus spent Himself for people and was busy non-stop with the needs of others. He was accessible to those from the top to the bottom of society whether it be Nicodemus, the rich young ruler, the twelve, other disciples, Lazarus, Mary, Martha, fallen men and women, or hated tax-collectors, such as Zacchaeus. Jesus was not a religious, recluse, monk, or sage who retreated to some hermit-like life. Instead He was constantly "on the move," very active in beneficent ways, expressing His compassion and grace through teaching, responsiveness to the needs of others, to their healing, and to the reorientation of their lives. He spent His life in doing the Father's will.

However, He also found it necessary every now and then, in-between activities, late at night or early in the morning, to be renewed in this relationship with the Father. During the day, He was in constant demand and therefore had little time for this bond with the Father. Thus, He often spent His nights in maintaining this relationship. Everywhere Jesus went, He looked to relate to people thereby relating them to God who seeks relatedness with them. Through Jesus, God is bent on a rescue-mission for people who have lost their way. Important also to mention that while Jesus enjoyed the company of others, He does not allow for intrusion into His inner circle. This is vital!

Jesus sought relationship with others before they associated His benefits and gifts with His person. Even though people came to Him with their pressing physical needs, they learned that He dealt with them individually, in a completely personal manner; thereby, they developed a relationship with Him, not merely as a benefactor but also as the Lord and Saviour. However, God is a person who seeks to be dynamically and relationally involved with people; He desires the best for humanity, whom He came to save in the person of Jesus.

Jesus argued that the starting point of religious activity is found in the new relationship with Him. He did not abrogate the Law, but expressed the necessary and responsible conduct in keeping with the new relationship. The Parable of the Two Builders (Mt 7:24-27) illustrates that the authentic response to Jesus' entire Sermon is *hearing* and *doing* His words.[34] In Matthew 5:19, Jesus says that whoever keeps one of the least commandments and teaches others to do so shall be called great in the Kingdom of Heaven. The language of *hearing* and *doing* presupposes the new relationship that He offers. So He emphasizes the truth that the new relationship is not based upon religious performance but upon divine grace for those who own up to their own bankruptcy (Lk 18:9-14) and upon *hearing* and *doing* His words. It shows that action stimulated by hearing the Word of God or by an attempt to fulfil God's will is a paramount requisite in this relationship.

---

[34] The verb "to do, practise" (ποιἐῖν) is found 19 times in the Sermon on the Mount.

Concluding this chapter on praying in Jesus' manner, it has become clear that both by words and example the prayer that Jesus taught us is not repeating routine words (Mt 6:7) or trying to impress those around us with our spirituality (Mt 6:5), but that prayer is meant to flow from close, vital, and continuous fellowship with Him. This fact therefore necessitates certain relevant personal questions:

Do I have any personal relationship with Jesus? How deep is that relationship when I pray? Do I pour my heart out to Him with complete confidence and trust in His help because I have come to know and experience His love? Do I know that it is almost impossible to be related to Jesus as a friend when He is regarded simply in causal categories? If I do not know, what am I doing about it?

This is not something we can start practising automatically, it takes effort and time, like any relationship. The more you spend time with Him, the more you will come to understand His ways, His heart, and His will as you pray. There is no substitute for taking time to study the Bible (which is the source from which one learns to know Him) and for allowing the Holy Spirit to teach you how to pray in a way consistent with God's will. Place His Word in your heart and mind, then the Holy Spirit will use those Scriptures as you pray to keep your life on track and consistent with God's will. This is so because as one begins to appropriate for oneself Jesus' experience, to enter into this archetype, this way of apprehending in faith His experience as the relationship of Son to Father, the person will establish the foundational balance for Christianity, most succinctly described by Hans Urs von Balthasar, when he wrote:

> Christ is the archetypal relationship of man to God, a relationship measured only by itself, and he is this as a true historical man.... The measure of being included in the original Christ-experience is at the same time the measure of the apostolic mission: the more a person participates (*teilnimmt*), the more must he (and can he), in turn, communicate (*teilgeben*), not out of a gratuitous generosity, but in virtue of the intrinsic teleology of the experience. In this way there arises a lively unity of descent and ascent.[35]

Personal Relationship with God: a Condition for Discipleship

Tertullian wrote, "Christians are made, not born," and the process by which Christians are made was identified as "catechesis." Each of us is made a Christian at baptism. We spend the rest of our lives involved in a process of becoming more Christian. That life-long process is one of catechesis. To be more precise, there are various distinctive, deliberate (intentional), systematic (related), sustained (life-long) processes which comprise this catechesis. Let me suggest three: formation, education, and instruction. Formation implies "shaping" and refers to intentional, relational, experiential activities within the life of a story-formed faith community. Education implies "reshaping" and refers to critical reflective activities related to these communal experiences. Then, instruction implies "building" and refers to the means by which knowledge and skills useful to communal life are

---

[35] Hans Urs von BALTHASAR, *The Glory of the Lord* (San Francisco: Ignatius Press, 1982), pp. 305-306.

transmitted, acquired, and understood. Formation forms the Body of Christ, education reforms it, and instruction builds it up. This is the general formula of the Christian catechesis.[36] The practical realisation of all these "shaping," "reshaping," and "building" takes place in our individual vocational states.

---

[36] In the New Testament, the word catechesis is used to signify teaching or instruction in the law of God (Acts 18:25; Rom 2:18; Gal 6:6). The practice of catechesis is referred to in Hebrews (5:12-14; cf. 1 Cor 3:1-3) as feeding children with milk rather than the solid food of justice. The primitive catechesis as revealed in the Epistles of Paul, Peter, and James in particular seems to have developed in two forms. The first, addressed to converts from Judaism, was based on the Holiness Code of Leviticus (17-19) and followed the lines of the Jerusalem apostolic decree that had prescribed baptism and abstention from uncleanliness and idolatry (Acts 15:19-21) as essential for entrance into the Church of Christ. This early catechesis emphasized adherence to the Word of God as truth in contrast with idolatry and stressed the requirements of fraternal charity. There are numerous indications in the New Testament of the use of catechetical formulas based on Christ's Sermon on the Mount and of lists of vices and virtues (Mt 5:3-11; Lk 6:20-23) that seem to have been formed into groups of texts for teaching.

Didache, an early second-century work and the letter of Barnabas supply examples of the primitive catechesis in the guise of the two ways, of life and of death (Didache), or of light and darkness (Barnabas' letter), and were based on Jewish synagogue practice. The Didache proclaimed the law of the love of God and of neighbour taken by Christ from the Old Testament (Dt 6:5; Lv 19:18) and the golden rule (Didache 1:2). It described the virtues (1:3-4, 14) and vices (5-6, 3) that characterize respectively life and death by way of preparation for baptism (7), and described participation in the Eucharist (9:1-5). See F. X. MURPHY (ed.), Catechesis, I (Early Christian), in *New Catholic Encyclopaedia*, Second Edition, vol. 3, Can-Col, (Washington, DC: Thomson Gale, 2003), pp. 227-228. Read also the successive article edited by M. E. JEGEN, pp. 228-232.

Consequently, vocation begins where we are and it is really all about the summons to go in search of ourselves in responding to God's call through Christ. In other words, our calling is to grow beyond the status quo. Vocation is to seek after and to become our true selves in God's sight.[37] From this status quo the religious is called and consecrated (deepening the initial consecration by baptism) to live Christ's life on earth, thereby living under the tutelage of Christ as is made evident in the Gospels. To know exactly what this "tutelage of Christ" entails, it is necessary to have a review of the nature of discipleship in the New Testament setting.

From a variety of biblical statements, it is clear that the relationship of Jesus to His disciples is that of teacher/ role model. It is instructive also to note that in the Jewish and Greek worlds, the teacher-student relationship "is predominantly characterized by the concept of *mimesis*. Teachers and students are bound together by a certain teaching and practice of life, and the student is recognizable in his imitation of the teachings and life of the teacher."[38] Therefore, the nature of discipleship is *mimesis* (imitation). Examples of this are many in the Scriptures, like in Luke 6:40 where Jesus affirms the traditional rabbinic notion that "a pupil is not above his teacher but everyone (each, in every case, without exception), after he has been fully trained will be *like his teacher.*" The expression "not above," suggests that the pupil normatively does not deviate from anything the teacher does. In the Gospel of

---

[37] Cf. Saint Irenaeus' statement: "For the glory of God is a living man; and the life of man consists in beholding God" (Against Heresies 4, 20, 7).

[38] H. WEDER, "Disciple, Discipleship," in *American Biblical Dictionary* (ABD), II (2009), p. 20.

Saint John, this pattern of rigidity in replicating Jesus' life is repeated in 13:34, 17:18 and 23, and 20:21, using the conceptual formula, "As I...so you." In John 13:15, Jesus states, "For I gave you an example that you also should do as I did." The continuation and imitation of Jesus' mission in His disciples is explicit in John 20:21: "As the Father has sent me, I also send you."

When we move into the Epistles, the theme of "discipleship" is every bit as strong as in the Gospels and Acts of the Apostles, only the vocabulary changes. Outside the narrative documents it appears that the terms "disciple" and "follower" are replaced with specific exhortations to live out the Christian life: to "walk" in the "way" of Christ, or "put on Christ" or be "in Christ" and so on.

Discipleship, however, moves to a third, fourth, and even a fifth generation in the New Testament. Saint Paul can require of his readers, for example, "Imitate me even as to the same degree and extent that I imitate Christ" (1 Cor 11:1). Four other times he exhorts churches to imitate him (1 Cor 4:16, Phil 3:17, 2 Thes 3:7 and 9, cf. Gal 4:12, Phil 4:9, Jas 3:1, 1 Tim 4:16, 2 Tim 3:4). At another place Saint Paul again says: "I exhort you to become imitators of me. For this reason I have sent to you Timothy, who is my son whom I love (an echo of Jesus' baptism)...who will remind you of my ways."

All the above examples are proofs that a Christian should have only one mentor and that is Christ. Christ is the only MASTER with whom one should constantly be comparing one's life. The call to Christian life is a call to be imitators of Christ. To know exactly what the Christian should be doing so as to be an imitator of Christ, let us first of all find out in the New Testament what a disciple is expected to do in order to be an imitator of a teacher/

rabbi. Before going into this, let us step back for a moment and view the big picture of the content of New Testament discipleship by asking five simple questions:

- What is it that the New Testament says that Jesus came to do?
- When ministering, with whom does He minister?
- What does Jesus tell His disciples to do?
- What actually is the motivation for Jesus' ministry?
- What is the consecrated religious (the "disciple of the disciples") expected to do?

The answers to these questions are going to be evident in the subsequent five sub-titles.

Opposition to the Reign of the Devil

Frequently, when the New Testament writers condense Jesus' ministry into a sentence or two, they show him in **opposition to the reign of the devil**, which appears as demonic possession, sickness, the disruption of nature, or sin: it was "for this purpose that Jesus appeared, to destroy the works of the devil" (1 Jn 3:8). Peter spelled out the result of Jesus' baptism and gave a summary of His mission on earth saying: "God anointed Jesus of Nazareth with the Holy Spirit and power…he went about doing good and healing all who were under the power of the devil, because God was with him" (Acts 10:38). Both of these verses confirm the programmatic statement about Jesus' mission in Luke 4:18:

> The Spirit of the Lord is upon me, for he has anointed me. He has sent me to bring the good news to the poor, to proclaim liberty to captives and to the blind new sight, to set the downtrodden free, to proclaim the Lord's year of favour.

Therefore Jesus came to oppose the reign of the devil made manifest in the lives of individuals and in nature.

Jesus Calls Disciples: "Follow Me"

Call is from the Latin verb *vocare* (to call). Each of the four Gospels records the call by Jesus of individuals to be apostles and disciples (Mt 4; Mk 1; Lk 5; Jn 1). The call was to leave all, including family members, and follow Jesus. This call often entailed significant sacrifice and commitment. On one occasion Jesus called a young man to be a disciple but the young man did not follow the call, because he had many possessions to which he had to attend to (Lk 18). Calling takes on a deep theological meaning in the writings of the apostle Saint Paul. Calling is a special election by God (Rom 11). Saint Paul writes eloquently of his own calling, making a case that he is an apostle equal to the other apostles called by Jesus (2 Cor 2). He also writes profoundly of calling or election as summons to salvation and an invitation to participate intimately in the redemptive activity of Jesus (2 Thes 2). Thus, calling for Saint Paul is an election by God for a deeply religious mission.

A call or a vocation in the Hebrew and Christian biblical traditions has four characteristics. They are:

- A person is called for a specific purpose to which he/she must make a commitment;
- The called person has a special gift for accomplishing this purpose;
- A vocation presumes a person who calls: God, Jesus; and
- Finally, to accept a vocation means to live a life of sacrifice, to live with faith in darkness.[39]

---

[39] See John L. ELIAS, "Reflections on the Vocation of a Religious Educator," in *Religious Education* 98, no. 3 (2003), pp. 297-310,

Jesus' command, "follow me," is an invitation to a relationship and obedience coupled with His faithful promise. The obedient response of such a call is well explained by Bishop Lucius I. Ugorji where he remarked:

> In responding to Christ's call the Apostles entrusted themselves to a role and a destiny which was much greater than anything they could foresee or understand themselves—a destiny which tried and tested them to their limits and in some cases, cost them their lives. At the heart of the life of an Apostle and a priest is selfless giving of oneself to a life that is not shaped by one's own needs, ambitions, conveniences and comforts.[40]

The religious, like the apostles and disciples, leave their occupations, families, homes and commit themselves fully to a new and unfamiliar experience, founded on a person (Jesus Christ) and a promise (I will make you fishers of men [Mk 1:16-20]). The apostles and disciples give themselves without reservation to this One who totally reorients their lives (also Jn 1:39, 43). In the process of this following, they discover that Jesus lays down conditions and rules for discipleship when He invites them into relationship. Some of the examples of such conditions are found in Mt 8:18-22: unsheltered lives and no security save in him; Lk 9:47-60: the least being the greatest; Mt 19:16-29: the rich young ruler, etc. In a fishing context, Jesus who knows nothing of fishing commands Peter—the expert fisherman—and Peter obeys the seemingly absurd

---

here p. 298.

[40] Lucius Iwejuru UGORJI, *Words from the Heart of a Shepherd* (Enugu: Snaap Press, 2015), p. 13.

command, even though it runs counter to his practicality as to the right time and place to fish. He will not disregard Jesus' presence and authority. Thus he says, "But at your word, I will let down the nets" (Lk 5:5). So Jesus ministers with the apostles and disciples whom He called, so that they can both be with Him and learn how to continue His ministry when He would no longer be with them.

Purpose of the Call: "To be with Him" (Companionship)

It is very important to underline the fact that Jesus' formal appointment of the Twelve begins with an explicit purpose statement, "to be with Him...he appointed Twelve; they were to be his companions and to be sent out to preach, with power to cast out devils" (Mk 3:14-15). It is only natural, then, that after their being "with" Him, Jesus would then send them out to replicate His own mission. So, relationship with Jesus precedes commission (Mk 3:14-15; Mt 10:5ff; Mk 6:7ff; Lk 9:1ff). Due to their relationship with Him, they obey and venture out into the hazardous task of proclaiming the Kingdom of God. They carry out His charge and are responsive to Jesus in "report-back" sessions when they are "with Him" again (Mk 6:30). In the same vein the purpose statement for our individual calling to the consecrated life is to be "with Jesus." In the process of being with Him, a transition of an inner union is realised and then there will be a shift from "being with Him" to "being in Him" (Jn 14:20). Because of this relationship of being with, one obeys and obedience to Jesus attracts God's love, "If anyone loves me, he will obey my word and my Father will love him, and we shall come to him and make our home with him" (Jn 14:23).

When people enter into relationship with Jesus at His invitation (Mt 11:28), they are promised a personal transformation, expressed well in Jesus' thanksgiving prayer (Mt 11:25-30). Thus, through his relationality with the Father, Jesus is empowered to share the story, nature, and relationality of the Father with others. Similarly, just as Jesus lives in an ever-so-close relationship with the Father, so the religious who is in the privileged position of "preferring nothing to the love of Christ" (*RB* 72:11), should be able to narrate the Jesus-story to humanity through his/her personal life. One who lives in this way, gradually learns that Jesus conveys a qualitative newness of life for those who have made a personal commitment to Him; they are promised a hundredfold now in present time—houses, brothers, sisters and mothers, children and lands (cf. Mt 19:29). Thereby, he points to the excellence of the new life, which is infinitely superior to what one has previously known.

Convinced of these promises, the consecrated person should also be aware that following Jesus not only means that one becomes the recipient of various forms of blessing, but it also enables one to deepen one's relationship with Him, apart from certain "benefits." Thus, one will learn what it means to drink His cup of suffering and share in His fearful baptism (Mk 10:35-40; Mt 20:20-23) quite apart from personal gain. Remembering also that when He promised us a hundredfold now in this present time, He added "not without persecution" (Mk 10:30). Therefore, what is important here is the awareness that to be a Christian consists precisely in offering oneself to the cross in union with Christ, the benefits notwithstanding. Christians encounter suffering and the cross, and are called sometimes to martyriological (quite often this is white martyrdom) witness precisely because they are the disciples of Christ Jesus. Indeed, a distinguishing mark of the Church is the possession of the cross in which Christians endure every misfortune and persecution by inward or mental pains, such as, sadness, timidity, fear, and outward miseries, poverty, contempt, illness, and weakness in order to become like their head, Christ. The only reason for such suffering is that they steadfastly adhere to Christ and God's Word, enduring this for the sake of Christ and in imitation of Him.

Indeed, if there is any analogy that exists between the religious and Christ, it is not established by growth in holiness but instead by suffering—we are being conformed to the image of the crucified.[41] Properly speaking, it is not we but God who makes us to be Christ's disciples, and it is a thing of joy which carries a big responsibility. Hence Saint Paul in Galatians 6:14 says that he takes glory in the cross of our Lord Jesus Christ. This can be a point of reflection for every religious to ask oneself: Where is my glory? In what do I glory in? Do I take glory in my glory, i.e., do I glory in my worldly achievement? Or do I glory in hardships that I go through in order to get things done for Christ in the person of my brothers/sisters in community, for the poor or the less privileged? His gifts and benefits are appreciated in greater ways when people are joined by faith in Him and share the cross with Him. But when on the contrary they hold tight only to the benefits thereby lying not only to human beings but also to God, the result is disastrous as with the case of Ananias and Sapphira (Acts 5:1-11). So, through numerous encounters, Jesus reveals

---

[41] See Marc LIENHARD, *Luther: Witness to Jesus Christ* (Minneapolis: Augsburg, 1982), pp. 120-121.

that the new life He embodies and offers begins with an attachment and relationship to His person, to be followed by growth in that relationship.

Jesus' Mission: Compassion

Compassion is a motivation for Jesus' teaching and ministry and therefore the stimulus for His summoning disciples to Himself with whom He could share both His life and His mission.[42] It is shown to the Jews as He teaches the masses, since they are "as sheep not having a shepherd" (Mk 6:34; Mt 9:36). Compassion goes hand in hand with activity, e.g., His healing ministry, teaching, and feeding miracles:

- "As he went ashore he saw a great throng; and he felt compassion for them, and healed their sick" (Mt 14:14).
- "And Jesus in compassion touched their (two blind men) eyes, and immediately they received their sight and followed him" (Mt 20:24).
- "I have compassion upon the crowd because they have remained with me three days and they do not have anything to eat" (Mk 8:2; cf. Mt 8:2).
- "And when the Lord saw her (widow of Nain) he had compassion on her and said to her, 'Do not weep'"(Lk 7:13).

It is striking to discover that J.L. Story was right when he observed that the verb "to feel compassion" (σπλαγχνίζεσθαἴ) "occurs 12 times only in the gospels alone and in each case refers to Jesus' emotive motivation for doing good. Once the people sense his compassion for them, they immediately pursue him for some evidence of

---

[42] See Mary Bride NJOKU, *Consecrated Life: A Renewed Insight* (London, 2016), pp. 222-232.

his compassion."[43] They assume that Jesus is willing to give advice or help them; sometimes they appeal to His will (Mk 1:40; Mt 8:2) and lay their requests before Him (Mk 1:40; Mk 2:1-12; 9:22ff; Mt 8:2; 8:8-9; Lk 7:8ff).

Instead of evangelization outlines, Jesus' missionary activities offer another approach, a style that speaks to the heart of people and to those in need of relationship with God, with their fellow human beings. God takes the full initiative in His gift of His Son, who personally approaches others and seeks to elicit responses of love, trust, and faithful obedience. He respects the freedom of others to make decisions and experience the consequences of their decisions.

Jesus never demands any reward or compensation for His help nor do the people respond with remuneration for His help. There are some instances where people express spontaneous gratitude (Lk 7:36ff; 17:16). However, Jesus clearly directs their attention away from the gift to the Giver (Mk 1:44; Mt 8:4; Lk 5:14; Lk 13:10-17). The love of Jesus is expressed as compassion and grace, i.e., His attitude and saving activity towards those whom He loves; correspondingly the recipients bring nothing to the helpful event that would in some way make them deserving of such blessing.

The early Church comes to appreciate that the whole of Jesus' life, ministry, death and resurrection express His

[43] See J. Lyle STORY, "Christology and the Relational Jesus," in *American Theological Inquiry*, vol. 1, no. 2 (2008), pp. 91-112, here pp. 100-101. J. Lyle STORY is Professor of New Testament and Biblical Languages of the School of Divinity of Regent University. He has taught at Regent University for the last twenty-five years, possesses special passion for the message of the four Gospels, and has produced the Greek to Me Memory System (textbook, flash cards, and multimedia CD-ROM).

love, grace, and compassion for the whole of humankind (Acts 10:38; Eph 5:21; 5:25; 1 Pet 1:8). His compassion is directed to persons, motivated by His deep desire to accept them and help them in their most pressing needs, irrespective of the relative worth or position of the recipient. People also experience and respond to the incredible love that Jesus expresses for them. Jesus is the one who knits together love for God and love for others in an indissoluble bond; such a dual-bond is the supreme commandment upon which all other commandments depend. Jesus accepts others where they are; He does not expect people to "get cleaned up" before He relates to them.

The stories of Jesus' compassion for the blind, the deaf, and the lame, for the ill and the grief-stricken, should be a decisive pointer to the Christian's mission of compassion for the world. His feeding of thousands, who are hungry, not only for bread but for the smallest morsel of hope, feeds also one's faith. His astounding compassion even towards those who crucified Him gives one a glimpse of the immensity of divine love. In all these ways, writes Andrew Purves, "Jesus' compassion becomes a window of access into the nature of God's vulnerability and willingness to suffer with us. Compassion reveals the inner nature of God."[44] When we open our hearts with compassion to anyone that

---

[44] Andrew PURVES, *The Search for Compassion: Spirituality and Ministry* (Louisville, KY: Westminster/John Knox, 1989), pp. 12 and 16. Andrew Purves is a Christian theologian in the Reformed tradition through the Church of Scotland (and later, the Presbyterian Church [USA]). He holds the Chair in Reformed Theology at Pittsburgh Theological Seminary. Originally a member of the Church of Scotland, Purves moved to the United States in 1978 and was ordained in 1979. He served as pastor of the Hebron Presbyterian Church in Clinton, Pennsylvania, until 1983 when he began teaching at

suffers, we are thereby enabled by grace to participate in God's compassion for the world.[45] Our compassion, in other words, does not arise out of our meagre resources but is grounded in God's own capacious suffering love. This theological grounding in God is critically important, because human compassion is not large enough to meet the depth of another's true need. God alone can meet the need of the human restless heart, hence the timeless Augustinian dictum: "Our hearts are restless until they rest in thee."[46]

Expectations: *"Learn from Me" (Mt 11:25-30)*

The consecrated person is expected to replicate the life and ministry of Christ in the Apostles. To be totally consecrated to God means that one ought to "seek," "desire earnestly," "rekindle," and "employ" certain "spiritual" gifts that helps one in imitating the Lord (1 Cor 12:31; 14:1). Jesus could direct the attention of all who wished to practise the traits of Christian discipleship to Himself because He is Master of these virtues. He could say, "Learn from me." He who learns from Him is His *mathetes*.[47] To

---

Pittsburgh Theological Seminary. Purves' primary concerns surround Christology. He continually argues for a vital connection between the person and work of the Lord Jesus Christ in His vicarious humanity and the Christian life; a connection founded upon the believer's union with Christ. He wrote many theological books but this very one: *The Search for Compassion: Spirituality and Ministry*, is a very wonderful book. In it, Purves sees compassion through the lens of being God's hands and feet to show people Jesus.

[45] Read Andrew PURVES, *The Search for Compassion*, pp. 60-81.

[46] Saint Augustine, *The Confessions*, Trans. PIGON, J.K., (Garden City, New York: Image Books), p. 43, (Bk. 1, Ch. 1).

[47] mathētés (μαθητής)—a disciple (from math-, the "mental effort needed to think something through")—properly, a learner; a disciple, a follower of Christ who learns the

preach the cross is no simple task and, humanly speaking, Saint Paul did it masterfully. But in order to bear the cross, we do not look to Saint Paul but to Jesus, the author and finisher of our faith, for He bore it with and in love.

Christ is our example as we live lives of service to others in the various offices which we hold in relation to others. The imitation of Christ is expressed not so much by living a unique, "holy" life, antithetical to the world, as that one lives as "little Christ or other Christ" right within the world, in the specific vocation which God gives. Living as other Christ in a consecrated religious life is possible only when the four pillars or four components of religious life—*Consecratio, Oratio, Comunio, and Missio*—are blended with the four forms of prayer: *Lectio Divina, Oratio Contemplativa, Liturgia Horarum,* and *Missa.*[48]

---

doctrines of Scripture and the lifestyle they require; someone catechized with proper instruction from the Bible with its necessary follow-through (life-applications).
See http://biblehub.com/greek/3101.htm.

[48] For more details on the four pillars of religious life, read Mary Bride NJOKU, *Consecrated Life: A Renewed Insight* (London, 2016), pp. 19-22.

The Expression and Nourishment of this Relationship through the Four Forms of Prayer

To say that personal relationship with God is nourished by means of the Church's four forms of prayer is a fact which this Part Two intends to demonstrate. It is in the imitation of Christ who demonstrated this relationship so much in His life that the Church developed so many forms of prayer. All these different forms can be condensed in the following four fundamental ways:

- the praying of the Scriptures (technically known as *lectio divina*)
- letting the Spirit of God pray in us (*oratio contemplativa*—contemplative prayer)
- the praying of the Liturgy of the Hours (as a duet with God)
- and the praying of the Mass (as a covenant in His Blood)

These four fundamental ways, connectedly form a quadrilateral armor for the spiritual journey in the life of Christians. Besides, all four are helpful means to the fulfilment of one's duty as a religious as is envisaged in the Church's Law (c. 663 §1), which says that "the first and foremost duty of all religious is to be the contemplation of divine things and assiduous union with God in prayer." To achieve union with God, the Church recommends the practice of some pious exercises like: adoration of the Blessed Sacrament (c. 663 §2), praying the rosary (c. 663 §4), annual retreats (c. 663 §5), and frequenting of the Sacrament of Penance (c. 664). In addition to these, canon 663 §2-3 indicate those "special situations" in which a deep encounter with God will normally take place, they are: praying of the Scripture, contemplation, celebration of the Eucharist, and celebration of the Liturgy of the Hours. These are going to be the focus of our research in this Part Two. All four forms of prayer have a common source, conjoint means, and a shared purpose.

Lectio Divina and Contemplative Prayer: Processes of Growth in Relationship

The first two forms, the praying of the Scripture (*lectio divina*) and contemplation, are more of a personal exercise. They offer individuals opportunity for a deepening of the second two forms of prayer which are always prayed communally and in a celebrative mood.

While everyone is familiar to some degree with liturgical prayers (i.e., the Mass and the Liturgy of the Hours) and with devotional prayers (i.e., the rosary, novenas, etc.), few Christians today know the dynamic power in the Bible, through the method of prayer called *lectio divina* (divine reading) and so many "shun" both the word and the practice of contemplation. Contemplation is not a specialty of those who live in monasteries nor of the consecrated religious and priests. It is a way of praying and being for every Christian.

The Word is a powerful means of self-worth, because "Man is being created as hearer of the Word, and only in responding to the Word rises to his full dignity. He was conceived in the mind of God as a partner in a dialogue."[49] Accordingly, he should maintain this partnership with a prayerful dialogue with God. All too often our prayer begins with our concerns being voiced to God, words of need and hope. This, however, should not always be the case. The ancient practice of *lectio divina* takes for granted that we begin our prayer first by listening to God speak to us. Then, after we have heard God speak, we respond. Sometimes we respond by thanking and blessing God for the divine goodness showered upon us. Other times, we respond with an acknowledgment of our weakness and sinfulness. Yet other times, God's word reveals to us our previously unknown needs, needs of which we have now become all too aware. Thus we can see how the Word of God itself teaches us to pray, shows us what our greatest needs are, and opens us to the mysterious transforming power that reveals to us our deepest longings and desires, which leads to the prayer of abandonment in contemplation.

---

[49] Hans Urs von BALTHASAR, *Prayer* (New York: Paulist Press, 1976), pp. 18-19.

Chapter Three: Praying the Scriptures (*Lectio Divina*)

The Latin phrase "*lectio divina*," literally means "divine reading," which is simply the term for reading of a "holy," "spiritual," or "divine" nature. It is both a practice and a process, and there are many ways of doing it, but it essentially consists of reading Sacred Scripture. This ideally leads to prayer, to active service, to closer bonds with God in the gift of Himself in Christ Jesus.

Fr. Jean Leclercq defined *lectio divina* as a reading "about God, who for us is Christ: a reading, therefore, about Christ."[50] He went on to elaborate this point more by saying that Christ as Word is the Book—containing all the treasures of the divinity, and Christ is also the Book as man—for through His incarnation the Word becomes readable in Him. Christ, then, is the exemplar of our reading and the model in whom, according to the authority of Scripture, all is contained: "In your book all human beings are written. For the correction of our behavior we must study the example of his life. All should study that book for their own instruction."[51] But these alone Leclercq says will never result in *lectio divina*, a Christian reading, a reading in the Spirit, a reading of Christ and in Christ, with Christ and for Christ. There must first of all be the experience of love. *Lectio divina* is an act of love, an activity of love. The experience of Christ was essentially His

---

[50] Jean LECLERCQ, *Lectio Divina*, p. 244.
[51] PL 152:805, quote in Jean LECLERCQ, *Lectio Divina*, here pp. 242-243.

awareness of being loved by the Father and His return of that love. It was an exchange of love. So also is our divine reading, too, an exchange of love. That is why *lectio* is presented as a dialogue. Through Scripture, through the Book Jesus Christ, God speaks to us and we answer Him. *Lectio divina* is this dialogue of love.

Saint Bernard once wrote: "Today we are reading in the book of experience."[52] This experience of encounter between ourselves and Christ is essential to us because of the experience Christ had of encounter with the Father in the Spirit. Through our own experience, we shall be able to read Christ the Book and, in Him, God the Father because the heart of Christ is the heart of the Father.[53]

Therefore, *lectio divina* is an approach to meditative reading and praying of the Scripture. It is a way of encouraging the Spirit to lead us into pondering the deep truths hidden in God's Word. It is not an attempt to acquire knowledge or obtain more information, nor is it an exegetical study of the Bible, but it is an experiential process of allowing the Spirit of God to breathe into us life-giving truths to transform our thinking, feeling, and understanding of God and ourselves. Through the method of *lectio divina*, we move beyond just the words on a page to an encounter with an actual person, the living God in Christ.[54]

---

[52] Cf. Super Cantica, 3:1, Sancti Bernardi Opera I (Rome, 1957), pp. 16-17.

[53] In Dedicatione Ecclesiae, 5:4-5, Sancti Bernardi Opera V, (Rome, 1968), 391; Super Cantica, 62:5, II (Rome, 1958), 158.

[54] Our experience with *lectio divina* can be understood by the following analogy: A poster art fad surfaced in the early 90s which was called "magic-eye art." This popular and modern expression was composed of lines that were either straight or wavy, which resulted in a multi-colored geometric design. At an initial glance, it remained rather abstract, but by gazing

The purpose of *lectio divina* is to come into contact with God and let ourselves be transformed by His love. The fundamental attribute of *lectio divina* is its Spirit-driven nature. There are no rigid rules or compulsive techniques. Just as human intimacy must be natural and dialogical, so intimacy with God must flow freely and peacefully.

Historical Background of *Lectio Divina*

The practice of *lectio divina* has waxed and waned throughout the centuries. The roots of this form of prayer have been traced back to Judaism. Devout Jews are expected to know Holy Scripture (especially the first five books of the Bible known as the Pentateuch or Torah), to study it, and to take it into their hearts. This is summarized in the *Shema*, a fervent declaration of the Oneness of God, based on Deuteronomy 6:4-9: The *Shema* reminds us that the reality of God's presence must be written within our very hearts, and God's word should be with us wherever we are and in whatever we are doing. Bearing the Word of God within the heart comes about through the process of interiorisation, that is, not only listening to the Scriptures but also allowing them to sink into our hearts and transform us. At one time every Jewish male was expected to write out a copy of the Torah, because copying helps the memorisation process.

---

deeply for a while, and adjusting your focus, you are able to see "hidden" in the overall picture a three-dimensional object (e.g., a winged horse or airplane or eagle). A common response upon this discovery is a fervent, "Wow!" The practice and experience of *lectio divina* can yield a similar effect with Scripture and the Spirit of God.

See http://authenticdiscipleship.org/.

The Israelites used the Torah to pray the Word of God (*lectio divina*). Their method consisted in reading it, explaining it to the people, and then praying with it (cf. Neh 8). The Book of Deuteronomy records that "the word is very near to us; it is in our mouths and in our hearts; and that one should give expression to this Word of God by living it out" (Deut 30:14). By really listening to Scripture as it is read slowly and deliberately, and letting it soak and sink into one's heart during a time of silence, one learns to tune one's heart to the "gentle whisper" of God as Elijah did (1 Kg 19:12-18).

Many people experience encounter with God in the Scriptures, and such encounters call for a more radical obedience. Such obedience is formative, giving new direction to their lives. In the same way, a daily reading or encounter with the Word of God ought to draw us into the same Paschal Mystery first experienced by the people of Israel and then lived most fully by Jesus. Jesus was formed by the Word of God He heard in the domestic setting of His home and in the communal setting of the synagogue. It drew Him into communion with God whom He called Abba, and eventually led Him through the mystery of the cross to the glory of the resurrection. That is how *lectio divina* complements the celebration of the Eucharist. In the early days of the Christian community, this Jewish practice of everybody reading and reciting the Scriptures continued among the followers of "The Way" (as Christianity was first known).

The Desert Fathers and Mothers of early Christianity were also avid readers of the Bible. They would memorize parts of the Bible in order to meditate on them and to allow the Word of God, inscribed within their minds and hearts, to form them and help them turn gradually into saints by the grace of God.

When commenting on the praying of the Scriptures, the early Church Fathers appealed to Saint Paul's letter to the Romans (10:8-10) where he talked about the presence of God's word in the believer's mouth and heart. "The word...is very near to you, it is on your lips and in your heart." The movement went from reading to probing the heart's response to Christ in the Scriptures. This practice, which was in existence before the birth of Christ, received a technical name "*lectio divina*" from Origen (c. 185-254), a Father of the Church. He affirmed that in order to read the Bible profitably, it is necessary to do so with attention, constancy, and prayer. He considered *lectio* as the necessary foundation of the entire spiritual life, of understanding, and of contemplation. He did not present praying Scripture as one way among others. Nor did he consider it just a pious exercise. It is the special, concrete presence of the *Logos*, the Word, in our history. It is the voice of Christ and it is intended for every faithful Christian.[55]

Origen's practice of *lectio divina* got taken up by Saint Ambrose, who wrote, "We speak to God when we pray; we listen to God when we read his words" (*De Officiis Ministrorum* 1, 20, 88). Saint Augustine, commenting on Psalm 85, wrote, "Your prayer is a speaking with God. When you read, God speaks to you: when you pray, you speak to God" (*Enarratio* in Ps 85:7). Saint Benedict eventually inaugurated this variant of private Scriptural prayer for his monks. Origen (AD 185-254) and Saint Ambrose (AD 340-397) were credited with establishing the practice within

---

[55] Read Ernest J. FIEDLER, "*Lectio Divina*: Devouring God's Word," in *Liturgical Ministry* 5 (1996), pp. 65-69, here p. 65.

their cultures. Saint Benedict (AD 480-543), however, promoted and refined its use.[56] Saint Benedict, in his Rule for Monks,[57] wrote that sacred reading or prayerful reading (*lectione divina)* should occur at specific periods of time (*RB* 48:1); that the monks should listen readily to prayerful reading and devote themselves to prayer (*lectiones sanctas libenter audire, orationi frequenter incumbere* [*RB* 4:55-56]), and pray/read the Psalms after Vigils (*RB* 8:3). In addition, Benedict specified that sacred reading should occur during meals (*RB* 38:1) and at intervals when the community gathers, like after Vespers or before Compline. In this way, Saint Benedict recommended both private and communal *lectio divina.*

As the practice of *lectio divina* developed, some people attempted to set down guidelines so that others would be confirmed in good practice. The most famous "method" of *lectio* was set out in the twelfth century by a Carthusian monk called Guigo, also known as Guigo II, in his book *Scala Claustralium* (The Monk's Ladder).[58] Guigo believed that the "ladder" of *lectio* consisted of four rungs or stages, of which the first stage was *lectio* (reading). This meant

---

[56] Cf. Norvene VEST, *No Moment Too Small: Rhythms of Silence, Prayer, & Holy Reading* (Kalamazoo, MI: Cistercian Publications, 1994), pp. 59-62.

[57] The two critical editions of the Rule of Saint Benedict are: HANSLIK Rudolphus, (ed.) *Benedicti Regula*, CSEL LXXV, Wien 1977 and NEUFVILLE Jean, (ed.), *La Règle de Saint Benoît,* (Sources Chrétiennes, 181-182), Paris 1972.

[58] See Lettre sur la vie Contemplative (L'échelle des Moines). Douze Méditations, ed. E. Colledge and J. Walsh, Sources Chrétiennes 163, (Paris, 1970). Guigo II De CASTRO, *The Ladder of Monks and Twelve Meditations*, trans. Edmund COLLEDGE, OSA, and James WALSH, SJ (Garden City, NY: Doubleday, Image Books, 1978).

listening to (not necessarily just reading) a passage from the Bible or another spiritual text several times. The second stage Guigo identified was *meditatio* (meditation). This meant reflecting upon the passage and its meaning. The third stage is *oratio* (prayer) inspired by the passage which turns us to God. Guigo said that the final stage of *lectio*—in fact the reason we do it at all—is *contemplatio* (contemplation). This is a stage that we cannot bring about by ourselves. Rather, we have to wait for that grace from God, and silence is often recommended as an aid to this.

This ancient practice of *lectio divina* has been preserved and kept alive in the Christian monastic tradition, and is one of the precious treasures of Benedictine monastics. But it was not meant only for monks and nuns nor is reading the Bible only for religious professionals. Monasteries have long been known as places for preserving valuable cultures; so also, they preserve practices like *lectio,* which became the main stream of their spiritualties. For example, every religious community in the Middle Ages practiced *lectio divina* in one form or another, though perhaps not always under that title. Religious regulations, including the Rule of Saint Benedict and the Carmelite Rule of Saint Albert, stipulated that the monk, friar, or nun should give time to holy reading, either on their own or in a group. Pioneers among such Bible meditation (*lectio divina*) were the Benedictine, Cistercian, and Carthusian Orders. Perhaps, because the monastic and desert life kept this Christian practice alive, some Church leaders at the time believed that reading the Bible was meant for religious professionals, and for a long time—particularly during the Reformation—bishops decided that ordinary people could not be "trusted" to read the Bible without supervision from trained clerics. For this reason *lectio divina* declined as a practice for many centuries and reading the Scriptures was wrongly seen as something uniquely "Protestant." In place of reading the Scriptures, devotions such as the rosary developed, (the recitation of the Hail Mary 150 times corresponding to the 150 Psalms). Other forms of devotional practices sprung up as a way of substituting the reading of the Bible. Vatican II and subsequent popes have brought back the fervor in the faithful and a new appreciation of the Word of God as a source of life and spiritual nourishment.

The Validity of the Traditional Stages of *Lectio Divina*

In the early Church, *lectio divina* was a common—often the most basic—form of personal prayer for the Christian people. In fact, it is perhaps one of the oldest forms of Christian prayers. It consists in reading the Divine Word and that is why it is called *lectio divina*. It is called "divine" because it deals with Holy Scripture. Moreover, for the ancient and medieval Church, Scripture is never separated from the interpretation given to it by tradition. So *lectio divina* deals not only with the Bible itself, but with the commentaries given and written on it by the Fathers, who are known as the *expositores*: they have explained the Bible. In the Middle Ages this same notion of *expositores* was used for contemporary authors—that is, the more recent ones, such as the Carolingians, Saint Bernard, and so forth.[59]

The first step of *lectio divina* is appropriately called **lectio** (reading). At this point, it is important to distinguish

---

[59] Read Jean LECLERCQ, "Meditation as a Biblical Reading," pp. 562-563.

between praying and reading. Quite simply, when we pray we speak to God, and when we read God speaks to us. Thus, *lectio* is not ordinary reading. It involves listening to or the hearing of Scripture; importance should be given to listening (*ausculta*) to the word rather than reading it. In other words, it is reverential listening. We need to realize that within the context of *lectio*, reading of Scripture is something different than what we normally do when we read a book. Often, we read a book for information or as a means of entertainment. But in *lectio* we personalize the words and understand them as God speaking at that moment to us. In practice, the readings of the day's Mass are a good basis for choice. Having a predetermined set of readings helps us to avoid choosing the passages that we like because they are "comfortable."

The second step is known as **meditatio** (meditation). It has been pointed out that in *lectio,* the content of the reading is the Bible. As regards the manner of reading, we have different ways in different periods in history. In biblical times, in the patristic period, and in the medieval era, meditation was an exercise of the memory which fixed a text into the memory by dint of pronouncing it, of pronouncing it again, and if necessary, again and again, in order to keep it in the mind, to taste it, to feel it and to savour it. This is exactly what underlies the saying: "*Sapientia: id est cognitio vel lectio sapida*" (Wisdom means a well-relished cognition or reading). In addition, until a relatively recent epoch, men used to read with the voice more than with the eyes. They understood a thing, not when seeing it written, but when hearing it pronounced by themselves. The lips moved, the body entered into action and took possession of the text by expressing it. This operation of pronouncing the words was the "meditation" proper.[60] To more fully explain this point, Fr. Leclercq quoted Psalm 36:30: "The just man's mouth utters wisdom and his lips speak what is right." This same Psalm verse appears as an Introit in the *Graduale Romanum* in a slightly varied form: "The *mouth* of the just man *meditates* wisdom, and his tongue utters what is right (*Os justi meditabitur sapientiam, et lingua ejus loquetur judicium)*. So in this varied form it is the mouth, *os, that* meditates the wisdom: "*Os meditabitur.*"[61] Even today, as a matter of fact, many of those who have not yet dissociated the activity of the eyes and the activity of the mouth still pronounce the words when they read them, and it is only when it is done this way are they capable of retaining them. For them, that is meditation. It works differently for different people.

Meditation has also been described as ruminating, pondering, and pronouncing the text.[62] Ruminating simply means chewing the cud. A cow, for example, regurgitates a mouthful of previously swallowed food and slowly chews it a second time. Thus, chewing the cud has come to mean recalling and thinking over the text so as to listen or search for connections, from the biblical context to our context. *Lectio* has given us information about this text, but the Word of God is the Word of Life, not just the word of knowledge. So now we have to let it touch our lives. In *lectio* we struggle to master the Word, but we do this only

---

60 Read Jean LECLERCQ, "Meditation as a Biblical Reading," p. 563.
61 Graduale Triplex, Solesmis (1973). The Introit is for *Commune Doctorum Ecclesiae*, p. 494.
62 Cf. Luke DYSINGER, O.S.B., "Accepting the Embrace of God: The Ancient Art of *Lectio Divina,*" Valyermo Benedictine (Spring, 1990), pp. XX-XXI.

so that the Word might master us. In *meditatio* we look for points of contact between the plans of God as it unfolds in the Bible and then in our lives as they disclose facts; these may be confirming, or they may be challenging. We need to listen to what God is saying to us, today.

The third step is **oratio.** If we keep in mind that the content of *lectio* is the Holy Bible and the work of *meditatio* is ruminating, pondering, and pronouncing the text of the Bible, then we are in the position to understand many ancient texts when they speak of *oratio.* Saint Benedict, for example, says that *oratio* has to be *"brevis et pura"* (short and pure [*RB* 20:4a]). Fr. Leclercq explained that the word *"pura"* (pure) means without distraction, according to John Cassian[63] and the traditional authors, who were the sources of Saint Benedict.[64] In order to keep prayer "pure," it has to be "short" because for most men, even in ancient times, it is impossible to remain a long time without distractions. Having spent enough time in *lectio* and meditation, prayer proper should be short. However, Saint Benedict went on to say that prayer could be prolonged under the inspiration of divine grace (*nisi forte ex affectu inspirationis divinae gratiae protendatur* [*RB* 20:4b]), meaning

---

[63] John Cassian (c. AD 360-435), was a Christian monk and theologian celebrated in both the Western and Eastern Churches for his mystical writings. Cassian is noted for bringing the ideas and practices of Egyptian monasticism to the early medieval West. His achievements and writings influenced Saint Benedict, who incorporated many of the principles into his monastic rule and recommended to his own monks that they read the works of Cassian. Since Benedict's rule is still followed by Benedictines, Cistercians, and Trappists monks, John Cassian's thought still exercises influence over the spiritual lives of thousands of men and women in the Latin Church. He died in 435 at Marseille.

[64] Jean LECLERCQ, "Meditation as a Biblical Reading," p. 564.

that it is only by God's grace that an undistracted prayer could be sustained for a longer period.

Moreover, having read and understood the Word of God, having reflected on it, and seen how it speaks to us, it is only natural that we should react to what we have discovered. *Oratio* is nothing but our reaction to the Word, and it is our turn to speak to God. It may be spontaneous repentance and a re-commitment, when we see how far our lives are from the values inherent in the Word. We may be struck by God's sheer goodness, and pray in thanks, or we may pray for forgiveness of the areas where we are lacking. The practice of *lectio* is not a *monologue* but a *dialogue* with God because it brings about a two-way conversation. It brings the words that our mind heard during the first two steps into the heart. Bringing the mind into the heart means bringing the Word of God into the innermost core of our lives. Thus, we link our heart to God. This will evoke a response from the deepest part of our inner being. Our response may include wonder, regret, surrender, and other feelings that will culminate in a yearning to be in relationship with God.

The last traditional step is **contemplatio.** The word "contemplation"—and the traditional tag attached to it—may make us want to reject it as a monastic or mystic specialty, but this is not the case, it is a method of praying for every Christian. In the previous steps, we have tried to understand the meaning of our text. Now it is time to let it engage our lives in the present, to let it encourage a response from God who has long ago begun a relationship with us. This is the point of *contemplatio*. There is nothing more that we can do, except to let God have His way, to be still and let Him do it. For materialistic minded people, this can be a difficult and sometimes apparently fruitless and useless discipline, but it is an essential prelude to action. We simply give God a chance to work within us—to sit still quietly and humbly in God's presence, allowing Him to touch us. *Contemplatio*, to the extent that it involves effort on our part, is our consent to God transforming us. It is characterized by an openness of the heart, by which the reader experiences God as the One who prays within, who allows the person in contemplation to know the Word wordlessly and without image.

So the first step of *lectio divina*, which began with reading the word, now ends with an astonishing intimacy with God. There is nothing left but to move to action— action that will bring healing to us and to others. This means that we need to let others see what we see, hear what we hear, feel what we feel, and be transformed as we are by a loving embrace that causes us to keep coming back to the practice of *lectio divina* again and again.

The additional fifth step is called **actio.** Strictly speaking, we need not consider *actio* to be a step in the process of *lectio divina*. It is, rather, an essential result of the encounter with God in the Sacred Scripture; that is, it is the renewal of life which is the entire purpose of *lectio divina*. As Pope Benedict XVI wrote in his Post-Synodal Apostolic Exhortation *Verbum Domini*: "We do well also to remember that the process of *lectio divina* is not concluded until it arrives at action (*actio*), which moves the believer to make his or her life a gift for others in charity" (*VD* 87). Having received God's love and grace, we go forth to serve others out of the love we have been given. Our transformation calls us to witness to others; it calls us to selflessly serve our brothers and sisters in Christ. These acts are done not so much out of a sense of duty, but out of the inspiration we receive from the acceptance in faith of God's love.

Equally, Fr. Hayden held that commitment to living the words of Scripture could be considered a fifth element in the process of *lectio divina*, because without it the whole process would be radically incomplete and a worthless effort. He says:

> The word of God is for transformation rather than information. It is for life and for living. Likewise, *lectio divina* teaches us not just how to pray, but how to live. While we need to devote specific times to it, *lectio divina* is not an activity which stands alone. The word of God cannot be a hobby or a special interest, but must touch our lives in a concrete and tangible way. Far from setting up a closed circuit, a cosy tête-à-tête between ourselves and God, praying the Scriptures opens us out, in a new and demanding way, to the world.[65] Prayer and action are completely inseparable. The words, groans and aspirations which make up our prayer need to translate itself into the warp and woof of our daily living.[66]

Consequently, having gone thus far to explain this gradual step-by-step process of *lectio divina*, it must be sincerely mentioned that *lectio divina* is not meant to be a kind of straitjacket, dictating the details of how we pray. Although there is the above mentioned traditional step-by-step manner presentation, any given period of prayer with the Bible may not be quite so ordered. In practice,

---

[65] Christopher HAYDEN, *Praying the Scriptures: A Practical Introduction to Lectio Divina* (London: St. Pauls, 2001), p. 106.

[66] Christopher HAYDEN, *Praying the Scriptures*, p. 19.

we will often be doing *meditatio*, reflecting on a passage, even as we read it. At other times, the first contact with a verse of Scripture may lead us straight into prayer. Again, there may be the odd occasion when, no sooner have we opened our Bible, than we feel moved to sit quietly in contemplation as experienced by some people at other times. When there is an effortless, inner movement in our time of prayer with the Bible, we should follow it, rather than anxiously trying to conform to a rigid, step-by-step pattern.

In view of this, it might be helpful to consider the different steps in *lectio divina* as components, rather than strictly as steps which must necessarily follow each other. Without a doubt, the "normal" route we follow will be a progression—or a struggle to progress—through the steps of *lectio divina*, but they are given to guide us rather than to bind us.[67] Summarizing the various steps, I would like succinctly to see them in this way:

- *Silentium* - be aware of God's presence
- *Lectio* - read the text
- *Meditatio* - chew it
- *Oratio* - pray it
- *Contemplatio* - be still and let God pray in you
- *Actio* - live it out in your life

At the end of the day, *lectio divina* remains for us a useful and very fruitful form of Scriptural prayer.

The Church in Modern Times and the Practice of *Lectio Divina*

We have demonstrated thus far that the Jewish and Christian experiences of God both follow the same pattern: Divine initiative and human response. This belief

---

[67] See Christopher HAYDEN, *Praying the Scriptures*, p. 77.

is well captured by the Johannine passage in 1 John 4:9: "We are to love because he first loved us." Even the creation story has the same pattern. Repeatedly it says: "God said, 'Let there be...' And so it was" (Gen 1). Scripture is the witness of God's dialogue with human beings. Hence the Letter to the Hebrews says: "At various times in the past and in various different ways, God spoke to our ancestors through the prophets; but in our own time, the last days, he has spoken to us through his Son" (Heb 1:1). Scripture contains God's Word. However, it is not just a document that records what has happened in the past. It is the Word of God for us.

The Dogmatic Constitution on Divine Revelation *Dei Verbum* of Vatican II was promulgated by Pope Paul VI in 1965. It is the Church's declaration on how God reveals Himself to His people. In *DV* 21, the Council Fathers stress that God turns to us in words of the Scripture, speaks to us and picks up the conversation with us. They, (Council Fathers) were intent on retaining and reviving this ancient tradition of praying the Word of God when they said: "Let them remember that prayer should accompany the reading of the sacred scripture, so that *a dialogue takes place between God and man.* For 'we speak to him when we pray; we listen to him when we read the divine oracles.'"[68] That extraordinary document *Dei Verbum* admonishes priests and those officially engaged in ministry to "hold fast to the sacred Scriptures through diligent sacred reading and careful study" (§25). The text then proceeds to exhort all the faithful to do likewise, learning the "excelling knowledge of Jesus Christ" (Phil 3:8) and to "gladly

---

[68] "The Fathers are in turn citing St. Ambrose," *De Officiis ministrorum* I, 20, 88: PL 16, 50.

put themselves in touch with the sacred text itself...and let them remember that prayer should accompany the reading of sacred Scripture..." (§25). *Optatam Optius* (the Decree on Priestly Training) says that those preparing to be leaders in the Christian community as priests should "be taught to look for Christ in...faithful meditation on God's word..." (§8). *Perfectae Caritatis* (the Decree on the Adaptation and Renewal of Religious Life) says that religious should first of all "take the sacred Scriptures in hand each day by way of attaining 'the excellent knowledge of Jesus Christ' (Phil 3:8) through reading these divine writings and meditating on them" (§6). Even these few brief references make clear to us that the Council Fathers urged primacy for assiduous *lectio* and urged that it be practised daily. All indicators seem to point to this method of prayer as basic to learning to pray and advancing in the life of the Spirit of Jesus.

A frequent personal contact with the Word of God is the basic receptiveness which ought to complement the divine self-revelation of God through the prophets and in the Son Christ Jesus (Heb 1:1-2). Together they open the door to the "surpassing knowledge of Jesus Christ," to a deep personal knowledge of God, which serves as a catalyst to loving the Father through the Son. In this way, the Church teaches us that the Scriptures are just as much part of the bread of life as is the Body of Christ in the Eucharist.

The Eucharist or Mass feeds us from both the reading of Scripture and the Body and Blood of our Lord. When we read the Scriptures at home, in addition to what we hear at Mass, *lectio divina* becomes a continuation of that feeding from God. Moreover, *Dei Verbum* has given us a vibrant spirituality of the word, teaching us to understand the Liturgy of the Word as a focal point of the celebration of the Sunday Eucharist. It speaks about the sacred liturgy nourishing the faithful from the table of both the Word of God and of the Body of Christ (*DV 21*).

In his Post-Synodal Apostolic Exhortation *Vita Conse-crata*, Saint John Paul II dedicated a whole paragraph on the importance of listening to the Word of God by every Christian faithful, especially by religious men and women.

> The word of God is the first source of all Christian spirituality. It gives rise to a personal relationship with the living God and with his saving and sanctifying will. It is for this reason that from the very beginning of Institutes of Consecrated Life, and in a special way in monasticism, what is called *lectio divina* has been held in the highest regard. By its means the word of God is brought to bear on life, on which it projects the light of that wisdom which is a gift of the Spirit. ...Meditation of the Bible *in common* is of great value. When practised according to the possibilities and circumstances of life in community, this meditation leads to a joyful sharing of the riches drawn from the word of God, thanks to which brothers or sisters grow together and help one another to make progress in the spiritual life. Indeed it would be helpful if this practice were also encouraged among other members of the People of God, priests and laity alike. This will lead, in ways proper to each person's particular gifts, to setting up schools of prayer, of spirituality and of prayerful reading of the Scriptures, in which God "speaks to people as friends (cf. *Ex* 33:11; *Jn* 15:14-15) and lives among them (cf.

> *Bar* 3:38), so that he may invite and draw them
> into fellowship with himself" (*VC* 94).

In his apostolic letter *Novo Millennio Ineunte* (39), Saint
John Paul II in reminding bishops, clergy, and lay people of
the old kind of Christian prayer, noted that "holiness and
prayer is inconceivable without a renewed listening to the
word of God... It is especially necessary that listening to
the word of God should become a life-giving encounter, in
the ancient and ever valid tradition of *lectio divina*, which
draws from the biblical text the living word which questions, directs and shapes our lives."

A hallmark of the pontificate of Pope Benedict XVI is
his call for Christians to return to a prayerful study of the
Scriptures. On 16 September 2005 in an address to the
International Congress commemorating the 40th anniversary of *Dei Verbum*, the Vatican II document on divine
revelation, Pope Benedict XVI said:

> I would like especially to recall and to recom-
> mend the ancient tradition of *lectio divina*: the
> assiduous reading of Sacred Scripture accom-
> panied by prayer brings about that intimate
> dialogue (colloquy) where, by reading, we listen
> to God who speaks and, in prayer, we respond
> to Him with confident openness of heart (cf. *DV*
> 25). This practice, if effectively promoted, will
> bring to the Church—of this I am convinced—a
> new spiritual spring. As a firm point of biblical
> pastoral ministry, *Lectio Divina* should for this
> reason be further encouraged, through the use,
> too, of new methods, carefully considered, that
> are fully up to-date. We ought never to forget

> that the Word of God is a lamp to our feet and a
> light to our path (cf. Ps 118/119:105).[69]

The Church today is very much intent on reclaiming this ancient practice of *lectio divina*. A good example of this is the theme of the 12th General Assembly of the Synod of Bishops (5-26 October 2008): "The Word of God in the Life and Mission of the Church." This is not just a partial reference to the importance of the Word of God—we might illustrate something of the growing *crescendo* by noting that the first discussion paper sent to the bishops (the *Lineamenta*) includes several references to *lectio divina,* and the working paper for the Assembly (the *Instrumentum Laboris*) also contains some references, and includes a full section (§38) on the topic. The Bishops' Message to the People of God at the conclusion of their Assembly (October 24) goes on to give a helpful description of Guigo's four stages of the traditional elements of *lectio divina* (read §9).[70] At the end of the synod the pope observes that praying Scripture draws us into a deeper encounter with the Living God through the Word.

> Let us now remain silent, to hear the word of
> God with effectiveness and let us maintain this
> silence after hearing, so that it may continue to
> dwell in us, to live in us, and to speak to us. Let
> it resonate at the beginning of our day so that

---

[69] Pope Benedict XVI to the International Congress on Dei Verbum, 16 September 2005.

[70] The various documents relating to the 12th Synod are available on the Vatican website. http://www.vatican.va/roman_curia/synod/ index.htm.

God has the first word and let it echo in us in the evening so that God has the last word.[71]

Furthermore, in his Post-Synodal Apostolic Exhortation *Verbum Domini* of 30 September 2010, Pope Benedict encouraged anew the Christian faithful on the importance of *lectio divina* and its capacity to bring about a personal encounter with Christ, the living Word of God. He therefore re-elaborated the four traditional stages of *lectio*. He said:

> I would like here to review the basic steps of this procedure. It opens with the reading (*lectio*) of a text, which leads to a desire to understand its true content: *what does the biblical text say in itself?* Without this, there is always a risk that the text will become a pretext for never moving beyond our own ideas. Next comes meditation (*meditatio*), which asks: *what does the biblical text say to us?* Here, each person, individually but also as a member of the community, must let himself or herself be moved and challenged. Following this comes prayer (*oratio*), which asks the question: *what do we say to the Lord in response to his word?* Prayer, as petition, intercession, thanksgiving and praise, is the primary way by which the word transforms us. Finally, *lectio divina* concludes with contemplation (*contemplatio*), during which we take up, as a gift from God, his own way of seeing and judging reality, and ask ourselves *what conversion of mind, heart and life is the Lord asking of us?* In the *Letter to the Romans*, Saint Paul tells us: "Do not

---

[71] Pope Benedict XVI, XII Ordinary Assembly of the Synod of Bishops, 27 October 2008.

be conformed to this world, but be transformed
by the renewal of your mind, that you may prove
what is the will of God, what is good and acceptable and perfect" (12:2). Contemplation aims at
creating within us a truly wise and discerning
vision of reality, as God sees it, and at forming
within us "the mind of Christ" (1*Cor* 2:16). The
word of God appears here as a criterion for dis-
cernment: it is "living and active, sharper than
any two-edged sword, piercing to the division
of soul and spirit, of joints and marrow, and discerning the thoughts and intentions of the heart"
(*Heb* 4:12) (*VD* 87).

The Church is bringing to the believer's awareness
the importance of *lectio divina,* and therefore she is
re-emphasizing its importance to every sector of the
Christian life. An example of this is that the Church con-
siders *lectio divina* to be an important form of continuing
catechesis. According to the *General Directory for Catechesis*, the Church desires that "the study and exploration
of Sacred Scripture, read not only in the Church but with
the Church and her living faith, should help to discover
divine truth, which it contains, in such a way as to arouse a
response of faith, and the '*lectio divina*' is an eminent form
of this vital study of Scripture"(*GDC* 71).[72]

Judged from this little expose, it is clear that *lectio
divina* has been recommended enthusiastically by Pope
Saint John Paul II, Benedict XVI, as well as the Pontifical
Biblical Commission and the Catholic *Catechism* (nos.
1177, 2708). Karl A. Schultz has also noted that *lectio*

---

[72] Congregation for the Clergy, *General Directory for Catechesis*
(1971).

divina has also been promoted by the Catholic Biblical Federation and Cardinal Carlo Martini, S.J., Archbishop Emeritus of Milan and a renowned biblical scholar. Of Cardinal Martini, Schultz said, "he has published over forty books on the subject and fostered awareness and practice throughout the world. He gave an outstanding presentation on *lectio divina* to the U.S. bishops at a conference in Collegeville, Minnesota in 1986."[73] If such Church's officials have spoken plausibly on *lectio divina*, it then shows that it is not only a monastic treasure but a pearl of priceless value for the whole Christian faithful. In fact Saint Augustine of Hippo's phrase "ever ancient, ever new" describes the renewed interest in praying with Scripture that has re-emerged in today's Church.

The Need for Both Private and Communal *Lectio Divina*

Once when I was challenging someone about the indispensable need for reading and praying the Bible (*lectio divina*) privately, he surprisingly, threw back an unexpected question: "Given that we encounter Christ in the liturgies of the Church, why do you Benedictines emphasize individual *lectio* in private as well as *lectio* in the community?" That was a clever question indeed. It could be said that someone who listens to the Word through the Liturgy in a prayerful manner has already done enough *lectio* for the day. That might be true. However, there are some reasons why private *lectio* is also important.

- The first is that private reading exposes us to more passages from the Bible than are possible from the

---

[73] Read Karl A. SCHULTZ, Catholic Diocese of Christchurch, https://chchcatholic.nz/.

snatches we hear in communal reading. We therefore appreciate the Bible in a wider context and are
more able to link our public worship of God to our
private relationship with God.

- The second is that Jesus wants to develop a direct
personal friendship with us individually. There are
things that Jesus wants to say to us personally in the
heart—and one of the surest ways for that to happen
is through our private meditation on the Scriptures.

- Thirdly, *lectio* at home on a daily basis enables us
regularly to be challenged, comforted, and inspired
at a personal level. *Lectio* is an aid to fostering conversation with the one whom we know loves us.

- The fourth reason is that *lectio* is the most wonderful experience and can very often lead to an emotional outpouring of some sort—whether that is
repentance at the recognition of some deep-rooted
sinful attitude or sheer joy. Tears are not uncommon
with *lectio* because it opens our hearts to the healing
presence of God, and tears can sometimes be more
easily shed in private.

- Listening to the Word of God in Scripture (*lectio
divina*) privately is a way of cultivating friendship
with Christ. It is a way of listening to the texts of
Scripture as if we were in conversation with Christ,
and He was suggesting the topics of conversation.
The daily encounter with Christ and reflection on
His Word leads beyond mere acquaintanceship to an
attitude of friendship, trust, and love. Conversation
simplifies and gives way to communing.

Besides the private practice of *lectio* in religious houses
today, *lectio divina* can provide a simple yet prayerful

method for faith sharing among Christians/religious at every stage of life.

The Word opens us to the voice of God beckoning each of us in a unique and wondrous way along the path to glory. Those who daily engage in *lectio* experience how recurring the movement is. As we read the Word in preparation for the Eucharistic celebration, its enrichment keeps drawing us back to daily reflection on the divine word. *Lectio divina* feeds and nourishes our celebration of the Eucharist, calling us back time and time again to experience its power to touch our lives in truly blessed ways.

Prayer is best understood as a dialogue or conversation between God and a person. All too often our prayer begins with our concerns being voiced to God, words of need and hope. The ancient practice of *lectio* takes for granted that we begin by first listening to God speak to us. Then after we have heard God speak, we respond. Thus the Word of God itself teaches us to pray, shows us what our greatest needs are, and opens us to the mysterious transforming power that reveals to us our deepest longings and desires. Reflecting and praying with these texts in the course of the week can then bring a powerful sense of prayer to the Sunday Liturgy.

While *oratio* is personal, it is not self-absorbed. It is personal, flowing from the Word of God, through us, and then back again to God. Communally, the Word of God is capable of providing answers to our problems, both communal and pastoral. Hence, Pope Benedict XVI stresses that the Word of God addresses life, and does so concretely:

> It is decisive, from the pastoral standpoint, to present the word of God in its capacity to enter into dialogue with the everyday problems which

> people face...we need to make every effort to share the word of God as an openness to our problems, a response to our questions, a broadening of our values and the fulfillment of our aspirations (*VD* 23).

To make this a reality, we need to abandon the potentially arrogant position of being a textual expert and become a disciple who not only reads but also prays with these words, who hears them not only in an auditory manner but also with the ears of the heart. The fruits of this being-with-and-in-the-text, flow forth in our actions; it becomes second nature and is reflected in our deeds, in our apostolates and pastoral ministries.

The Crucial Need for *Lectio Divina* in the Life of Christians

A story was once told of a poor widow whose only son left home to make his fortune in America. She never complained about how little she had and cheerfully accepted assistance from people in her small town. From time to time, people would ask her, "Can't your son help you in your need?" She always defended him. One day she opened up to someone and said: "You know, my son is a good boy, but he needs his money. He writes me twice a month and sends me some pictures of men I do not even know. I keep them in my Bible." This person asked to see the pictures. It turns out that the pictures were money. By then she had plenty of money to live lavishly the rest of her life. She had a treasure and did not even know it.

Analogically, this is exactly how some Christians are living their lives; they have a treasure that they are not even aware of—the Bible—nor do they value it. Imagine that God is transmitting a radio signal to the world. In order to hear it, you would have to have a radio. Not only that, you would have to tune it to the proper channel. Besides, you would have to turn on the radio and actually listen to it. How wonderful that would be. The fact is that God has done just that in the Bible. It is God's living word that has an amazing power to change our lives. It is not enough to have a Bible in our home, we have to use it and pray it. Praying the Bible, i.e., *lectio divina,* is one of the most effective ways of using the treasures in our hands.

Today, consecrated men and women, priests and lay faithful are facing delicate challenges. While our personal experiences make us sense the need for a prayerful reading of the Bible and the people look to us for direction, we still have difficulty in giving a response because we ourselves were never given a preparation for reading the Bible as prayer. There are many difficulties in our apostolates as religious, and pastoral pressures often lead us to read the Bible more for others than for ourselves. We have too little time to stop and allow the Word to penetrate into our own lives. Often, our way of reading smacks more of study and discussion than of meditation and prayer. Also, there is a certain rationalism in us and some forms of fundamentalism, which disturb us with questions like: Did it really happen that way? How could God allow that to happen? All of this makes peaceful attention to the Word of God more difficult.

Along these same lines, the Scriptures speak of Mary as having the openness to the Word of God as it unfolded in her life. At the visit of the shepherds in Bethlehem, "Mary treasured all these things and pondered them in her heart" (Lk 2:19). After finding Jesus in the temple with the elders, the text tells us that, "his mother stored up all these things in her heart" (Lk 2:51). When something speaks to the heart, it raises probing questions, moves us to wonder deeply, to think intensely, and to pray passionately. That is exactly how the Scriptures are meant to speak to our hearts.

Lectio divina is an urgent task if we are to be faithful to what God is asking of us today. It is something like curing the veins so that the blood which keeps us alive is able to flow.

To this end we offer some suggestions:

- It will do us good to read what the Dogmatic Constitution *Dei Verbum* says, directly and indirectly, about *lectio divina*—the prayerful reading of the Bible (§25).
- For personal and daily reading of the Bible, each person has to gradually develop his/her own way of communicating with the Word of God.
- When doing *lectio* communally, it is advisable to follow the traditional stages of *lectio, meditatio, oratio,* and *contemplatio,* just for the sake of maintaining unity and keeping the group focused.
- *Lectio divina* can provide us with the consistent opportunity and necessary time to return to the essentials, to the cornerstone which is Christ, and to search for God who is the real reason for Christian life in the first place.
- Taking time to reflect on the Scripture passages assigned for the Sunday celebration can greatly enhance one's participation.
- It must be emphasized that the practice of *lectio divina* has no direct apostolic utility, like homily preparation. It is solely meant to have an enriching effect on one's personal life. As one reads and invites

the Word to become a transforming lens that brings the events of daily living into focus, one can come to live more deeply and find the presence of God more readily in the events of each day.

Lectio divina is a way of prayer and because prayer is always a very personal and intimate activity, *lectio* will itself take on a very personal character proper to each person who makes use of this method. For this reason, each person must discover the way that works best for him or her. The needs of different individuals are different, and indeed, the needs even of the same individual are different at different times.

To contemplate the Word and to make it present in our lives is one of our greatest challenges. To pray with the Word is also to proclaim it. The Word prayed is not only for me: I must share it, I must make it live. Besides, we must not forget that biblical prayer should finally centre us on the person of Jesus. Jacques Guillet remarked that:

> In our listening to the Gospels, the most profound and rigorous knowledge of the gospel's words is insufficient and deceptive without our gaze being fixed on the living Person, without the direct contemplation of the Lord. The irreplaceable value of the gospels, the mark of their authenticity, is precisely that they always prevent us from separating the words from the Word.[74]

---

[74] Jacques GUILLET, cited by Brother Álvaro Rodríguez Echeverría, Superior General of the Lasallians, "Reading reality in the light of the Word: *Lectio Divina* for Lasallians," Secretariat "Being Brothers Today," La Salle Generalate (Rome, Italy, 2009).

Lectio divina runs counter to our modern tendency to view the Bible scientifically, that is, as a document to be read like studying for a test and trying to remember the facts. The goal is to experience God's presence, not for me to get data to use. It is to let the text shape us as we read it. The reading of the Scriptures is an essential part of daily life; hence, it is the pathway to *conversatio morum* (conversion of life), and for an ongoing formation which is part and parcel of every Christian life. Reflection on the Word of God, if done intensely and prayerfully, possesses the power of calling people to continual conversion of life. This is so because there is dynamism in the Word of God that is capable of renewing, re-creating, and forming us by its unique and mysterious power. This is the reason why *lectio divina* has something wonderful to offer anyone who practises it. *Lectio divina* is a way of praying the Scriptures so that we listen carefully, each day, to what God wants to say to us—personally and as a community—about our life and our work.

The Difference Between Studying the Scriptures and Praying the Scriptures (*Lectio Divina*)

Before noting the difference between studying and praying the Scriptures, we must first say that there is a time and place for both, but one way should not be substituted or forgotten in favour of the other. The studying aspect might typically happen on first reading. For example, we may be reading an essential text only as a study, after which we might shift our attention towards a particular word or sentence that shines out to us. Such reading can provide us with divine, direct disclosures that at once reveal and conceal the overall plan of God for our lives. The following chart should make the complementarity of these two ways clear.

Studying the Scriptures	Praying the Scriptures (*Lectio Divina*)
Point of Comparison: *Modus operandi*	
In studying the Scriptures, one tries to take in as much as possible, to fill up, and to devour voraciously. In a word, its *modus operandi* is quantitative.	*Lectio divina* in the real sense follows a "method-less method," because, one chews the word over and over again, being open to moments when God Himself immediately directs His Word suddenly to one's attention. Sometimes the text seems to jump off the page and touches one's heart in a deep spot. Within this meditative stage, the key distinction is how the application arrives: one does not derive or devise the application from the passage; rather, it is something that comes to a person, from the text, directly from the Spirit of God alone. The Spirit breathes wherever and whenever He wills, one cannot ascribe any method to the ways and dictates of the Spirit of God. The sooner one senses the Spirit's moving in one's heart, the better the one can discern a true case of this divine movement rather than one's human machinations.

Tempus	
Here it is regulated by the clock. One has only a given amount of time to get it in and only this much time to get out the meaning of what one has read.	A shift takes place here from *chronos* (cosmic time or time in general) to *kairos* (proper time).[75] One is not looking for anything in particular. One does not have a set purpose in mind. One is open to what may come. One lets God take the initiative through the text.
Character	
Here the Bible is seen as a treasure trove of doctrinal truths and as a catalog of God's utterances.	It is primarily communication of God—communication in the literal sense: God Himself communes with us. He wants us to experience communion with Him.[76] As one comes to God's Word, one is not just studying recorded history, but is engaged in a personal communication and communion with God.

---

[75] Christian reflection on time has been influenced by the distinction in classical Greek thought between two kinds of time: *chronos* and *kairos*. *Chronos* translates the experience of time as duration, as chronological progression and continuity, while *kairos* refers to time as opportunity or occasion; it is a time that has a special significance or potential—the "right time," a favourable moment, or critical period, a time of grace. Cf. J. WHITEHEAD, "An Asceticism of Time," in *Review for Religious* 39 (1980) 3-17, here p. 6.

[76] See Gerhard MAIER, *Biblical Hermeneutics*, trans. Robert Yarbrough (Wheaton, IL: Crossway, 1994), p. 55.

Key	
Here the key to understanding the Bible is more of human mind and intelligence and not necessarily the heart.	According to the Bible, as far as human responsibility is concerned, the key to interpreting all forms of divine revelation is found in the heart, not in the mind. The religious leaders of Jesus' day studied the Bible more than anyone, but because of the condition of their hearts they never heard God's voice at any time (cf. John 5:37). Humility, not intelligence, has always been the heart quality that moves God to speak to us and enables us to hear Him clearly. It is the humble, not the smart, that God guides and teaches (cf. Ps. 25:9).
Attitude towards the Text	
It is possible to regard this kind of reading as a finished product. It is one's task as a Scripture scholar to unload all the treasures and meanings, exegetically, historically, and analytically. One does so in order to acquire knowledge for oneself and for others, to be used as homiletics, as teaching equipment, and for pastoral purposes.	The divine exegete is the Holy Spirit who teaches one the meaning of the text personally. *Lectio* is not so much about reading a book as about seeking Someone and being sought after by Someone. It emphasizes the value of interior examination. The text is like a keyhole through which one gazes upon endless spiritual horizons. One can never hope to reach them all. One sees that the treasure of the text is inexhaustible. *Lectio* demands response, the response of a life that embodies the values of the Word of God.

Approach	
The words "Bible study," "exegesis," and "hermeneutics" are associated with this approach of studying the Scriptures, in which one brings questions to the text and analyses it in order to gain knowledge of the truth. Analytical reading highlights the use of one's God-given mind to master the public meaning of the God-given written text, an essential process to discern the objective truth of God's special revelation. One wrestles with the written text to winnow out the author's intended meaning resident in the text to know the truth. One is on a mission to ply the text with questions until one discerns the answers. This *modus* can be categorised as "exploring" and "researching."	Here one patiently waits and listens for God to speak to him/her personally. One's purpose is not to master a certain portion of Scripture, but to read a few verses, slowly, prayerfully, meditatively, vocalizing each word, and monitoring one's heart to sense God's movement to highlight a certain word, or phrase or sentence for one's attentive reflection and rumination. In *lectio divina* there is no hurry to read so many verses, to pose questions of the text, no need to control or direct one's reading. One wishes to be ready for God to speak to him/her personally. With David, one invites God to expose the depth of one's soul, "Search me, O God, and know my heart; test me and know my thoughts. See if there is any offensive way in me, and lead me in the path of life eternal" (Ps 139:23-24). And with the child Samuel, one opens oneself to God with submission, "Speak, Lord, for your servant is listening" (1 Sam 3:10). So this approach can be considered as "listening" and "hearing."

Kind of Receptivity	
When studying the Scriptures, one's powers of mastery come to the fore. Reading is more utilitarian and functional. One receives but with a singular purpose in mind: "What I can get out of this text."	In *lectio divina*, one places oneself in a context of openness to the mystery of God, with no real agenda, as He seeks to touch the person's life in the deep places. For, if one wishes to seek a personal word from God, nowhere else can one be as certain of hearing God's voice as when one is listening to the very words of God in Scriptures. One comes to the Scripture as a conversation with God and within the context of a dynamic and growing relationship with the God who is personal.
Result	
Thanks to the studying of the Bible, one is better equipped to tell others what one has learned. The person becomes more of an expert in the topic chosen. One builds one's life as a professional, Scripture scholar or exegete, able to serve family, Church, and society more competently and effectively.	Thanks to prayerful reading, one learns to sit still and listen to what is being told to one personally by way of divine direction and disclosures in the text (contemplation). One no longer just reads to solve problems or to deal with a current difficulty or issue. One may learn to live with dissonance and to see in it a call to deeper consonance. One result of prayerful reading is that it allows one to transcend difficulties and to descend to the deeper meanings of life.

These two modes—studying and praying the Scripture—involve, I believe, a complementary relationship and are so distinctly different that they may seem almost mutually exclusive. As Peter Toon notes, "the separation of the scholarly pursuit from the devotional use of the Bible is not inevitable, but it is common."[77] It would be helpful if the Christian would begin to recognize the need for both approaches, yet the question is how do these approaches relate to each other? For me, it is difficult to practice both simultaneously if I desire to be true to the dictates of each format. I prefer to engage them in a cyclical process, now studying the Bible and at other times pausing to engage in *lectio divina*. It is advisable to have a time set apart for each, most especially for *lectio divina*.

The separation of the two approaches is necessary because on most occasions one might have one's "questioning/research" tendency (studying the Scripture) and would not be ready to stop, receive, and listen to a word or a sentence that stands out to the person. It demands a strong disciplined willpower for one who is engaged in a questioning/research approach to consciously decide to stop the questioning mode and enter into a time of meditation. Yet, someone might also decide to give him/herself permission to pursue a question and then later return to meditation. In whatever way it is done, through such repetitive movement the one seeks to understand truth and welcome God's penetrating and personal touch in one's life. We need both *lectio divina* and studying the Scripture if we wish to be fully responsive to God's transforming work in our lives through His Word. One key disposition

---

[77] Peter TOON, *The Art of Meditating on Scripture* (Grand Rapids: Zondervan, 1993), p. 73.

to fostering *lectio divina* is a letting-go of "control-centre me" combined with a humble willingness to be led, often where we would not go, by the mystery.

Concluding the chapter on *lectio divina,* the hope is that we grow in our relationship with Christ and arrive at that contemplation which is the duty of every Christian. Therefore, we are encouraged to read the passage slowly, prayerfully, listening to what is being read (*lectio*). We are encouraged to muse on the passage by reading it over and over again, slowly, lingering on a word or phrase, where our hearts are touched (*meditatio*). We are to converse with God, on a personal, intimate, and open way regarding the deep and secret places that have been touched, whether they be what are regarded as "positive" or "negative" ones (*oratio*). Perhaps we may sense God drawing near, an increasing longing for God, an awareness of our specific need for God's grace, (cf. Phil 4:6-7, Rev 3:20). We should pause, now and then, for a time of stillness, waiting, bowing before God (*contemplatio*). One might be overwhelmed by feelings of reverence, awe, wonder, worship, mystery (Ps 62; Jn 14:21, 23). At any point, praying may lead back to reading, contemplating back to meditating. Reading could lead directly into contemplation. There is no strict order in the way the Spirit of God moves in our lives. Over time, this way of reading Scripture can become second nature and spill over into other areas of life. One can "read" a situation, a world event, a personal crisis, or a relationship in this manner.

Chapter Four: Contemplative Prayer (*Oratio Contemplativa*)

One cannot adequately write about contemplation today without respecting the authority of Thomas Merton.[78] Merton was a prolific writer and, as Fr. James Conner[79] rightly noted, one can say that everything that he wrote was a development of his basic theme: "What is Contemplation?" Whether he was explicitly writing on prayer, monastic life, liturgy, and the Psalms, or on civil

---

[78] Thomas MERTON, OCSO, (31 January 1915 – 10 December 1968), was a Trappist monk of the Abbey of Gethsemani, Kentucky, in America. He was a prolific writer, a mystic, a poet, social activist, and student of comparative religion. In 1949, he was ordained to the priesthood and received the name Father Louis. Merton wrote more than 70 books, mostly on spirituality, social justice and a quiet pacifism, as well as scores of essays and reviews. Among Merton's most enduring works is his bestselling autobiography, "The Seven Storey Mountain" (1948), which sent scores of World War II veterans, students, and even teenagers flocking to monasteries across America and was also featured in National Review's list of the 100 best non-fiction books of the century. Merton was a keen proponent of interreligious dialogue and understanding. He pioneered dialogue with prominent Asian spiritual figures, including the Dalai Lama, the Japanese writer D.T. Suzuki, the Thai Buddhist monk Buddhadasa, and the Vietnamese monk Thich Nhat Hanh, and authored books on Zen Buddhism and Taoism. In the years since his death, Merton has been the subject of several biographies.

[79] Fr. James CONNER, OCSO, is a fellow monk of Gethsemani Abbey, and was a student of Thomas Merton. He worked with Merton as under-master for novices. He has also written on Thomas Merton in *Cistercian Studies, The Merton Annual* and in the volume *Thomas Merton Monk: A Monastic Tribute*.

rights, peace and war, nuclear disarmament or ancient cultures, he was expressing the fullness of the nature of contemplation. This is because contemplation for Merton was not simply one aspect of life, still less some esoteric phenomenon attainable by only a few in life. For him, contemplation was the fundamental reality in life. It was what made life real, alive, and fulfilling. It was what makes us to be truly human. In his *New Seeds of Contemplation*, Merton writes:

> Contemplation is precisely the awareness that this "I" is really "not I" and the awakening of the unknown "I" that is beyond observation and reflection and is incapable of commenting upon itself.[80]

According to Thomas Merton, nothing could be more alien to contemplation than the *cogito ergo sum* ("I think, therefore I am") of Descartes. This is the declaration of an alienated person, in "exile from his own spiritual depths."[81] He believed that if a person's thought is necessary as a medium through which he or she arrives at the concept of his existence, "then he is in fact only moving further away from his true being."[82] By reducing ourselves to a concept, it becomes impossible for us to experience directly *the mystery of our own being*. Therefore for the contemplative, says Thomas Merton, "there is no *cogito* ("I think") and no *ergo* ("therefore") but only *sum*, "I am." Not in the sense of a futile assertion of our individuality as ultimately real, but in the humble realization of our mysterious being as

---

[80] Thomas MERTON, *New Seeds of Contemplation* (London – New York, 2003), p. 17.

[81] Ibid.

[82] Ibid.

persons in whom God dwells, with infinite sweetness and inalienable power.[83]

Contemplation does not arrive at reality after a process of deduction, but by an intuitive awakening in which our personal reality becomes fully alive to its own depths. Above all, contemplation does not result from our choosing to wake ourselves, but from God who chooses to awaken us. So it becomes vital and necessary to say that contemplation is not a mental gymnastics nor is it a mystical experience but a simple awareness of "self" as the *templum* of God. We are that sacred space (*templum*) where God dwells and operates.

To prove this point we need to look into the root of the word "contemplation" from the Latin word *contemplatio* which can be traced back to the Latin verb *contemplare.* *Contemplo* is a compound word consisting of the prefix *con* and the word *templum*. The prefix *con* (with) expresses simultaneity, a joint action. While the word *templum* was used to denote the defined area of the sky or land within which a seer would perform his auspices. Such a seer was a Roman priest who during augury would interpret the messages from the gods through observance of occurrences within the predefined space or *templum.* The augur also defines places with his divining rod for sacred buildings to be built, from where *templum* came in use to refer to temple buildings as well.[84]

---

[83] Ibid., pp. 17-18.
[84] See John AYTO, *Word Origins: The Hidden Histories of English Words from A to Z* (London: A & C Black Publishers, 2005), p. 129, under "contemplate"; Hensleigh WEDGEWOOD, *A Dictionary of English Etymology* (New York: Macmillan & Co., 1878), p. 169; *Oxford Latin Dictionary* (London: Oxford University Press, 1968), pp. 426-427.

From the biblical perspective *templum* is the human body. This is made clear where Jesus said to the Jews: "Destroy this temple, and in three days I will raise it up... But he spoke of the temple of his body" (Jn 2:19, 21). Similarly, Saint Paul in his first letter to the Corinthians describes who we are, using the same word: "Do you not know that you are God's temple and that God's spirit dwells in you? If anyone destroys God's temple, God will destroy that person. For God's temple is holy, and you are that temple" (1 Cor 3:16-17).

According to the New Testament, both the individual Christian (1 Cor 6:18-20) and the corporate Body of Christ (i.e., congregations of true believers; 1 Cor 3:16-17 and Eph 2:19-22), function essentially as temples of the Holy Spirit.[85] Biblically, a temple is by definition a place of divine presence, a sanctuary where the presence of God is manifest and approachable. On one level, this is who and what we are, individually and corporately, in Christ. The foundation for understanding this New Testament principle and its implications is laid in the Old Testament. As God said to Moses at the burning bush (theophany on the mountain of God), "the place where you are standing is holy ground" (Ex 3:5b). Any place where God manifests his special presence is a holy place and therefore a temple.

If we are God's temple then it becomes imperative that what the seer does in his sacred space, in his *templum*,[86]

---

[85] See the extensive discussion in Harold W. HOEHNER, *Ephesians: An Exegetical Commentary* (Grand Rapids, MI: Baker, 2002), pp. 396-415.

[86] The seer interprets the message of the gods by observance of the elements and occurrences within that sacred space (*templum*). Such elements are like chickens; the seer would pay equally much attention to spontaneous appearing elements, such as for instance birds, within the templum.

is what God does in us. Can we not then see that contemplation is not about us? It is about God. We become part of it by means of the preposition *con* (with). The prefix *con* denotes a joint action.[87] "Our vocation is not simply *to be,* but *to work* together with God in the creation of our own life, our own identity, our own destiny...we should not *passively exist* but *actively participate*"[88] in God's creative freedom of our own lives and in the lives of others, by choosing the truth. We are even called to share with God in the work of creating the truth of our identity and of our destiny.[89]

The great weakness of today's spirituality is that it is all about us: contemplating on God, fulfilling our potential, getting the blessings of God, expanding our influence, finding our gifts, getting a handle on principles by which we can get an edge over the competition. The more there is of us, the less there is of God. Christian spirituality is not a life project for becoming a better person. It is not about developing the so-called inner life. We are in/on it, to be sure, but we are not the subject, nor are we the action. We get included by means of a few prepositions: God *with* us (Mt 1:23), Christ *in* me (Gal 2:20), God *for* us (Rom 8:31). With, in, for, and through—they are powerful, connecting, relation-forming words, but none of them makes us

---

[87] Now what is joined in action in a contemplation is first of all the dispersed attention. Normally attention is fragmented in many external occurrences and in meaningless thoughts. In contemplation all these diverse attentions are gathered and joined in the action of contemplating that one predefined subject. Moreover, "joint action" may also refer to the shared participation in contemplation of the contemplator and the contemplated, i.e., in this sense between us and God.

[88] Thomas MERTON, *New Seeds of Contemplation*, p. 32.

[89] See Thomas MERTON, *New Seeds of Contemplation*, p. 32.

either the subject or the predicate. We are the tag-end of a prepositional phrase. Sooner or later in this life, we get invited or commanded to do something. But in that doing, we never become the subject of the Christian life, nor do we perform the action of the Christian life. We are invited or commanded into what could be called "prepositional participation." The prepositions that join us to God and God's action in us within the world are the *with*, the *in*, the *for*, and the *through*. They are very important, but they are essentially a matter of the ways and means of being in/on and participating in what God is doing.

These ways and means are the second basics in the Christian life that are also counter to our today's spirituality. Ways and means must be appropriate to ends. For example, we cannot participate in God's work but then insist on doing it in our own way. We cannot participate in the building of God's Kingdom but then use the devil's tools and nails. Christ is the way, as well as the truth and the life. When we do not do it His way, we mess up the truth and we miss out on the life. It is all God's business. Our role is to make sure that this business does not collapse in our hands—and this is done by letting Him do it, in, with, for, and through us.

Who is it that prays in us?

Since we are the *templum* (temple) of God, we are therefore neither the subject nor the predicate of contemplative prayer. The question then is: Who is it that prays in us? If prayer is to be the voice of the superficial mind, the result would be nothing but an endless inner chatter. But prayer goes deeper, it issues from an eternal well within us. The presence that prays within us is the soul and this happens when we pray *in* the Holy Spirit. The preposition "in" suggests how we are suffused with the Holy Spirit, and our participatory role in the action of the Holy Spirit in us. Our body is the temple of the Holy Spirit and the deepest level in us is our individual spirits. So our spirit, which is the true image of God, is in constant dialogue and communication with the Spirit of God. The Divine is in continuous conversation with Itself within us. For this reason Saint Paul in his Letter to the Romans (8:16) says that the Spirit Himself and our spirit bear united witness that we are children of God.

Meanwhile, our mystery is never fully present to us. Our prayers in wishes and words are always partial and often blind; the deep prayer of the heart—which in another word is called contemplation—continues within us in a silence that is too deep for words (Rom 8:26). In contemplative prayer, the Holy Spirit is the *moving* and *guiding* power that moves and guides our spirits to pray. We pray by His power and according to His direction. In a word, He is the one praying *in, with, through,* and *for* us. Saint Paul in his Letter to the Ephesians (6:18) expresses it thus: "Pray all the time, asking for what you need, praying in the Spirit on every possible occasion." It is obvious here that "praying in the Spirit" is not a special form of prayer, like speaking in tongues as the members of the Pentecostal movement would interpret and believe. This point is clear because Saint Paul tells us to pray in the Spirit at all times and on every occasion. So having the Spirit praying in us is the way all prayer is to be offered. In other words, the contemplative dimension of the Christian life is basic and from there other different types of prayer emerged.

In Romans 8:26, Saint Paul writes: "For when we cannot choose words in order to pray properly, the Spirit himself expresses our plea in a way that could never be put into words." The Spirit chooses the words for our prayers, the Spirit guides our prayers, and we venture to pray by the power of the Spirit. The role of the Holy Spirit in the Christian life is fundamental. Further examples of this role of the Holy Spirit are found throughout Saint Paul's letters: Galatians (5:16) says, walk by the Spirit; Romans (8:13) says, put to death the deeds of the body by the Spirit; First Corinthians (12:3) says, we can say Jesus is Lord by the Spirit; Philippians (3:3) says, worship by the Spirit, etc. These references show that we are to live and act in a way that it is the Spirit who is doing and acting through us.

As human beings we are endowed with the responsibility for action, but God Himself is the decisive actor. Our action is dependent. So we are told to "walk" (Gal 5:16), "fight sin" (Rom 8:16), confess the Lordship of Jesus (1 Cor 12:3), worship (Phil 3:3), and pray (Jude 1:20) in the Holy Spirit. We perform all these actions in a way that shows indeed that it is the Holy Spirit who is doing them *in, with, for,* and *through* us. This is faith in action that produces a life permeated by the Spirit. When the different cords in a person's life find a common source in the Holy Spirit, that person is said to be spiritual and, therefore, a contemplative.

John O'Donohue demonstrated how our lives are profoundly engrained in this indwelling Spirit of God to which we are supposed to be attuned to. Hence he writes that

> the roots of all intimacy and belonging are planted powerfully in the invisible spirit. You belong ultimately to a presence that you cannot see, touch, grasp or measure. When you forget or repress the truth and depth of your invisible

> belonging and decide to belong to some system,
> person or project, you short-circuit your longing
> and squander your identity. To have true integ-
> rity, poise and courage is to be attuned to the
> silent and invisible nature within you. (...) True
> prayer in the Holy Spirit keeps the graciousness
> and the splendor of that vulnerability open.[90]

To attune to this Spirit of God both in our prayers and in our day-to-day life is undeniably contemplation, which in another word is congruence or unison of life.

Contemplation Means Congruence of Life

If there is a single word that identifies the contemplative life, it is congruence: congruence between ends and means, between what we do and the way we do it; congruence between who we are and what we do, between *being* and *expression*, between prayer and life. It is the same harmony we see, when, for example, we admire an athlete whose body is accurately and gracefully responsive and totally submissive to the conditions of the event. There is no dissonance between word and spirit, no pretence but *realness.*

I always use the word "contemplative" with consid-erable apprehension, fearing that you will associate it with the kind of living that is done best in monasteries, in mountain retreats, or in desert caves. I am apprehensive that you will disqualify yourself on the grounds that you work in a noisy office, live in a dysfunctional family, or do not have much interest in the kind of life that is called "contemplative life."

---

[90] John O'DONOHUE, *Eternal Echoes: Exploring our Hunger to Belong,* p. 199.

Unfortunately, conventional teaching is such that this word has always been connected with a quiet life of withdrawal, which no doubt carries with it a gross harmful effect of alienating the majority of Christians from that deep prayer which transcends complexity and restores unity. The conclusion drawn from the "false understanding of the Church's contemplative dimension distorts the explicit teaching of the New Testament, namely, that the call to sanctity is universal."[91] In light of this, there is urgent need for a renewed understanding that the call to prayer, to deep prayer, and in a word, the call to congruence of life is a universal call. "Our authority as disciples is our closeness to the Author"[92] of our life, THE MASTER. We cannot say that the contemplative function of the Church is limited exclusively to those who dedicate themselves to it entirely; it is for all the disciples that Jesus prays to the Father "that they may contemplate my glory" (Jn 17:24). The privileges are granted to those who live and serve the Lord in spirit and in truth, who do not fear the hour of the manifestation of glory which is the hour of the manifestation of the cross (Jn 17:1).

Therefore, contemplation, I believe, is a word that defines the way Christians—every butcher, baker, trader, farmer, priest, brother/sister, in a word every single Christian—can live to the glory of God. I want to free the word "contemplative" from its captivity in Buddhist and Trappist, Carmelite and Benedictine monasteries and reclaim it for every baptised Christian—married, single, ordained, consecrated and so on. Gerard Manley Hopkins[93]

---

[91] John MAIN, *Word into Silence* (London, 1989), p. viii.

[92] Ibid., p. ix.

[93] Born into an artistic middle-class family, Gerard Manley Hopkins (1844-1889) won a scholarship to Balliol College,

beautifully brought out this fact of contemplation and congruence as a reality achieved in us (every Christian) by Christ "to the Father through the features of men's faces," i.e., it is achieved *in* us, *with* us, to the Father, in his poem entitled *"As kingfishers catch fire"*:

> As kingfishers catch fire, dragonflies draw flame;
> As tumbled over rim in roundy wells
> Stones ring; like each tucked string tells, each hung bell's
> Bow swung finds tongue to fling out broad its name;
> Each mortal thing does one thing and the same:
> Deals out that being indoors each one dwells;
> Selves—goes itself; myself it speaks and spells,
> Crying **What I do is me: for that I came**.[94]

> I say more: the just man justices;
> Keeps grace: that keeps all his goings graces;
> Acts in God's eye what in God's eye he is—
> Christ—for Christ plays in ten thousand places,
> Lovely in limbs, and lovely in eyes not his
> To the Father through the features of men's faces.[95]

Oxford, where he was a "star" before converting to Catholicism under the influence of the Oxford Movement and Cardinal Newman. Hopkins entered the Society of Jesus and lived and worked thereafter as a priest, mostly teaching until his early death from typhoid fever. The poetry was communicated to friends but two attempts at publication were rejected. Nothing was known until 1918, when Hopkins' boyhood friend, Robert Bridges, then poet laureate of England, collected the poems and published a volume.

[94] What I *do* is *me* (unison of contemplative-active life).

[95] Gerard Manley Hopkins, *Poems and Prose* (Penguin Classics, 1985). The title of the poem is "As kingfishers catch fire," but I changed it to be, "What I do is me," extracted from the last phrase of the first stanza.

This poem is a wonderful invocation of contemplative life. Hopkins piles up an incredible accumulation of images to fix our attention on this sense of lightness and of wholeness, of grace and of harmony that comes together when we realize the utter congruence between what a thing is and what it does: kingfisher, dragonfly, a stone tumbling into a well, a plucked violin string, the clapper of a bell sounding—what happens and the way it happens are seamless. He then goes on to us men and women—"each mortal thing does one thing and the same"—bodying forth who and what we are. But what kingfishers and falling stones and chiming bells do without effort requires development in humans, formation into who we truly are becoming, in which the means by which we live are congruent with the ends for which we live.

Hopkins does not talk about achieving this congruence. He talks about it being achieved in us. That is what we have been saying about contemplation. In the process God is in charge, achieving it *in* us, *with* us, *for* us, and *through* us. What the plucked string, the dragonfly, and the kingfisher do as determined by biology or physics happens with us when Christ lives in us, Christ living the Christ-way in us, in the truth of our lives, playing through our limbs and eyes to the Father. I love that final image: Christ plays in ten thousand places, lovely in limbs—your limbs, my limbs—lovely in eyes—your eyes, my eyes: the contemplative life, living the Christ-life in the Christ-way.

The words of Jesus that keep this in focus are: "I am the way, the truth and the life" (Jn 14:6). Only when we do the Jesus *truth,* in the Jesus *way,* do we get the Jesus *life.* But this is not easy. It is easier to talk about what Christians believe—the truth of the Gospel formulated in creeds and doctrines. For example, in the Church today we have a magnificent roster of eloquent and learned theologians who can teach us to think carefully and well about the revelation of God in Christ through the Holy Spirit. It is easier to talk about what Christians do, the behaviour appropriate to followers of Jesus codified in moral commandments and formulated in vision statements and mission strategies. We have never lacked for teachers, preachers, and parents to instruct us in the mores and manners of the Kingdom of God. But what counts most is the Christian life as lived, lived in this sense of congruence between who Christ is and who we are right now at this job, this apostolate, this work. In other words, how is Christ seen in my life? It has always been more difficult to come to terms with Jesus as the *way,* than with Jesus as the *truth.* More difficult to realize the ways our thinking and behaviour get fused into a life of relational love and adoration with neighbour and God, God and neighbour. There are a lot of people talking about God but seldom to God, just as there are a lot of people who are talking at us, but seldom to us. There are no shortcuts to becoming the persons we are created to be. The contemplative life is a life in which Jesus' way and Jesus' truth are congruent, where one's being and one's doing are congruent, and where "kingfishers catch fire, dragonflies draw flame."

Consequently, it is a fallacy to believe that a contemplative way of *being* inhibits an active way of *doing,* or vice versa. This mistake has corrupted our spiritual life for far too long. It is high time we claim the heart of our Christian faith, which is an authentic relationship with Jesus; a relationship that requires a veritable melt-down of the ego and a readiness to create a new being, as the apostle Saint Paul observed centuries ago. Without that, we fail to receive the fruits of the *way* forged by Christ Himself.

What I Do Is Me

The nature of the Christian vocation is *being* and *doing*, as Hopkins' poem brought out. Therefore, one's essence is something to be fulfilled, not ascribed. Each living thing under God's reign, though in constant flux should "act in God's eye what in God's eye he is—Christ": congruence, harmony between *Esse et agere* (being and doing). The greatness of the Christian vocation is found in the word "entire"—to be whole in each thing. Put all that you are into the least you do.[96]

The second stanza in the poem extends this concept of "wholeness" and "entirety" from object to man with tautology of lines such as "the just man justices" and "Acts in God's eye what in God's eye he is." This suggests that to live out God's will is to live one's essence. The person is most him/herself when he/she manifests Christ, and part of realizing oneself as a human being is realizing Christ. God bestowed grace to man, which reveals itself in all his daily activities. He acts before God as the being that God sees him to be. It is the beauty lent by Christ's presence that makes "the features of men's faces" lovely in God's sight.

This poem turns from a physical first part to a spiritual, moral, or theological second part. More specifically, the poem shifts its focus from *being* (the mere passive possession of essential, defining characteristics) to the more active notion of *self-expression*, and then to action itself. Hopkins first draws on the physical being of kingfishers, dragonflies, and stones: each aspect he describes as a part of the unchanging nature of the object. However, the sound of the bell moves us more into the realm of deliberate self-expression. The inevitable process for the

---

[96] Quoted in John O'DONOHUE, *Eternal Echoes*, p. 224.

objects described takes on a different character when applied to man. The process is complicated for human beings, because human beings possess moral capacity. It is not enough for us to be what our nature intends. We are created in the image and likeness of God so we have to be like our Creator, meaning that we have to be holy. This holiness is more than being human, it is more than humanity. "If we are never anything but human, never anything but people, we will not be saints and we will not be able to offer to God the worship of our imitation, which is sanctity."[97] Thus the enacting of the self cannot happen unconsciously or automatically. Rather, it means becoming one's highest self or acting to the highest of one's capacity. Thomas Merton has a wonderful way of presenting this same undeniable fact when he commented that "for me to be a saint means to be myself. Therefore the problem of sanctity and salvation is in fact the problem of finding out who I am and of discovering my true self."[98]

In line with Merton's assertion, Hopkins states that a man is not just until he behaves justly. The implication is that he is not fully a man unless he fully realises himself as intended by God. That is, being just is part of the essence of man insofar as the striving for moral perfection is part of his basic existence. Hopkins then extends this concept to the theological idea of God's immanence in the world, and the Christian belief that Christ dwells within the hearts of men. It is by the grace of God that humans are what they are; more specifically, it was through divine grace that Christ came to redeem men from sin. Hopkins therefore asks that men "keep grace." This phrase describes the

---

[97] Thomas MERTON, *New Seeds of Contemplation*, p. 31.
[98] Ibid.

humble acceptance of God's grace that is the first gesture of Christian life. This acceptance will lend grace to their everyday comings and goings, and will allow man to act "in God's eye what in God's eye he is"; that is, to become one with Christ and so fulfil his destiny.

The Hypocrisy of Christian Life: Living "As If"

In Matthew (6:1-6 and 16-21), it seems as if we are taught that "hypocrisy" is a terrible thing. But what is giving alms without anyone knowing, if it is not saying one thing and doing another? What is praying in secret, unless it is pretending to be something you are not? It is then clear that what we have here is not the choice between acting and integrity, but between two kinds of acting. It is not about avoiding "hypocrisy," but about choosing what kind of "hypocrite" you want to be. Some kinds of hypocrisy are inevitable, even desirable. This is because the world we live in is open to multiple interpretations. There is much good, yet there is real evil. One can say that there is no reward for good, and act accordingly: the cynic is never disappointed. Or one can say that there is reward for good, but wholly or largely in another world. This is faith. It calls the disciple to live, at least part of the time, *as if he/she were already in the next world,* a world where all share freely and constantly commune with God, in short, a life of love. But this requires the disciple to be an actor, a hypocrite, by seeming to live in this world when deep down he believes in the next.

The Greek word for actor is hypocrite.[99] We are all actors on a stage or in a theatre. This is not a theatre of

_____

[99] The word *hypocrisy* comes from the Greek ὑπόκρισις (hypo-krisis), which means "jealous," "play-acting," "acting out,"

spectacle or display, but a secret theatre. In the drama of salvation, God is the actor and the disciple is the spectator. But in the drama of holy life, the stage is a locked room, the secrecy of your heart, the actor is the disciple and the audience is God. The place of encounter between God and His people is not only the temple made of wood and bricks, the great theatre, the Holy of Holies. It is now the temple of your body, the locked room (where the disciple meets God one on one).

The child of God wants to be noticed, respected, and admired. The child—and we are all children—wants to

---

"coward," or "dissembling." (Read *Pocket Oxford Greek Dictionary*, ed. Morwood and Taylor, Oxford University Press, 2002.) The word *hypocrite* is from the Greek word ὑποκρίτης (*hypokritēs*), the agentive noun associated with ὑποκρίνομαι (hypokrinomai κρίση, "judgment" κριτική (kritiki), "critics") presumably because the performance of a dramatic text by an actor was to involve a degree of interpretation, or assessment. Alternatively, the word is an amalgam of the Greek prefix *hypo-*, meaning "under," and the verb *krinein*, meaning "to sift or decide." Thus the original meaning implied a deficiency in the ability to sift or decide. This deficiency, as it pertains to one's own beliefs and feelings, informs the word's contemporary meaning. (See Online Etymology Dictionary, "Hypocrisy," accessed 28 March 2013, https://www.etymonline.com/.)

Whereas *hypokrisis* applied to any sort of public performance (including the art of rhetoric), *hypokrites* was a technical term for a stage actor and was not considered an appropriate role for a public figure. In Athens in the fourth century BC, for example, the great orator Demosthenes ridiculed his rival Aeschines, who had been a successful actor before taking up politics, as a *hypokrites* whose skill at impersonating characters on stage made him an untrustworthy politician. This negative view of the *hypokrites*, perhaps combined with the Roman disdain for actors, later shaded into the originally neutral *hypokrisis*. It is this later sense of *hypokrisis* as "play-acting," i.e., the assumption of a counterfeit persona that gives the modern word *hypocrisy* its negative connotation.

be the centre of people's attention. We can have that if we want it, or we can be the centre of God's attention. We choose our audience. If we choose the crowd, we have our reward already. If we choose God, we receive another thing a child loves: we get to share a secret. The secret of holiness that is between God and the disciple is not the stuff of newspaper revelations or talk-show speculation. It is a bond that time and death will never break. Behind these two theatres—the theatre of the crowd and the theatre of the locked room—lies a significant irony. Every theatre is a kind of game, a kind of suspended disbelief with an agreed set of rules. The players in the game are called the actors.

If these alternatives seem difficult, one can reduce or mitigate one's risk by gaining what reward this life has to offer, and at the same time gesturing towards the next. It is this last option that Saint Matthew's Gospel condemns so heavily, and describes as "hypocrisy"—though a better description might simply be lack of faith. A person who lacks faith settles for the majority verdict—playing to the gallery and having the good esteem of the crowd—while the disciple who has faith knows there is only one verdict that matters: the judgment of God. The faithless disciple aims for both heaven and earth and gets neither. But the disciple with faith receives an unexpected bonus. Secret almsgiving, prayer, and fasting have an additional political and eschatological dimension. The disciple who can fast, who can depend on God for sustenance for a whole day or two, will not be an easy prey to purveyors of instant gratification and immediate solutions, or to advertising, which dominates the contemporary world, with its promise of rapid and empty reward. The disciple who can pray, who can depend on God's judgment rather than the world's valuation, will not be at the mercy of popularity or fashion.

A true disciple is a stranger to worldly ways (*RB* 4:20); there is distinctiveness in his/her bearing, in both being and doing. When the Scripture speaks of renunciation of the world (Rom 12:2; Jas 4:4; 1 Jn 2:12; Lk 16:15), it is talking of "*behavioural distance*"[100] and not physical distance. Fr. Michael Casey notes that when Maximus the Confessor wishes to distinguish between monks and worldly people, his criteria was not where they live, what they wear, nor even what they do, but what fills their minds. "Worldlings," he said, "are those who allow their minds to rest in material things.... A monk is one who separates his mind from material things and by self-mastery, psalmody and prayer, devotes himself to God."[101] So here the difference in identity and action is determined by the contents of the mind and heart. "Where your treasure is, there will your heart be also" (Mt 6:21).

Earthly life for every Christian is transitional. We all exist in it as pilgrims, wayfarers, in the world but not of the world. The Christian wavers between two worlds—the sacred and the profane—without being part of either. Christian life has taken this fact very seriously and turned it into a permanent way of life. The Christian is therefore seen as one who has "died to the profane world." In itself, this view of life as transitional is not unusual for anyone, but what makes it very unusual is that for the Christian it has been institutionalised; it exists as an integral and essential feature of Christian life—this is vividly seen in the Christian's eschatological orientation—a daily

---

[100] Michael CASEY, "Strangers to Worldly Ways: RB 4.20," in *Tjurunga: An Australasian Benedictine Review*, no. 29 (1985), pp. 37-46, here p. 38.

[101] Maximus the Confessor, "Centuries on Charity," 2.53-54, cited in Michael CASEY, "Strangers to Worldly Ways," p. 38.

re-affirmation of the gratuitousness and non-utility of a life totally dedicated to God.

A Contemplative Christian Lives "As If"

> What I mean, brothers and sisters, is that the time is short. From now on those who have wives should live *as if* they do not; those who mourn, *as if* they did not; those who are happy, *as if* they were not; those who buy something, *as if* it were not theirs to keep; those who use the things of the world, *as if* not engrossed in them. For this world in its present form is passing away (1 Cor 7:29-31).

"As if" is a Pauline technical term that prepares the *eschaton* (end) of each condition, whatever it might be. In this sense, each condition is relativized. For the fact that Saint Paul says it while talking about the different vocations is also an indication to this "universal call to contemplative life." The human existence is already a *proleptic* sign of the Kingdom, though some are intensely called to be this sign, yet we are all living in this strong tension of *already and not yet*, continuously moving into the future. The vocation of every Christian is a messianic vocation, meaning that it is a potentiality that one can employ, and yet never possess. For the contemplative, each condition (freedom, slavery, marriage, celibacy, circumcision, un-circumcision, all according to one's vocation) can be used, but it can never be owned. A life lived "as if" cancels the hold that the world can have on each one of us, not by revolting against it through *fuga mundi* but by simply cancelling it. However, this can only truly happen if the Christians are truly either contemplative-actives or active-contemplatives.

Dealing with the world is inevitable and important—
we need to deal with it well for the sake of our families,
our nation, and ourselves. But we need to maintain an
"eschatological reserve," knowing that this is not all
there is, for we look to the eternal beyond of that which
is passing away. Basic to this thinking is that one is to
disengage from the world, for all is transitory. There is no
point in becoming consumed or even entangled with the
world and its concerns, for the "present form of this world
is passing away." In the light of the eschatological nature
of the Christian vocation, in every situation of life they are
to live without their relationship to the world being the
determining factor, but instead with their relationship to
Christ determining their attitudes and decisions. Christians are to be in the world, but the world is not to dictate
their present existence. The contemplative Christian or
the eschatological person "has nothing, yet possesses all
things" (2 Cor 6:10; cf. 1 Cor 3:22).

The contemplative power to infuse every moment and
every act with singular importance and the ironic power
to behave "as if," is a constant invitation to work "as if"
our works, in Teilhard de Chardin's words, are "eternal-
ized." The present occupation, duty, work and so on have
no value except when weighed from the eternal perspective. This "end" is what Christians look forward to, and
are called to pursue with intensity, living on earth "as if,"
thereby giving every assignment and every engagement
an eternal orientation. There are so many ways of doing
this. The consecrated men and women, for example, have
decided to counteract with their lives the very things that
have brought the initial misery of man (in the narration
of original sin). Thereby they choose to celebrate Christ's
life with and in their own lives, making present the earthly

life of Christ through the promises of the three traditional Christian values of poverty, chastity, and obedience.

The revelation of the mystery of God in the man Jesus also becomes the revelation of the world and its precariousness, implying a theological conception of the things of the world and therefore of human history. Christian revelation evolves in this tension of beginning (*protology*) and end (*eschatology*). The Christian, representing humanity in this case, is born into this theological tension of *proto-escato-logical*, the beginning (original sin) and the end (final judgment).[102] Man's freedom and salvation is found in this tension, and it is this tension that Christianity most illuminates in her teachings of the Christian's total submission to the divine pedagogy. This divine pedagogy is summed up for us by Jesus in Matthew 12:30-31—commandments of love as a "custom of liberty" in that way breaking ourselves free from the "culture of the temporary,"[103] living on earth "as if" we are already in heaven. Such an attitude of the mind makes the believer enter the secret temple of his/her deepest belonging. It is only in this temple that our hungriest longing finds stillness and peace. This approach finds its harmony in the Divine directive of Psalm 45:11: *Agite otium,*[104] *et agnoscetis quia ego Dominus* (Be still, and know that I am God).

---

[102] Cf. Stefano Pasini, *Il metodo nel diritto: Il rapporto tra teologia, filosofia e diritto nella riflessione canonistica contemporanea* (Rome, 2002), p. 361.

[103] Pope Francis meeting with seminarians and novices.

[104] The word *"otium"* (still) has always been an ambivalent word because it is often mistaken to be *otiositas* (RB 48:1), which means idleness. For this reason, to this biblical quotation Saint Augustine added an explanatory phrase: *"non otium desidiae, sed otium cogitationis, ut a locis ac temporibus vacet."* (See *De vera religione* XXXV, 65: CCSL 32, p. 229.) (Not the stillness

To be still is to have a spiritual leisure or contemplation, which normally adapts itself to the personality and circumstances of different people; but one thing that is sure: it cannot exist nor occur in the context of a loveless life. As lovers of the eternal, a true contemplative reminds us all of the most precious testimony that if it is necessary to save anything in this world, it is above all this love that God has given first to man—a love that surpasses, amazes, and unsettles us. The texts of the Eastern liturgy refer to

---

of doing nothing, but the stillness of thought independent of locations and times.) However, the Greek word for *otium* (leisure) is σχολή (*schole*), which passed on to the Latin as schola and into English as school. To be occupied with work is ά–σχολή, translated into Latin as *neg-otium*, i.e., a negation of leisure or, in one word, "*unleisurely.*" In the first chapter of his metaphysics, Aristotle says that *otium* is one of the foundations of Western civilization. For the Greeks, the seat of culture or of cultural formation means *otium*. In this sense σχολή does not mean school in the way we use it, but *otium* (leisure). (Cf. J. Pieper, *Otium e Culto* [Brescia, 1956], p. 33.)

In general the word *otium* denotes a general idea of tranquillity and peace, for the individual and for society. It is the absence of war. This primitive concept of *otium* is unfortunately unknown to our programmatic, activist world; instead, *otium* and *acedia* are termed to be synonymous. But for the medieval mind, *acedia* means principally the renunciation of aspirations natural to man's dignity: his blunt refusal to be what God wants him to be. *Acedia* is the sprawling of weakness, lack of initiative in both spiritual and economic life. *Acedia*, in its ancient meaning, is far from being the equivalent of *otium*. (Cf. Joseph Pieper, *Otium e Culto* [Brescia, 1956], pp. 33-35.) *Otium* is a spiritual attitude, which springs from adhesion to the person of Christ and the service of His Kingdom. (Cf. Romano Guardini, *Meditation before Mass*, pp. 5-6.) It is not inactivity, not similar to quiet or to interior quietude; rather, it is similar to the conversational silence of lovers nourished with intimate agreement. Such stillness is the womb where contemplative presence comes to life and becomes in our existence the wellspring of action.

this love as *"theos philanthropos"* (the man-loving God).[105] Such love should necessitate personal reflection of one's standing before God. Pope Francis has a wonderful presentation of such reflections:

> We may ask ourselves: am I anxious for God, anxious to proclaim him, to make him known? Or do I allow that spiritual worldliness to attract me which impels people to do everything for love of themselves? We consecrated people think of our personal interests, of the functionality of our works, of our careers. Well, we can think of so many things... Have I, so to speak, made myself "comfortable" in my Christian life, in my priestly life, in my religious life, and also in my community life? Or do I retain the force of restlessness for God, for his Word that makes me "step out" of myself towards others?[106] (CICLSAL, "Rejoice!" Question from Pope Francis, no. 5).

The end product of living "as if" is evident: restlessness for God, for His Word and work and therefore for others. Where such is evident, the change is seen in the person's outlook. The competitive attitude, the desire to amass power, to be in control, to possess, disappears. At the same time, concern for excellence in personal relations and in all that one does increases. This outlook also manifests in one's concern that things be done well for their own sake and for the sake of others. Social ranking ceases to function in a credible way for the contemplative, who treats each person equally with the respect that would be shown,

---

[105] Paul Evdokimov, *The Sacrament of Love*, p. 79.

[106] Pope Francis, Homily for the Opening of the General Chapter of the Order of St. Augustine (Rome), 28 August 2013.

in a ranking mentality, to those of the highest rank.[107] All these because he/she is living here on earth "as if" he/she is already in heaven. This way of living for Love brings us closer to our end (*eschaton*). While looking forward to this end, the joy and happiness which emanates from our adhesion and attention to Christ in his service radiates to others.

In view of this "end," we must resist any effort to define ourselves and our work as merely instrumental, as merely useful. For, as Teilhard says, "...everything which diminishes my explicit faith in the heavenly value of the results of my endeavour, diminishes irredeemably my power to act."[108] Contemplation is a form of resistance! It is resistance at a level of human life and response that is so elemental that the thoughtless will not notice.

Thomas Merton brought out the idea very well when he writes: "In all the cities of the world it is the same. The universal modern man is the man in a rush (i.e., the rhinoceros), a man who has no time, who is a prisoner of necessity, who cannot understand that a thing might perhaps be without usefulness."[109] The contemplative way of being and mode of consciousness enables the worker to reclaim pleasure in work, to breathe value into the simplest tasks, to savour the very simplicity of work, and to approach the complexity of work with calm.

This process involves awakening to the presence of the transcendent in our actual here-and-now situation. It is as if we live simultaneously in two orders of reality:

---

[107] Beatrice BRUTEAU, "From *Dominus* to *Amicus*: Contemplative Insight and a New Social Order," in *CrossCurrents*, vol. 31, no. 3 (1981), pp. 273-284, here p. 281.

[108] Pierre TEILHARD de Chardin, *The Divine Milieu*, p. 58.

[109] Thomas MERTON, *Raids on the Unspeakable*, p. 21.

the invisible and the visible, the infinite and the finite, the eternal and the temporal. In short, the integration of heart and mind, of inspiration and incarnation, is the hidden goal of contemplative life. More and more we sense that the temporal is pierced by the Eternal. It is "as if" we live standing simultaneously on two planes of reality— one foot in time, and the other in eternity. But what has first priority for us is the invisible horizon—the unseen, because it speaks through the visible. There is no moment that cannot be read as a message from on high, as an epiphany. We can then read God's presence everywhere as immanent and transcendent. We are then in the best position to meet the Mystery in our lives and in the lives of our brothers and sisters.

Christian Life Is Essentially Contemplative-in-action and Active-in-contemplation

Any split in ministry between the contemplative and the active life, between *oratio and missio*, between prayer and participation, in the working places of family, convents, monasteries, church and society is simply an illusion. A sincere appraisal of the Gospel truth would show that we must never separate Mary, who rested at the feet of Jesus, from Martha working busily in the kitchen (Lk 10:38-42). This is so because the Lord, who went off to a quiet place to pray, is the same worker of wonders who fed the five thousand with five loaves and two fish (Mk 6:30-44). This is a sign that Christian spirituality and Christian mission (*oratio–missio*) are two sides of the same coin. It is only when I am growing inwardly in faith, hope, and love can I serve outwardly with unselfish commitment all those entrusted to my care.

There are several instances in Scripture revealing that Jesus paused to pray (in receptive contemplation of the Father's will) before he ministered to those in need of healing (in donative action). Some examples of this in the Gospels are:

> Mk 1:35: "He...went off to the lonely place and prayed there."

> Mt 14:23: "He went up into the hills by himself to pray."

> Mt 26:36: "Stay here while I go over there to pray."

> Lk 3:21: "Jesus after his own baptism was at prayer."

> Jn 6:15: "Jesus escaped back to the hills by himself."

He is the model of Christian life in general. Unfortunately, the concern and anxiety is that our society has given functionality (*missio*) so much priority over spirituality (*oratio*). Why has our sense of accomplishment for Jesus' sake taken precedence over the awed recognition that without Him we can do nothing? This reflection should shed instructive light on the link between love for the Lord and fruitfulness of service. The priest/religious, or better the Christian, should be able and capable of abandoning him/herself to the mystery before engaging in ministry. Such is the key to becoming a contemplative-in-action and an active-in-contemplation. This total abandonment enables us to cope with seemingly meaningless and disappointing events and their unpredictable outcomes. This contemplative vision enables us to appreciate with grateful hearts any manifestation of the mystery in our ministry. We try our best to strike the balance between form-reception (contemplation) and form-donation (action).[110]

---

[110] Read Susan MUTO, "Living Contemplatively and Serving God in the World: Two Sides of the Coin of Christian Ministry," in

The medieval master, Saint Bernard of Clairvaux (1090-1153), names the ebb and flow of contemplation and action as two movements of the Holy Spirit in the baptized soul, these being *infusion* and *effusion*. As the abbot of one of the largest monastic centres in Western Europe, it was Saint Bernard's hope that his monks and everyone inspired by them would learn the art and discipline of being contemplatives-in-action and active-in-contemplation. *Infusion* has to precede *effusion*; otherwise one's best efforts may result in no more than an "empty yawning." In Sermon 18 of his eighty-six sermons on the Song of Songs, he writes:

> The man who is wise, therefore, will see his life as more like a reservoir than a canal. The canal simultaneously pours out what it receives; the reservoir retains the water till it is filled, then discharges the overflow without loss to itself... Today there are many in the Church who act like canals, the reservoirs are far too rare. So urgent is the charity of those through whom the streams of heavenly doctrine flow to us, that they want to pour it forth before they have been filled; they are more ready to speak than to listen, impatient to teach what they have not grasped, and full of presumption to govern others while they know not how to govern themselves.[111]

Journal of Spiritual Formation and Soul Care, vol. 6, no. 1 (Biola University, 2013), pp. 82-92. Here p. 82.

[111] Bernard of CLAIRVAUX, *Sermons on the Song of Songs I*, vol. 3 of Works of Bernard of Clairvaux, trans. Killian Walsh (Kalamazoo, MI: Cistercian Fathers Series, 1971), p. 134.

In other words, receptivity to the will of God in prayer must revitalize the activity required of us in any ministerial situation. Mere activism must be avoided at all cost. In writing on this topic, Susan Muto expressed this well:

> What good would it be to grow the Church of Christ without growing the spiritual life of every person in the congregation? How can we expect work to have any efficacy without its being grounded in worship? How can labor be effective without leisure? The risk we take by neglecting this rhythm of infusion and effusion is that Christian service may degenerate into a corporate enterprise unmindful of the call to holiness.[112]

A twelfth-century Benedictine monk, Peter of Celles, experienced in himself the conflict between action and contemplation and finally came to the conclusion that both *oratio laboriosa* (active or laborious prayer) and *oratio devota* (devout or contemplative prayer) as he called them, are necessary. None of them comes to the throne of grace without the other.[113] There should be a harmonious and organic balance between action and contemplation. Both are necessary. Martha and Mary are sisters and, as Peter of Celles said, none can approach the throne of God without the other.

This rhythm of recollection and participation is an essential feature of Christian commitment. Whatever

---

[112] Susan MUTO, "Living Contemplatively and Serving God in the World: Two Sides of the Coin of Christian Ministry," p. 86.

[113] Read *De Disciplina Claustrali*, 22, PL 202:1129. See also Thomas MERTON, *Contemplative Prayer* (London, 1973), pp. 70-73.

we happen to be doing—cooking a meal, writing a letter, teaching a class, scrubbing and cleaning a home, nursing the sick—we do it out of love for God and a desire to make this love manifest. We want to help others see Christ's face in every person, event, and thing. This is what it means as Christians to be contemplatives and missionaries. Missionary duty is not limited to evangelizing work in foreign lands, nor is contemplative vocation limited to separation with high walls and strange customs. It is what we are to do every day in our homes and professions. Whether we are involved in teaching, law, nursing, medicine, or social work, whatever our position or profession, we have to remain faithful disciples despite daily pressures. As the renowned Baptist preacher and chaplain to scores of soldiers, Oswald Chambers[114] expresses it:

> The tendency today is to put the emphasis on service. Beware of the people who make usefulness their ground of appeal. If you make usefulness the test, then Jesus Christ was the greatest

---

[114] Oswald Chambers was born to devout parents in Aberdeen, Scotland. At age 16, Chambers was baptized and became a member of Rye Lane Baptist Chapel. Even as a teenager, Chambers was noted for his deep spirituality, and he participated in the evangelization of poor occupants of local lodging houses. Oswald married Gertrude in May 1910, and on May 24, 1913, Gertrude gave birth to their only child, Kathleen. In 1915, a year after the outbreak of World War I, Chambers was accepted as a YMCA chaplain. He was assigned to Zeitoun, Cairo, Egypt, where he ministered to Australian and New Zealand troops, who later participated in the Battle of Gallipoli. Soon his wooden-framed "hut" was packed with hundreds of soldiers listening attentively to his messages. Chambers was stricken with appendicitis on October 17, 1917, but resisted going to a hospital on the grounds that the beds would be needed by men wounded in the long-expected Third Battle of Gaza. On October 29, a surgeon performed

> failure that ever lived. The lodestar of the saint is God himself, not estimated usefulness. It is the work that God does through us that counts, not what we do for God.[115]

The point is that in contemplation one should not allow one's occupations to become one's preoccupations.[116] A wise novice master once advised some young novices about their behaviour during recreation and in the chapel, he said: In the chapel you should behave as during recreation: relaxed. And during recreation you should behave as in the chapel: with dignity. So it all boils down to what has been said earlier; contemplation is nothing mystifying but simply congruence of life, be yourself, be real, and be entire.

The Paradox of Contemplation

The enigma in contemplation is that while it is as such God's work that calls us to remain still, passive, and receptive, there is perhaps nothing that calls for greater commitment and effort on our part than simply remaining still in God's presence. If contemplation is relatively rare,

---

an emergency appendectomy, but Chambers died November 15, 1917, from a hemorrhage of the lungs. He was buried in Cairo with full military honours. Gertrude, for the remainder of her life, published books and articles for him edited from the notes she had taken in shorthand from his sermons. Most successful of the thirty books was *My Utmost for His Highest*, which has never been out of print and has been translated into 39 languages.

[115] Oswald CHAMBERS, *My Utmost for His Highest: Selections for the Year* (Uhrichsville, OH: Barbour Publishing, Inc., 1963), August 30th.

[116] Cf. E. Borne & F. Henry, *A Philosophy of Work*, translated by F. Jackson (London, 1938), p. 206.

that is not because it is terribly high-flown, but because it is terribly ordinary. Some who remain faithful to prayer over a long period of time may have remarkable experiences in contemplation, but for the most part, contemplation is nothing more—and nothing less—than remaining quietly and humbly in God's presence, allowing Him to work in whatever way He chooses. One text from the Scripture that is used to describe the authentic state of contemplation is found in Psalm 37:7: "Be still before the Lord and wait in patience" (*Agite otium et expecta eum*).

In practice, our role in contemplation, the participatory role which we play, hence the "*con*" (with)—and *templum*—is the Christian's struggles to achieve some inner stillness. It will not necessarily—nor even usually—be a time of sweetness, light, and delight, but a time during which the Christian seeks to be open, in faith, to what the Lord now wishes to say, and to do within him/her. For this reason, we do not "do" contemplation, rather we make effort to let God "do" the work in us. Practically, this involves whatever we can do to "be still" in His presence. In Revelation 3:20, we read: "Listen! I am standing at the door, knocking; if you hear my voice and open the door, I will come in to you and eat with you, and you with me." So the Lord constantly knocks at the door of our hearts and mind; the effort made to give our attention to the Lord in *contemplatio* is equivalent to the Christian inviting Him in. Of course, if we let him in, an automatic transformation will follow. Because once He is there, He cleans and cleanses us and we become new creatures.

Finally, because the contemplative-active and active-contemplative Christian prays the way he/she lives and lives the way he/she prays, the whole of life becomes a training to pray. In this sense, therefore, prayer becomes the means of transformation and transcendence of the self. This intermingling of life, work, and prayer is well presented by the giant of Christian mysticism, Meister Eckhart, when he said:

> One should learn to work with this contempla-
> tion in him, with him, and emerging from him,
> so that one allows his inner life to break into his
> activity and his activity into his inner life so that
> one becomes accustomed to working collectedly.
> If they can both happen in him, that is best of
> all, for then he becomes a fellow workman with
> God.[117]

Prayer is a two-way process. It is not just human souls whispering to God. It passes over into communion, with God who is active in us, as well as we active towards God. A specific state of expectancy, of openness of soul is laid bare and receptive before the Eternal Goodness. In quietness we wait, inwardly, in unformulated expectation.[118] The fruit of this inward waiting or in another word this stillness is happiness and satisfaction. Pope Francis confirmed this during his meeting with seminarians and novices in Rome in 2013. The gratuitousness of life has joy as its reward.

> Joy is born from the gratuitousness of an encoun-
> ter... And the joy of the encounter with him and
> with his call does not lead to shutting oneself in
> but to opening oneself; it leads to service in the
> Church. St. Thomas said: *bonum est diffusivum
> sui*. Good spreads. And joy also spreads. Do not

---

[117] Quoted in Douglas V. STEERE, *On Beginning from Within* (New York: Harper & Brothers, 1943), p. 86.

[118] Read Thomas KELLY, *Reality of the Spiritual World* (Walling-ford: Pendle Hill), pp. 30 & 36.

> be afraid to show the joy of having answered the Lord's call, of having responded to his choice of love and of bearing witness to his Gospel in service to the Church. And joy, true joy, is contagious; it is infectious... it impels one forward.[119]

So joy and happiness are fruits of that encounter, that relationship with the Author of joy and happiness. A further indication that happiness consists in some kind of contemplative activity is that the angels and the saints are blessed and are happy at the highest degree and what kind of actions are we to attribute to them if not "the worship of the Lamb," following Him wherever He goes (Rev 14:4). With this, we have identified the deepest root of contemplation, i.e., worship. The angels and saints find existence and realities in their world in agreement, hence they praise their Creator. For us human beings who are still in the world of sin, the highest conceivable form of approval of the world is found only in the worship of God, in the praise of the Creator, in liturgy and in life.

Contemplation as a Duty of All Christians and Not a Goal

In our accomplished-oriented society[120] we have the tendency of approaching everything as a project, something

---

[119] Pope Francis meeting with seminarians and novices, Rome, 6 July 2013. Reported in the recent document "Rejoice!" a letter to consecrated men and women (CICLSAL, Rejoice 10), Congregation for Institutes of Consecrated Life and Societies of Apostolic Life. Year of Consecrated Life *Rejoice!* "A letter to consecrated men and women: A message from the teachings of Pope Francis," 2 February 2014.

[120] This "accomplished-oriented" tendency is a twin brother to what social psychologists call the "achievement-oriented lifestyle. They are basic for so many evils in our society today.

to be done and accomplished, with a determined measurable finished product. In this accomplished-oriented mentality, contemplation is seen as the goal of prayer or goal of Christian life, i.e., because either prayer or the Christian life is conceived as a project. But the Church's law calls contemplation a "duty" and not a "goal." Every religious (mind you, here it is both the so-called "active religious" and the "contemplative nuns"), has a duty to go through contemplative experience in his/her quest for God. So, contemplation is a way of prayer open to anyone who truly seeks God. To this reality Fr. Basil Pennington writes:

> It is the type of prayer experience that will ordinarily best help one to make progress in the Christian life, to be purified and illumined, and to abide more integrally in union with God in and through all. It is therefore, not something to be worked towards, a goal, but simply a way to be entered into, and experience that can be enjoyed—and struggled with—by all who seek God.[121]

This is to say that the experience of contemplation is open to development. The contemplative experience of God which ought to be in harmony with the whole growth of Christian life, is to become daily fuller and richer. What the Christian is seeking in contemplation is harmony and compatibility, which are other words for congruence of life. Through contemplation, the Christian seeks to be who he/she is and what he/she really is. In the words of Thomas Merton: "creatures, who come forth from God's love, one with the rest of creation, wholly oriented to finding the

---

[121] Basil PENNINGTON, *Centering Prayer: Renewing an Ancient Christian Prayer Form* (Doubleday, 1980), p. 114.

fullness of life and love in him; and Christians, who have been given the Christ nature, oriented to be, in Christ, with the Spirit, a complete 'yes' to the Father."[122] These experiences of who and what we are, are ineffable. Every description falls short of the reality. The mystery of God in us and us in God is beyond words and experiences. Verbalization either spoken or written can at most only approximate what these dynamics really mean. Still we must respect the word, even if the experience it attempts to capture is paradoxical. After all, the greatest paradox of all is the incarnation. Here is Jesus, God and man, who manifested His glory by washing the feet of His disciples. The same Jesus whose nature we have been given, teaches us that instead of seeking power, we should hunger for holiness. Instead of living hedonistically, we should welcome persecution, poverty, and purity. Contrariwise, if we are accustomed to being in charge of our lives, not being a complete "yes" to the Father, it is not going to be easy to give up everything and follow Him. Yet, only if we let go of ego and arrogance, and acknowledge our profound nothingness before God, can we appreciate anew these foundational directives for contemplation. It is only when contemplation becomes an avenue of joyful Christian living can it fulfill its purpose as a way to union with God, for not only will it touch our hearts, it will also help to transform our world. In other words, contemplation is "a way" of being a complete "yes" to God, it is a way of being "entire" in imitation of Christ who is whole and entire.

Moreover, the greatness of the Christian vocation is to be found in *"Entire"*: *"being"* (*esse*) and *"doing"* (*agere*). What makes a Christian a Christian is the person of Christ,

---

[122] Ibid., p. 123.

and Christ is real and whole; therefore he is entire. Prayer is a call to greatness. It is often the space where the poor and the oppressed re-claim and express their nobility and graciousness. There is a poem by Fernando Pessoa which articulates this:

> **To be Great, be Entire**
>
> To be great, be entire:
>
> Of what is yours nothing exaggerate or exclude.
>
> *Be whole in each thing.*
>
> *Put all that you are into the least you do.*
>
> Like that on each place the whole moon shines for she lives aloft.[123]

This is a beautiful prayer poem—to put all that you are into the least that you do. When you hold back, you avoid the truth of situations, you diminish what a prayerful experience can become. The prayerful presence transfigures everything.

The Liturgy of the Hours and the Eucharistic Sacrifice: The Common Prayers of the Church

The Liturgy of the Hours and the Eucharistic sacrifice have five things in common:

- Both are liturgy in the etymological sense of the word as a social or public service rendered to God.
- Both take place in a celebrative mood and celebrate the person of Jesus, His life birth, passion death, and resurrection.
- Both are celebrated by crossing a threshold.

---

[123] Quoted in John O'DONOHUE, *Eternal Echoes*, p. 224. The emphasis done in italics is mine.

- Both are necessarily a public action of Christ and His Body, the Church.
- Both demand harmony of the mind and voice (*Mens nostra concordet voci nostrae* [*RB* 19]).

1. Liturgy: When we say that the Liturgy of the Hours (*LH*) and the Eucharistic sacrifice (Mass) are both liturgies, what do we mean? What is liturgy?

From its very origins, the notions that were at the base of the Greek term *Leiturgía* were those at the etymological root of the word "people" (*laòs*) and "work" (*érgon*). Liturgy meant "action for the people." It was a work, a service in favour of the community (the city or the state). In classic Greek culture, the word liturgy was exclusively used with a civil meaning: an honourable service assumed by a citizen or a family in order to organise plays and feasts, and in such a case it was called an ordinary or cyclical liturgy. It became extraordinary liturgy when it was an emergency as in war.[124] Liturgy is therefore etymologically the immediate meaning of the compound word *leitourgía,* a "public service,"[125] work of the people. On the other hand, from the Scriptural point of view,[126] which is where the early

---

[124] Cf. S. Marsili, "Liturgia" in *Nuovo Dizionario di Liturgia*, Domenico SARTORE and Achille M. TRIACCA (eds.) (Paoline, 1988), pp. 726-727; See also D. Mosso, "Liturgia," in *Dizionario Teologico Interdisciplinare*, vol. 1 (Torino, 1977), pp. 67-88, here p. 67.

[125] Cf. S. Marsili, "Liturgia" in *Nuovo Dizionario di Liturgia*, pp. 726-727.

[126] In the New Testament, the word *leitourgía* has different meanings. Its first meaning is service in general, which is evident in Rm 13:6; 2 Cor 9:12; Heb 1:14. The next meaning is service as in the Old Testament liturgical ritual that also can be verified in Lk 1:23; Heb 8:2, 8; 9:21; 10:11. Liturgy as a Christian ritual worship has only one reference in the Scriptures: Acts 13:2, and liturgy as spiritual worship in Rom 1:9;

Christians got their particular notion of liturgy, it means a spiritual worship. It is from this early Greek notion of liturgy combined with its spiritual sense from the Scriptures that Saint Benedict has the idea of calling the Liturgy of the Hours *Opus Dei* (work of God).

From this etymological root of liturgy being a public service, action for the people which the Christians adapted and gave a spiritual meaning of being a public service of God, one can then understand that such a prayer is not and cannot be a private prayer. However presented, it remains the Church's own social offering of praise to God, and all those who take part in it, whether publicly in Church, in the seclusion of a hermit's cell, or on a sick bed, join in it not as private individuals only but always as members of the universal choir, in the audience chamber of the Most High God, and in the presence of the angels—*In conspectu Angelorum psallam tibi Deus meus.* One thing that is necessary is for one to bear in mind that in our prayers we should be consciously united with that "great multitude which no man can number (count) out of every nation standing before the Throne."

The same thing is true of the Mass. While a priest may celebrate Mass alone, he is in effect performing the action of Christ before the angels and saints and for the whole Body of Christ.

2. Celebration: One of the words most used in talking about liturgy is the word "celebration." This word has a certain vagueness about it that is inevitable. Since we are dealing with something which is easier to experience

---

15:16; Phil 2:17. As was emphasized in the first centuries of the Church's history, the word *leitourgía* is to be taken as a spiritual worship.

than to describe in exact terms, it is a condition common to many of our most profound human realities. When we reflect upon the things that we call celebrations in our ordinary experience, we find that there are elements there which help us to appreciate what we mean when we speak of our liturgy as a celebration, indicating the type of activity it is. Besides, it has to be made clear that all celebrations, far from being of human contrivance, have their origin in a divinely given rhythm. As Josef Pieper[127] has acutely stated,

> While man can make the celebration, he cannot make the festive occasion and the cause for celebrating. The happiness of being created, the existential goodness of things, the participation in the life of God, the overcoming of death—all these occasions of the great traditional festivals are pure gifts. But because no one can confer a gift on himself, something that is entirely a human institution cannot be a real festival. [128]

When we get together to celebrate—be it an anniversary, a birthday, a homecoming or whatever—it is always an appreciation of something or someone. When we celebrate, we joyfully acknowledge and recognise the presence

---

[127] Josef PIEPER (1904-1997) was a German Catholic philosopher, at the forefront of the neo-Thomistic wave in twentieth-century Catholic philosophy. Pieper studied philosophy, law, and sociology at the universities of Berlin and Münster. After working as a sociologist and self-employed writer, he became ordinary professor of philosophical anthropology at the University of Münster and taught there from 1950 to 1976. As professor emeritus, he continued to provide lectures until 1996. He died in 1997.

[128] J. Pieper, *In Tune with the World: a Theory of Festivity* (New York: Harcourt-Brace, 1963), p. 46.

of someone, something, or a delightful achievement. The desire to celebrate is the longing to enter deeper into the mystery of actuality.[129] On a twenty-fifth wedding, profession, or priestly anniversary, we come together to appreciate the life of married couples, of the sister/brother, or of the priest, their personal value to us and what they have achieved. It is a genuine moment of appreciation. This celebration, this appreciation, is not about nothing. It is about the real value we see in those people, it is about the life they have lived together, the achievement in their family life, in their ministries, and in their apostolate and also the achievement which they are in themselves. It is, in a sense, an appreciation of what has gone before, of what has led them to this moment.

In the course of this celebration, we use all sorts of gestures, words and things to express our joyful appreciation because there is always a sense of joy and happiness in celebration. We greet the couple, the sister/brother, or the priest in a way that expresses our congratulation, be it in a handshake, a hug, a kiss, a tap on the back or whatever. However, in a sincere celebration, we express our appreciation of those we are celebrating. Even though we appreciate them all the time, in a celebration we express our appreciation in special ways.

The make-up of these celebrations is varied: we eat and drink. Could one in fact imagine any sort of party, occasion, or celebration without eating and drinking? We

---

[129] See John O'DONOHUE, *Eternal Echoes: Exploring our Hunger to Belong* (London, 1998), p. 75. John O'Donohue was an Irish poet, author, priest, and a Hegelian philosopher. He was a native Irish speaker, and as an author is best known for popularising Celtic spirituality. He died in 2008.

have music and perhaps songs and dance. We create a festive atmosphere with our fine clothes, our specially set tables, our candles, flowers, or other decorations. Our time of special appreciation takes place in a whole atmosphere that brings about a sense of uniqueness of the occasion. This atmosphere is joyful, it creates enjoyment, but it is also serious. It is a serious occasion we have gathered for and not a frivolous one.

All of these elements will fail to make sense, however, if there is not a group of people present who mutually appreciate the person or persons they are celebrating, and who interact with one another, who know how to get on together and enjoy the atmosphere together. If they do not really get on together, then the celebration cannot but be a failure. Consequently, one recalls the passage in the Scriptures where Jesus says: "I tell you solemnly once again, if two of you on earth agree to ask anything at all, it will be granted to you by my Father in heaven. For where two or three are gathered together in my name, I am there in the midst of them" (Mt 18:19-20). Mutual agreement is indeed necessary for an authentic and fruitful celebration, whatever type of celebration it is.

Likewise, to speak of the Liturgy of the Hours or the Eucharist as a celebration means to use all the above-mentioned elements in the working out of the prayerful gathering of such celebrations. We do not just take these elements over into our liturgy, but we use these basic human celebrative words, gestures, and actions and fit them to the Eucharist and to the Liturgy of the Hours. We celebrate the Eucharist for what it is and so we have to tailor these elements to fit its depth of meaning, its fundamental structure, and its supreme dignity. If we are to have a serious celebration and not just the carrying out of rubrical prescriptions, we need these elements of human celebration. We need to be able to enflesh the basic structure, the basic design of the Eucharistic liturgy with these elements that we find in our moments of heightened appreciation of one another. There should also be the element of "a group of people present who mutually appreciate" the life, death, and resurrection of Christ, and who are also ready to celebrate their own lives while commemorating and making present the very life of Christ.

So in our liturgy we use gestures in prayer and towards one another. We give a sign of peace which ought to be human and most especially, sincere and Christian. We use lights and vestments, and special books and music, and song and solemn words. We are there to celebrate and appreciate Christ and we bring to bear all the elements we use in appreciating one another to appreciate what the Father has done for us, to appreciate what He means for us and for all humankind.[130]

3. Crossing of a Threshold: What actually makes a liturgical celebration different from other types of celebrations is that liturgical prayer involves a crossing of a threshold. We must leave behind many of our normal activities and go to a place apart. We need this move or shift in order to be able to connect to our glorified brothers and sisters. This transition is beautifully highlighted in the monastic customs of having *statio*[131] and wearing a special

---

[130] Read F. O'LOUGHLIN, "Celebration," in *New Liturgy of Summer* (1976), pp. 2-3.

[131] Etymologically, the Latin word *statio* was used by the early Christians in two senses, both of obscure origin. Fundamentally the Latin *statio* is derived from the verb *stare* (to stand, halt, take up a position), and it came to mean a gathering at a fixed place for any fixed purpose. *Statio* was certainly used to describe a strictly liturgical assemblage in the Luciferian

choir garment for the liturgical celebrations especially for the Hours of Lauds and Vespers (major hours) and for the Mass. The same sense of crossing a threshold applies to the priest dressing appropriately for the celebration of the Holy Mass: the surplice, the alb, amice, and the chasuble. All these double and several attires re-emphasize the sacredness of the act which the priest is about to perform. They are an indication that something unusual, which belongs to a different realm, the realm of the Spirit and beyond the human depth and manoeuvre, is about to take place.

Thus the Christian makes this transition from profane to sacred space, ritually crossing all the various thresholds he/she encounters each day, from sleeping to being awake, from home to Church, from intimate to communal participations. In the same sense, church doors are usually heavy and large, so that one has to enter purposefully. Church doors have no half measures, such as screen doors in domestic buildings, which permit a degree of

---

Libellus precum of 384 (see *Patrologia Latina* 13:83). Whether the convocations of clergy and laity called *stationes* by Cyprian and Cornelius were liturgical gatherings is not so clear. Cyprian, Epistle 44.2; 49.3 (*Corpus scriptorum ecclesiasticorum latinorum* 3.2:598, 612). Read the *New Catholic Encyclopaedia*, Second Edition, vol. 13, *Seq*, The Thomson Gale in association with the Catholic University of America (Washington, D.C., 2002), p. 498. In the Monastic tradition, the practice of *statio* acknowledges the importance of times between and within times, and the value of space between and within space. The practice of *statio* is meant to centre us and make us conscious of what we are about to do, who we are about to celebrate, before whom we are about to stand, and make us present to God who is present to us. *Statio* is the desire to do consciously what one could otherwise do mechanically. *Statio* is in other words the capacity for recollection and the virtue of presence.

privacy to be combined with a degree of openness. When entering a sacred space, one is either in or out, and what occurs inside is thus protected from inquisitive and casual attention. It is appropriate to the intentions of commerce that the doors of shops open without our touch, but the doors to the sacred must be pushed open physically and intentionally.

The sense of crossing a threshold is extended by the use of the holy water font. This is a ritual remembrance of the Sacrament of Baptism through which one enters Christian life. Thus, with each entry to the church, one physically re-enacts his spiritual entry into the divine milieu. The sign of the cross, the holy water, the genuflection or bow—all ritually express the crossing over into sacred space. Since the space calls for action, once the believer has entered the church, he/she begins his/her journey forward. His/her imagination leads the way, as the interior world of the sacred reveals visibility. The altar gives an emotionally and visually satisfying focus to the journey. For it is there that the Eucharist is celebrated and witnessed, there the believers both observe the ritual and participate in it. Then the altar becomes a point of departure for a reversed journey out into the world again. Crossing the threshold, one enters a sacred space which evokes a response of forward movement, a spiritual journey towards communion, celebration, and the gathering together of all one's experience into an integral meaning, which, to be transformed, must be offered up at the altar, and then directed out into the world again.

Liturgy transcends human activity. It belongs to the sphere of the spiritual, so we should approach it with awe and trembling. We are out of our depths, we are rather operating in a zone of faith and mystery that does not yield its fruit to mere rationality as in other human ordinary celebrations. In coming to liturgy, we leave the world of space and time and enter the halls of eternity where we are joined with the angels and saints in worshipping the Creator of the universe. This fact is brought out very well in the passage of the Bible where it says:

> What you have come to is nothing known to the senses: not a blazing fire, or a gloom turning to total darkness, or a storm; or trumpeting thunder or the great voice speaking which made everyone that heard it beg that no more should be said to them. (...) But what you have come to is Mount Zion and the city of the living God, the heavenly Jerusalem, where the millions of angels have gathered for the festival, with the whole Church in which everyone is a first born son and a citizen of heaven. You have come to God himself, the supreme Judge, and been placed with spirits of the saints who have been made perfect; and to Jesus, the mediator who brings a new covenant and a blood for purification which pleads more insistently than Abel's (Heb 12:18-24).

So the Christian experience of God in the liturgy could be comparable to the experience of the awesome theophany at Mount Sinai in Exodus 19-20. The Christians gathered for the worship of God "have come to Mount Zion, to the heavenly Jerusalem, the city of the living God, to the Church of the firstborn, whose names are written in heaven, to God, the judge of all men, to the spirits of righteous men made perfect" (Heb 12:22-23). Therefore, "since we are receiving a kingdom that cannot be shaken, let us be thankful, and so worship God acceptably with reverence and awe, for our 'God is a consuming fire'" (vv. 28-29).

Worship is at the heart of genuine response to God's presence. Moreover, reverence and awe towards God are, in turn, central to worship. We do indeed serve an awesome God. Worship is one of the most transforming activities that we engage in as Christians. True worship happens when we get a glimpse of God—who He is and what He is about—and just stand there in awe of Him, being overwhelmed and transformed down to the very depths of our being by the magnificent vision of the glory of our heavenly Father.[132]

God's family is one but in two locations and two different situations. One is glorified and the other is in the process of glorification, hence Saint Paul says that every family whether spiritual or natural takes its name from God the Father (Eph 3:15). This one family in two different states comes together in every liturgical celebration. What we do during the liturgical worship of the Church is *plugging into* a supernatural realm where angels and saints are continuously praying and adoring God day in day out. So we are part of something bigger. The family of God in the process of glorification joins and unites with the glorified members of the same family in praise and worship. The Psalmist in Psalm 137 says: "in the presence of the angels I will sing to you," and to this Psalm Saint Benedict then adds: "let us consider, then, how we ought to behave in the presence of God and his angels, and let us stand to sing the psalms in such a way that our minds are in harmony with

---

[132] Read Richard E. AVERBECK, "Spirit, Community, and Mission: A Biblical Theology for Spiritual Formation," in *Journal of Spiritual Formation & Soul Care*, 1 (2008), pp. 27-53, here pp. 37-38.

our voices" [*RB* 19:6, 7]). The crossing of a threshold is an indispensable condition for this re-union of the family of God: the glorified and the yet to be glorified. The General Instruction on the Liturgy of the Hours did not hesitate to stress the unity that ought to exist between the family of God on earth and that in heaven, especially when the Body of Christ is gathered to offer praise:

> When the Church offers praise to God in the liturgy of the hours, it unites itself with that hymn of praise sung throughout all ages in the halls of heaven; it also receives a foretaste of the song of praise in heaven, described by John in the Book of Revelation, the song sung continually before the throne of God and of the Lamb. Our close union with the Church in heaven is given effective voice "when we all, from every tribe and tongue and people and nation redeemed by Christ's blood (see Rv 5:9) and gathered together into the one Church, glorify the triune God with one hymn of praise."[133]

So the reunion of God's family (the Church in heaven and on earth) is noticeable in the way churches are built. Whereas pagan temples were built for the gods only, Christian churches were designed to make a home for God and His people. Thus, the threshold, the path, the centre and the altar transmit the existential meanings of Christianity to the environment as a whole.[134]

---

[133] General Instruction of the Liturgy of the Hours (Congregation for Divine Worship, February, 1971), n. 16.

[134] Cf. G. DAVIES, *Temples, Churches, and Mosques* (New York: Pilgrim Press, 1982), p. 96.

4. Action of Christ and His Body the Church: In the Eucharistic celebration, the sacrifice of Jesus and that of the Church come together into a single sacrifice. The Church has its own part in the action of Christ. She receives this action, but she does it in an active way, since by participation in Christ's actions, the Church becomes a living body. The commitment of the Church with her sacrifice to the sacrifice of Christ is so deep that "both of these sacrifices flow together; they are fundamentally one."[135] It is in the Eucharist that the Church accomplishes the maximum of the worship Mystery[136] because it is then that the sacrifice of Christ becomes the sacrifice of the Church. In the celebration of the "mystery," the two of them, Christ and Church, merge into one offering of love to the Father.[137]

In the Liturgy of the Hours, it is Christ who prays with, for, and in us, His Church. To this effect the Vatican

---

[135] Odo CASEL, *The Mystery of Christian Worship*, Burkhard NEUNHEUSER (ed.), Introduction written by Aidan KAVANAGH (New York, 1999), p. 13.

[136] The term "worship mystery" is the Caselian terminology found in his mystery theology where he explained the difference between the mystery of Christ and the mystery of worship. The Mystery of Christ, he said, is Christ Himself, meaning the revelation of God in His incarnated Son, revelation that has as its highest peak the sacrificial death and the glorification of the Lord. While the Mystery of Worship is the presentation and the ritual reproduction of the Mystery of Christ by which it is made possible for us to enter the Mystery of Christ Himself. The Mystery of worship represents for the Christian, the way of living in the Mystery of Christ Himself. Odo CASEL, *The Mystery of Christian Worship*, Burkhard NEUNHEUSER (ed.), Introduction written by Aidan KAVANAGH (New York, 1999), p. 37-38, and a letter from the 20th of April 1943, in André GOZIER, *La porte du ciel: réactualiser le mystère avec*, Odo CASEL, O.E.I.L. (Paris, 1987), p. 91.

[137] Odo CASEL, "Le Sacrifice mystique du Christianisme," in *Revue Liturgique et Monastique*, 12 1/1926, p. 10.

II document *Sacrosanctum Concilium* (83) declares: "Jesus Christ, High Priest of the New and Eternal Covenant, taking human nature, introduced into this earthly exile that hymn which is sung throughout all ages in the halls of heaven. He attached to himself the entire community of mankind and have them join him in singing his divine song of praise." The whole theology of the Liturgy of the Hours is summarised in this passage. It means that the Liturgy of the Hours is a mystical moment because it is a moment of union between Christ and His Church.

Christ is indeed the protagonist of liturgical prayers (*LH* and Mass), hence Saint Benedict calls the Liturgy of the Hours *Opus Dei,* (work of God): the work of God in us and our work for God. The liturgical celebration is therefore a *trait-d'union* between the Christian faithful and Christ, the head of the Church. This is so because the liturgical prayers are said in union with Christ, praying to the Father, as a result, prayer means living in communion with God. There is only one way to this communion with the living God: Jesus Christ (cf. Jn 14:6). *In, through,* and *with* Jesus, and through the working of the Holy Spirit, we become sons and daughters of our Father in heaven. In this way, we participate in the life and the love of the triune God. "Through him and with him, and in him," we hear in the Doxology, the concluding prayer of praise in the Eucharistic prayer.

This is another reason why the Eucharist is the source and summit of the Church's life. In the celebration of the Eucharist, we come into unique and direct contact with the mystery of Christ. Everything becomes present: His humanity and divinity, His sacrifice on the cross, and His resurrection. The same is also true of the Liturgy of the Hours. As we celebrate the Hours, the whole life of Christ is made present. When we receive the Eucharist, He Himself comes to us and we become one with Him. This is why the Eucharist is an altogether unique form of prayer, which cannot be replaced by any other.[138] However, the Liturgy of the Hours is complementary to the Eucharist in as much as it helps us to remain constantly in a prayerful attitude. Pope Benedict VI remarked that "we celebrate and live the liturgy well only if...we remain in a prayerful attitude, uniting ourselves with the Mystery of Christ and with his conversation as Son with the Father."[139] This is what the Liturgy of the Hours helps us to do.

5. Harmony of Mind and Voice: One cannot help but appreciate the insight of Saint Benedict on this point, with his marvellous dictum: "*Mens nostra concordet voci nostrae*" (Let our mind be in harmony with our voice [*RB* 19]). After regulating the Liturgy of the Hours in detail, he speaks of what the monks are to do during each hour of prayer. For Saint Benedict, the liturgy is mental prayer: *mens nostra*. But this mental prayer consists in consenting to what our voice proclaims, namely, the words of God, the text of the Bible. We have to accord our mind to what the Church asks us to say. The Church has chosen for us; we must accept, consent, thank, and obey. This is the liturgy. Liturgy is obedience, it is renouncement, and that is why it is worship: it is perfect sacrifice. "Let us obey the song

---

[138] Read Andreas SCHMIDT, *We Have Come to Adore Him: An Introduction to Prayer at the School of Benedict XVI*, #5, The New Evangelization Series (Washington: Knights of Columbus, 2013), p. 18.

[139] Pope Benedict VXI, General Audience, 26 September 2012.

of the Wisdom of God, and let us renounce even to choose our words ourselves."[140]

This unison of mind and voice mentioned by Saint Benedict had a great influence on the many documents of the Church regarding the liturgy in general. The General Instruction (GILH 19) making an explicit reference to the Rule of Saint Benedict (*RB* 19) and to *Sacrosanctum Concilium* (90) notes:

> Mind and voice must be in harmony in a celebration that is worthy, attentive, and devout, if this prayer is to be made their own by those taking part and to be a source of devotion, a means of gaining God's manifold grace, a deepening of personal prayer, and an incentive to the work of the apostolate.... Seeking Christ, penetrating ever more deeply into his mystery through prayer they should offer praise and petition to God with the same mind and heart as the divine Redeemer when he prayed.[141]

The same Chapter 19 of the Rule of Saint Benedict led Pope Benedict XVI to a marvellous observation and explanation of the fact that ordinarily thoughts come first before words but in the Liturgy of the Hours the reverse is the case. The words are already provided, the individual needs to unify his/her thoughts with those words. He wrote:

> In his Rule Saint Benedict coined the formula "*mens nostra concordet voci nostrae,*" (our minds

[140] Jean LECLERCQ, "The Unity of Prayer," in *Worship* 33, no. 7 (1955), p. 414.

[141] General Instruction of the Liturgy of the Hours (Congregation for Divine Worship, February, 1971), n. 19.

must be in accord with our voice), *RB* 19:7. Normally thought precedes words: it seeks and formulates the word. But praying the Psalms and liturgical prayer in general is exactly the other way round: the word, the voice goes ahead of us, and our mind must adapt to it. For on our own we human beings do not "know how to pray as we ought" (Rom 8:26)—we are too far removed from God, he is too mysterious and too great for us. And so God has come to our aid: He himself provides the words of our prayers and teaches us to pray. Through the prayers that come from him, he enables us to set out towards him; by praying together with the brothers and sisters he has given us, we gradually come to know him and draw closer to him.

In Saint Benedict's writings, the phrase cited just now refers directly to the Psalms, the great prayer book of the people of God of the Old and New Covenant. The Psalms are words that the Holy Spirit has given to men; they are God's Spirit become word. We thus pray "in the Spirit," with the Holy Spirit. This applies even more of course of the Our Father.[142]

Liturgy is therefore humility because in the liturgy we retire behind the prayer of the Church, behind the words of God. In the liturgy, God is the chief actor and we have only to say, "Yes, Amen," to sing "Alleluia," as the angels and saints in heaven do, according to the Apocalypse. That "our mind accord with our tongue" means that it accords with

---

[142] Pope Benedict XVI, *Jesus of Nazareth: From the Baptism in the Jordan to the Transfiguration* (New York, 2007), p. 131.

the mind of God, with the words of God, with the mind of the Church. We understand now why, when dealing with divine services, the ancient writers speak so much of reverence in prayer. Saint Benedict has a chapter "On Reverence at Prayer" (*RB* 20). Reverence is a general attitude of presence to God, of admiration, of fear—in the biblical meaning of the word, which includes love and humility.[143]

In liturgical prayer one prays in spirit and in truth, prays with one's whole being, otherwise it is only an empty chatter, and the person is divided within. Like what our Lord said in Matthew 12:25: "Every kingdom divided against itself is heading to ruin; and no town, no household divided against itself can stand." If one is divided within oneself, the mouth praising God while heart and mind are elsewhere, one's prayer becomes ineffective. Because of this let us unite our minds with what our voice says. In the liturgy we are called upon to bring our mind in harmony with what the Church does for us and says to God. And the best way to hear these words is to pronounce them. Saint Bernard wrote in a concise but marvellous formula, "*Sola quae cantat audit*" (Only the soul that sings truly hears).[144] In order to hear the words of God in the liturgy of the Church, let us sing them; it is in singing that we hear. It is in this unison that our prayers are heard.[145]

---

[143] Cf. Jean LECLERCQ, "The Unity of Prayer," p. 414.

[144] *Sermones super Cantica*, I, 11. Ed. J. LECLERCQ, etc. (Rome, 1957), Vol. 1, p. 8.

[145] The following story brings out the truth of this fact: *Their heart is not in it...*
"A man died recently and went to heaven. He was very happy up there, as he wandered about, exploring the place. One Sunday morning he bumped into Jesus. Jesus called him over to show him something. He opened a sort of trap-door in the floor of heaven, so that the man could look through, and see

The active participation, which was so much high-lighted by the Conciliar document, entails not only par-ticipation in terms of singing and responding but also an interior fervour of a liturgical piety wherein the mouth, and the whole body are in unison with the heart, mind, and will. This is indeed the meaning of "full, conscious and active participation in liturgical celebrations which is demanded by the very nature of liturgy...and which is the primary and indispensable source from which the faithful are to derive the true Christian spirit" (*SC* 14).

---

even as far as the earth below. Eventually, Jesus got to focus his attention on a church, his own local church at home, where there was a full congregation at Mass. The man watched for a while, and then something began to puzzle him. He could see the priest moving his lips, and turning over the pages. He could see the choir holding their hymnals, and the organist thumping the keyboards. But he couldn't hear a sound. It was total silence. Thinking that the amplification system in heaven had broken down, he turned to Jesus for an explanation. Jesus looked at him in surprise. 'Didn't anybody ever tell you? We have a rule here that if they don't do those things down there with their hearts, we don't hear them up here at all!'" Jack McARDLE, in *And that's the Gospel truth!* cited by Fr. Jude BOTELHO, at www.NetForLife.Net.

Chapter Five: Liturgy of the Hours:
A Sharing in the Prayer of Christ

Before proceeding, it is expedient to mention briefly that this prayer of the Church is known by so many names: The Canonical Hours, The Breviary, The Divine Office, The Sacrifice of Praise, The *Opus Dei,* and The Liturgy of the Hours.

- *Horae Canonicae,* Canonical Hours: This is the oldest of the names. Derived from the Greek word *Kanon* which literally means, a level, a ruler, rule or regulations. Showing that from its earliest times, the different Hours were subject to rule and had to be recited at stated times.[146] It shows that we live with time and are in time. The Canonical Hours provide an efficient way to consecrate to God each "hour" of the day in view of consecrating the whole "hours" of the day and make them holy.

- *Breviarium* meaning "abridgement," because in the late Middle Ages Pope Innocent III (1198-1216) approved a shortened form of the older numerous manuscripts of the Divine Office for his curia. This book was adopted with modifications by the Franciscan order. This version made a rapid expansion in Europe. In 1568 Pope Pius V (1565-1572) in collaboration with the Council of Trent (1545-1552; 1562-1563) issued this breviary as *Breviarium*

---

[146] Read Vilma G. LITTLE, *The Sacrifice of Praise: An Introduction to the Meaning and Use of The Divine Office* (London, 1957), p. 23.

Romanum in a revised form and imposed its use on the Latin Church.

- ***Officium Divinum,*** Divine Office, from *ob* and *facio*, meaning that which one does for another. That is to say, it is a service whether voluntary or obligatory: a duty, a charge or a function, the performance of which in its wider sense, means "the church's office or duty" to praise God. In its narrow sense, the prayer in its official form is considered as the special duty of the ordained ministers and religious bodies or groups. So the word "Divine Office" should daily remind us that the vocal worship of God is a duty, hence the etymological meaning of the word "liturgy."

- ***Sacrificium laudis,*** the Sacrifice of Praise. In the book of Hosea 14:2 we read: "We will offer you our words of praise," and some translations said: "We will offer in sacrifice the holocaust of our lips." The Letter to the Hebrews 13:15 says: "through him (Jesus Christ) let us offer God an unending sacrifice of praise, a verbal sacrifice that is offered every time we acknowledge his name." The word *sacrificium* derives from *sacrum* (sacred) and *facere* (to make). In all forms of sacrifice throughout the ages, there is some aspect of life being made over to the deity whom it is desired to honour or to propitiate. Thus, the "essential core of sacrifice lies in the return of life to its author in a conscious, voluntary act of adoration and acknowledgement of its source."[147] A complete sacrifice therefore comprises *being* and *doing.* To call the Liturgy of the Hours a sacrifice

---

[147] Ibid., p. 25.

is very illuminating and very challenging. Vilma Little superbly explained in practical terms what this means: "In this liturgical offering, presented in words, the life principle is the breath, which in vocal worship, is being constantly consumed and used up in the service of God, winging its flight back to the mysterious Breathing which first set it in motion."[148] Little explained further that it was in this sense that Saint Augustine could say, "*Qui cantat bis orat*" (He who sings prays twice), not for any additional quality or beauty but because of the greater quantity of breath used up in the praise of God. In sacrifice, the identification of the offerer with what is offered can be either physical or mystical.[149] So when one participates befittingly in the Liturgy of the Hours the person is offering God both a sacrifice of praise and a sacrifice of the person's life.

- *Opus Dei* by Saint Benedict, meaning the work of God. The Christian/monk has a duty to do the work of God, which is the praise of God. It is our duty to praise God. Praise increases our capacity to live and grow in love and holiness. Praise draws us into the abundant life in which God created us to live. In this sense, therefore, *Opus Dei* becomes God's work in us. Another aspect of work of God is that work of vocal praise which Jesus unceasingly carries out on earth through the lips of those who have obligation to it like the ordained ministers and the religious persons.

---

[148] Ibid., p. 26.
[149] Cf. Ibid., p. 26.

- ***Liturgia Horarum (LH),*** the Liturgy of the Hours, used by the Second Vatican Council to replace the Divine Office and Breviary. The new term designates the official prayer of the Christian community gathered in the liturgical assembly under the ordained minister.

The present work is going to abide by that used by the Second Vatican Council, the Liturgy of the Hours, with the acronym (*LH*) where necessary.

It was demonstrated in Chapter Four that *lectio divina* is the first moment in the dialogical intimate sharing with God. The present chapter, however, is meant to establish that the liturgical prayer of the Church is not so much a dialogue with God as it is a duet with Him. It does not consist so much in asking questions and receiving answers, in alternating our words with the words of God, as in bringing our voice into accord with the voice of God in the Church and in us. It is agreeing in singing with Christ and His Church, with the Spirit and the Bride, in harmonizing our voice with theirs. Consequently, what prevails here is harmony of voices and therefore harmony of mind, heart, and of life.

Theologically, there are two ways of seeing this harmony:

1. The understanding that in the *LH* Christ prays *with*, *for*, and *in* us.

2. The understanding that the *LH* is a moment of salvation. Through this sacred time and space, of the liturgical celebration, Christ is rendered present and that "hour" in which it is celebrated and that "sacred space" where it is celebrated becomes a moment of salvation.

These two theological ways are also the two principle dimensions of the *LH*: one Christological and the other Soteriological. They are the two hinges on which the theology of the *LH* hangs. We shall start with the Christological dimension.

Christological Dimension: The understanding that in the *LH* Christ prays *with*, *for*, and *in* us

The Liturgy of the Hours is a mystical moment between Christ and His Body the Church in as much as He prays *with, for, through,* and *in* her. These prepositional tags are also the same tags that unite the soul with Christ in contemplation. This means that there is something contemplative about the Liturgy of the Hours.

Liturgy of the Hours: A sharing in the intercessory prayer of Christ

In order to understand this most important point, one needs to know what Jesus has been doing since He ascended into heaven. Anyone who remembers the Apostles' Creed will immediately think and imagine the Risen Saviour seated at the right hand of the Father. However, there is something too passive about the Redeemer seated for eternity. The Letter to the Hebrews and its description of the heavenly priesthood of Jesus (Chapters 4, 8, 9) offers a significantly more dynamic, post-ascension ministry for the Risen One: He stands forever before the throne of the Father making intercession for all. In this way, it is clear that Jesus is not simply a model for how Christians ought to pray, rather, He is the prayer (the One who prays) and it is we who share in His one prayer.

Jesus Christ's present ministry today is mainly inter-cessory; He prays for believers from heaven (Rom 8:34; Heb 7:25). Theologically, Jesus' *intercessory ministry* involves His praying which prevents our falling before temptation and our failing because of weakness. Then His *advocate ministry* consists of pleading our case with the Father after we sin (1 Jn 2:1). Nevertheless, both types of praying involve intercessory prayer. The Holy Spirit also intercedes for Christians (Rom 8:26-27). He articulates our deepest feelings to the Father when we struggle to express ourselves. Even when we cannot express how we feel, the Holy Spirit knows and translates those feel-ings into prayers that the Father understands. Although Christ's work of saving the world was completed on the cross as can be proven by His cry "it is finished" (Jn 19:30), yet His care for His redeemed children will never finish. Hence, He is very active in heaven interceding for us. He only requests that we join Him in prayer.

This basic element of the *LH* being the Church's partic-ipation in the intercessory prayer of Christ gives the key to understanding and appreciating many of the Psalms. We repeat with Christ the words of the Psalms, some of which we would never say were we to pray as an isolated person who stands in the centre of the action, and the prayer is more or less individualized. But being the prayer of the Church, the Bride of Christ whose objectives are the objec-tives of Christ's redemption, it automatically becomes our personal interests and objectives too. Therefore, in the Psalms we weep too, or rather the Church weeps through our tears together with those who weep, rejoices through our joys together with those who rejoice, and does penance with the repentant. All the sentiments of Holy Mother

Church find their echo in our heart. This gives a deeper content to our prayer; we spread out far beyond ourselves.

Moreover, in praying the Psalms, we pray not only as a community but personally. We do this by praying a first-person "I" prayer along with many other "I's." The Psalms are almost always first-person prayers. They use "I" and "me." They equip me with a Word *from* God *to* speak to God. For example, in the verse that reads: "I was punished, I was punished by the Lord but not doomed to die" (Ps 117:18), this verse might not in any way mirror my situation at the time I will be saying it. Yet, I pray it, because I am part of the Body of Christ, the Church. Saint Paul says that we are "individual parts of one another" (Rom 12:5) and that we should therefore "rejoice with those who rejoice and be sad with those in sorrow" (Rom 12:15). So the Psalms stretch us beyond our current situation and ask us to join with other members of the Church who are in that condition. This indeed frees us from being overly focused on how we are feeling and invites us to get involved with other people's needs and worries. Sometimes it reflects our situation and at other times it is prayed with a sense of solidarity or compassion for others.

On the other hand, the Church and thereby the individuals praying on behalf of the entire Church use many Christological Psalms. This is possible by virtue of this mystical union of voices, minds, and words. For example, in Psalm 16 (verse 3), "You search my heart, you visit me by night. You test me and you find in me no wrong. My words are not sinful as are men's words." Who can dare say such a prayer if not the spotless Lamb that was slain? But by virtue of Him whose prayer we share, the Church can with audaciousness use the same words of Christ. There are so many other Psalms like that. Other examples are Psalms 25, 138, etc. There is not enough room within the narrower confines of our own personal experience to sound all the rich variety of sentiments and moods and affections that these Psalms contain. It is through the Liturgy of the Hours that we participate in the official ministry and care of souls.

So the Liturgy of the Hours is not a private but a corporate prayer, it is a prayer with the whole Church which shares in the intercessory prayer of Christ.[150] Not only does the Church share in the mission of Christ to proclaim and effect the mystery of salvation, she is also involved in the joyous task of giving endless praise and thanksgiving to the Father. Since the Christian prayer is primarily the action of Christ Himself joined by the entire community, therefore, whenever possible, the Liturgy of the Hours and most especially the major hours, should be celebrated in common.

---

[150] This is one of the reasons why we do not need to meditate and ruminate when we are reciting the Psalms in the Liturgy of the Hours. It is Christ who prays with, through, and in us. Understood in this sense, it is not vital to the efficacy of the Liturgy of the Hours that all who take part in it should understand fully in every detail what they are singing or saying, and it is not essential for us to feel any personal joy or satisfaction in the offering. Otherwise, everyone should then choose a Psalm of his/her choice that best appeals to his/her sentiments and moods. What is essential is the carrying out in the name and by the authority of our Lord Jesus Christ this sublime function of rendering perpetual praise and glory to the Holy Trinity. Because the Church is the prolongation in time of the Word Incarnate, the Church's prayer here and now becomes *Per Ipsum, et cum Ipso et in Ipso*. It is also very important to always bear in mind that the real starting point of worship is a sense of duty which we owe to God as creatures of His. We are able to love Him because He first loved us says Saint John (1 Jn 4:19). This point is basic in building a firm foundation for a solid and lasting relationship with God in Jesus.

Contemplative Character of
the Liturgy of the Hours

If in the Liturgy of the Hours Christ prays with, for, and in us, it then means that liturgical prayer is meant to be contemplative prayer. Without doubt, liturgical worship, which is essentially and at once internal and external, is directed to such contemplation as to its proper internal perfection. In other words, in order that true worship may exist in him/her who participates in it, a corresponding internal conformity must accompany all participation in liturgical worship. Contemplation is therefore not something adequately distinct from liturgical worship (as if the latter consisted only in external participation), but it is merely its internal aspect which has attained its perfection.[151]

Among the chief characteristics of liturgical contemplation are the capacity for living out the dual realities of "community-individual" and the awareness that for the Liturgy of the Hours community prevails—it is the community, the Body of Christ who prays. There is also the capacity for living out the binomials—object-subject, God-man, grace-human effort. Here again is the realisation that one begins with the object, with God and with grace. Thus there is a special balance in which the various dual realities and binomials are lived in proper hierarchical relation to each other. This is what exactly is demanded by liturgical contemplation.[152] Beginning with the object, it is clear that the substance of the Church's prayer is broader,

---

[151] Cf. Cipriano VAGAGGINI, "Liturgy and Contemplation," in *Worship* 34 (1960), pp. 507-523, here p. 509.

[152] Read Cipriano VAGAGGINI, *Il senso Teologico della Liturgia* (Roma, 1957), Balsamo Milano 19996, pp. 517-533.

i.e., all the needs of God's Kingdom here on earth. In liturgical prayer, the individual feels more like a member of a great community, like a little leaf on the great living tree of the Church. He/she shares in her life and her problems. Christ is praying through my mouth, I offer Him my tongue to pray with Him for all the great objectives of redemption, and for God's honour and glory. The necessity for understanding this liturgical mystical union between Christ and His Church through the individual persons praying, was one of the basic reasons behind the teaching of the theologians of the Liturgical Movement. Cipriano Vagaggini, one of the theologians of the Liturgical Movement writes:

> In order to lead the faithful to live the liturgy in a full way, including eventually its mystical summits, it is indispensable to form their religious sensibility in a communitarian sense until one has brought them to feel completely at ease when they participate, in a normally active way, in the liturgical and communitarian action. And *it is necessary to educate this sensibility so that the ontologically communitarian character of the liturgy is never, psychologically, lost sight of,* even when, in some cases, by reason of extrinsic and less than ideal circumstances, this communal character is not externally expressed as it is by nature would require: e.g., in the case of Mass celebrated alone, or the private recitation of the breviary.[153]

Without such formation of religious sensibility and of religious psychology in a communitarian sense, it is

---

[153] Cypriano VAGAGGINI, "Liturgy and Contemplation," p. 516. The italics is mine.

impossible to enter fully into the world of the liturgy and consequently it is not possible to dispose oneself properly for liturgical contemplation. The Liturgical Movement has always instinctively sensed this fact, and therefore it regarded this formation as one of the first tasks of its mission. Therefore, the Liturgy of the Hours can be a perfectly mystical moment if one properly participates in it. Vagaggini in another place[154] explained the perfect harmony which can exist between contemplation and the Liturgy of the Hours, even with a normally active and communitarian participation. To demonstrate this further to those who are not convinced, those who attribute contemplation only to a passive silent prayer, he added the testimony of some people whose life practically testifies the co-existence of a normal communitarian and external participation in the liturgical action and contemplation.[155] The generally false conception of the word "contemplation" is such that people often find it hard to open their eyes and see that the Lord Jesus meets us anywhere and at any time once we are in unison with His will. We can therefore intuit how much more He is united with us when we pray in the company of the whole angelic hosts.

It might psychologically be difficult to be fully attentive during a long service without distractions. A general attitude of reverence and a humble and sincere devotion are very necessary for a contemplative liturgical celebration

---

[154] Cipriano VAGAGGINI, *Il senso teologico della liturgia*, pp. 517-33. To explore further on contemplation and liturgy, read Cipriano VAGAGGINI, "Contemplazione nella Liturgia e Contemplazione fuori della Liturgia," in *Rivista di ascetica e mistica,* Fiesole, VII (1962), pp. 8-34, with an amplified bibliography.

[155] Read Cypriano VAGAGGINI, "Liturgy and Contemplation," pp. 517-518.

to take effect. Moreover, the ensemble of texts and actions of which the liturgy consists and the singing of the Psalms and hymns creates a marvellous atmosphere of prayer, of poetry, of a high spiritual tenor that embraces the whole person, soul and body, and this is contemplation. Fr. Jean Leclercq, citing Fr. Georges Goyau who calls some of the ways of praying *"une grande distraction vers le ciel"*[156] (a great distraction towards heaven), comments on such paradoxical and significant formulation. He stated:

> What is required in the liturgy is a form of piety which sometimes, for at least some of its participants, excludes an actual attention to the words: the master of ceremonies, the choirmaster, the sacristan, and others must keep attentive to a number of things in a way that recalls the words of our Lord, "You are solicitous about many things." But in this case those many things are indispensable for the perfect expression of the *unum necessarium*, the one thing necessary. This latter involves all the words, the songs, and the actions.[157]

Prayer is indeed a profound unified mystery and liturgical prayer is a culminating moment of prayer in as much as it is a more ecclesial and communal moment which at the same time has to be individual and personal. Both realities are co-joined by contemplation.

---

[156] Jean LECLERCQ, "The Unity of Prayer," p. 415.
[157] Ibid.

Soteriological Dimension: The Liturgy of the Hours as Salvific Moments

In the Liturgy of the Hours, the praise of God, thanksgiving to Him, and above all the memory (*anamnesis*) of the mysteries of salvation are extended throughout different "Hours" of the day. This salvation is strictly connected with time: in order to save us, God came down and took on our human and mortal flesh thereby entering into the human history. In this way, salvation entered into time and the human time in turn became a sacred time in a sacred history. There are powerful "moments" in this time of salvation and these moments are marked with sacramental celebrations and with the different "Hours" of the Liturgy of the Hours. They therefore became powerful "moments" of the time of salvation.

Liturgical Time

The liturgical time is the succession of the significant "times" of a symphony. In a symphony the instruments are integrated to produce one sound, so it is in the liturgical times. The liturgical time is a time adorned with double draping: cosmic and salvific. These two moments, cosmic and salvific, symphonically consent to one another forming the Christian time thereby acknowledging the transcendent unity of eternity.[158] It is the liturgical hours with their specific mysteries that give rhythm, colour, style and tune to the Christian time, because of this, liturgical "time" is never neutral or purely chronological. It is a time

---

[158] Cf. Hans Urs von BALTHASAR, *The Truth is Symphonic: Aspects of Christian Pluralism* (San Francisco, 1987), p. 9.

either of mourning or of joy, of election or of penance, of expectation or of welcoming.

Time has no specific pace and quality. We can testify to this fact if we consider what happens in our personal lives. Whenever we are living in buoyancy, the time seems to pass quickly, and when we are tired or bored, it drags. This assures us that time takes its qualities and colouring from the events and experiences that occur in it. When these events and experiences are deeply meaningful or satisfying, a very strange phenomenon occurs: time does not simply pass quickly but comes very near to disappearing altogether.[159] Ecstatic and blissful moments seem to give us a taste of eternity in which time has ceased to exist.[160] What we would like, of course, is to live in a time that is always highly coloured, vivid and intense, a perpetual spring, a perpetual youth, and a perpetual sunny morning. C. Smith remarked that: "Meister Eckhart once observed that all things become young the nearer they are to their source, who is God. So by continually bringing the flow of time back to God through regular periods of prayer we are rejuvenating it, giving it life and colour and meaning by relating it to its origin."[161] So through the Liturgy of the Hours, time is brought back to the eternity of God, its source. The *LH* uses time to free us from time. By participating actively and reverently in the Liturgy of the Hours,

---

[159] Cf. the unpublished part of the dissertation of Mary Bride (Thecla) NJOKU, *Liturgy as Human Experience of Divine Mystery: Salient Features of Liturgical Renewal and Present-day Monasticism: A Review of the Works of Romano Guardini, Odo Casel and Cipriano Vagaggini* (Rome, 2005), p. 211.

[160] Cf. C. SMITH, *The Path of Life: Benedictine Spirituality for Monks and Lay People* (York: Ampleforth Abbey Press, 1995), p. 126.

[161] Ibid.

we are responding to the Scriptural imperative to "redeem the time" (Eph 5:16).

The Christian tradition has in its long history made a constant connection between the different Hours of the *LH* with the various moments of the mystery of salvation, which is the mystery of Christ. The hour of Lauds celebrates the resurrection of Christ, and Vespers celebrates His redemptive sacrifice. One who fails to understand such connections with the mystery of salvation, will not be able to understand the beauty of the Liturgy of the Hours, especially Lauds and Vespers. This fact brings out the importance of the principle of "time" and "hour" of the Liturgy of the Hours: one cannot pray the prayer of Lauds in the evening and Vespers in the morning, otherwise its authenticity is emptied and the mystery lost. It is called the Liturgy of the Hours because we are called to consecrate a determined moment or hour of the day which has a particular relationship with the mystery of salvation. The Hours are so arranged that every three hours of the Christian's journey through this arid desert, one is encouraged to stop and go to the oasis that offers the waters of grace and the cool refreshing shade of heavenly assistance. In order to understand what these arrangements and divisions of the day are supposed to mean, a brief look into the history of their development is indispensable.

The Origins of the Liturgy of the Hours

The Liturgy of the Hours owes its remote origin to the inspiration of the old covenant. God commanded the Aaronic priests (c. 1280 BC) to offer a morning and evening sacrifice (Ex 29:38-42). During the Babylonian Exile (587-521 BC), when the Temple did not exist, the synagogue services of Torah readings and Psalms and hymns developed as a substitute for the bloody sacrifices of the Temple, a sacrifice of praise. The inspiration to do this might be in fulfilment of David's words, "Seven times a day I praise you" (Ps 119:164), as well as, "the just man mediates on the law day and night" (Ps 1:2). Moreover, the first definite record of an organised daily choir office started with King David, the sweet singer of Israel in 1 Chronicles 16:4ff. Reading the whole of chapter 16 one observes how David established a morning and evening service of praise. In verses 40-43, he says "to offer holocausts to Yahweh unfailingly, morning and evening," with different people being assigned to give praise to God, "for his love is everlasting," and others assigned to play the instruments. Here, in this daily office of praise and thanksgiving, which consists of the chanting of Psalms, reading of the sacred books and certain prayers, is found the source of our Liturgy of the Hours.[162]

So the daily offices of prayer have roots in ancient Judaism and were practised by Jesus. Jesus began a day with prayer while it was still very dark. The Gospel of Mark states: "In the morning, while it was still very dark, he got up and went out to a deserted place, and there he prayed" (Mk 1:35). The Psalmist did the same, "I rise before dawn and seek your promises; I put my hope in your words. My eyes are awake before each watch of the night that I may meditate on your promises" (Ps 119:147-148).

These prayers were continued by the early Christians such as Peter, John, and Cornelius. "One day Peter and John were going up to the temple at the time of prayer—at three

---

[162] Read the whole of 1 Chronicles 15 and 16. Read also Vilma G. LITTLE, *The Sacrifice of Praise*, pp. 3-5.

in the afternoon" (Acts 3:1), and, "At noon the next day, as they were on their journey and approaching the city, Peter went up on the roof to pray" (Acts 10:9). And Cornelius said: "Four days ago, unto this hour, I was praying in my house, at the ninth hour, and behold a man stood before me" (Acts 10:30). The daily offices of prayer have continued throughout the centuries.

A subsequent, four main stages[163] can be distinguished in the evolution of Christian prayer, which led to the present structures of the Liturgy of the Hours.

a. Christian Prayer of Private Devotions

Apart from the witnesses of prayer that were recorded in the Bible, the earliest document that recorded an establishment of the custom of interrupting the course of the day with prayer was the *Didache,*[164] at the end of the first or the beginning of the second century. It recommends that Christians recite the "Our Father" three times a day, though it did not specify the moments at which this

---

[163] Much of these historical stages follow the idea of Juan MATEOS, "The origins of the Divine office," in *Worship*: Volume 41 (1967), pp. 477-485.

[164] The *Didache* means "Teaching." It is the short name of a Christian manual compiled before AD 300. The full title is *The Teaching of the Twelve Apostles*. Some Christians thought *Didache* was inspired, but the Church rejected it when making the final decision of which books to include in the New Testament. *Didache* contained instructions for Christian groups, and its statement of belief may be the first written catechism. It has four parts: the first is the "Two Ways, the Way of Life and the Way of Death"; the second explains how to perform rituals such as baptism, fasting, and Communion; the third covers ministry and how to deal with traveling teachers; the fourth part is a reminder that Jesus is coming again, with quotations from several New Testament passages which exhort Christians to live godly lives and prepare for "that day."

prayer was to be recited.[165] Clement of Alexandria (d. before 215) notes the custom that some Christians had of praying at the third, sixth, and ninth hours, besides at morning, evening, and night prayer. He does not agree with this custom of establishing definite times for prayer during the day, because a true Christian, praises God "all through his life in every place, whether he be alone by himself or have some who share his belief."[166] Concerning this private prayer, an early witness that can be cited is Tertullian of the African Church (d. after 220). Others at the beginning of the third century are Hippolytus of Rome (d. 235), Origen (d. 253),[167] and Saint Cyprian of Carthage (d. 258).[168]

These prayers were basically recited in private and occasionally in common. They were prayers said at the *third hour* (9:00 a.m., which corresponds to today's praying of Terce), *sixth hour* (noon, corresponding to Sext or mid-day prayer), and *ninth hour* (3:00 p.m., corresponding to the praying of the None). Clement of Alexandria told us that these prayers were recited by the Christians besides the normal morning (Lauds), evening (Vespers), and night prayers (Compline). Of all these prayers, two were of particular importance for the early Christians and these are morning (Lauds) and evening (Vespers) prayers and they

---

[165] *Didache*, 2-3. Cf. J. P. Audet, *La Didache*. Instructions des Apôtres (Paris, 1958), pp. 234, 171-73. Reported by Juan MATEOS, "The origins of the Divine office," pp. 477-485.

[166] Stromata, VII, 7 PG 9:455. Cited in Juan MATEOS, "The origins of the Divine office," p. 478.

[167] *De Oratione* 12, 2 (ed. Paul Koetschau, GCS II, 324-25).

[168] *De Oratione Dominica* XXXIV (PL 4:541). For a more elaborate history of this private prayer in the early Church, read Juan MATEOS, "The origins of the Divine Office," pp. 477-485.

were called *legitimae orationes;* prayers prescribed by the Law and therefore were mandatory.

b. The Office of the Egyptian Monks

The Egyptian desert tradition was born and practised in the wilderness without any regard for secular Church usages. The desert monks had only two offices each day: one at the beginning and the other at the end of the day. Certainly, these two praying times was an influence from the ancient practice of private morning and evening prayers. One thing was remarkable with the Egyptian monks, a very important novelty, "they practised these two prayers as a community celebration."[169] It was impossible for the monks themselves to arrive at an agreement on a suitable number of Psalms for the common celebration of these two offices. There was a divine intervention[170]

---

[169] Cassian describes these celebrations in his well-known work, *De Institutis Coenobiorum II, 3, I and III, 5* (ed. Petschenig, *Corpus Scriptorum Ecclesiasticorum Latinorum XVII*, pp. 19, 40). He calls these two monastic offices or *synaxes: legitimae orationes*, as described in Tertullian, for he says: "In Egypt and Thebaid…we see the prayers prescribed by the Law preserved in the evening assemblies and night vigils." The "night vigil" is an early morning prayer.

[170] A story was told that one day as the monks were discussing how many Psalms should be said for the offices, evening arrived before a solution had been agreed upon. Since the time for the evening prayer had come, all returned to the church to celebrate it in common. From the midst of the group one monk arose and recited eleven Psalms, interposing the customary prayers between them. Finally he intoned a twelfth Psalm with alleluia. Then he disappeared. The Fathers agreed that this was a divine intervention to put an end to their controversy. Cf. Juan MATEOS, "The Origins of the Divine Office," pp. 481-482. This story is also the genesis of the six Psalms of the first nocturne and another six of the second nocturne that was prescribed by Saint Benedict in his Rule for the monks.

that put an end to their controversy and from that time on, the length of the community's prayers was established as twelve Psalms at each praying time. This explains the reason why the norm of twelve Psalms has ever since been called the Rule of the Angel. From what was transmitted to us, the Psalms recited in these Egyptian monastic assemblies were not chosen neither for their content nor spirit; that is, they were not connected to any mystery as we have them today. They had no connection with either the time of day or the type of celebration. The Psalms were probably recited in numerical order in the morning and evening. The psalmody was done by a soloist who recited the Psalms slowly in a loud voice.

c. The Ecclesiastical Offices

From the beginning of the fourth century, the secular Churches started organising public offices for mornings and evenings. These *legitimate orationes,* which before the Egyptian monks were an important private devotion of Christians, were now celebrated in community as among the Egyptian monks. At this point the Psalms were not sung in their numerical order, as was the practice with the Egyptian monks. Instead the Psalms were chosen according to the hour, the purpose, and the mystery of the hour. Eusebius of Caesarea (d. 339) explains that the morning office is one of hope in the mercy of the Lord (praise and thanksgiving), while the evening prayer is penitential (a confession of faults).[171] There were many witnesses to the existence of such a community prayer in the fourth century. Examples are Saint Epiphanius (c. 315-403) in

---

(Read *RB* 9, the number of Psalms at the night office, and *RB* 11, the celebration of vigils on Sundays.)

[171] In Ps 97:2-3 (PG 23:1169-72).

his treatise *Against Heresies,*[172] Saint John Chrysostom (d. 407), and the *Apostolic Constitutions* (c. 380).[173] These sources explicitly mention these two offices.

d. Urban Monastic Tradition

The liturgical tradition of the late fourth-century monasteries in contact with the towns and cities developed by making use of already existing practices. Unlike the desert monks of Egypt, the urban monks were in contact with the secular Churches and adopted their morning and evening celebrations. Later on, they incorporated the Sunday vigil of the resurrection as well. The urban monks also celebrated together the ancient hours of private prayer, of praying at the third, sixth, and ninth hours, besides at morning, evening, and night prayers, thereby creating the offices of Terce, Sext, None, Compline, and the office of midnight. The urban monastic office, therefore, is deeply rooted in the popular Christian tradition. Almost all the rites now practised in the Church follow the daily cycle of the urban monastic tradition at least in some periods of the liturgical year. So, the Liturgy of the Hours as we know it today contains elements of diverse origin; it has integrated prayers which belonged to the early Christians with others which are exclusively monastic.

Observations

From the brief history above, certain observations can be made:

1. It should be clear that the Liturgy of the Hours does not owe its origin to monasticism. Instead, it

---

[172] *Adversus Haereses* III, 23 (PG 42:829).
[173] 28II, 59, 2-4, ed. Funk, pp. 171-72; VIII, 35-38 Wid., pp. 545-47.

originated from ordinary Christians starting from the time of David. Due to the popular Christian origin of the Liturgy of the Hours, the Church desires it to be the prayer of everyone as it was from its very beginning and not something reserved for clergy and religious. What monasticism later did was to put form and structure into it. It is indeed the prayer of all the people of God (every baptized Christian) though the clergy and the religious have a special obligation to it. One might say that for the clergy and the religious it is an *obligation,* while for the faithful people of God there is *need* for it. The remote sources of the Hours therefore run thus:

a. From every evidence that we have, it stands out that Vespers and Lauds are the oldest Hours of the *LH* and their origin can directly be traced from the liturgical worship of the temple at Jerusalem. There is an uninterrupted link, though with much development.[174] The office of the lighting of the lamps at sunset is named *lucernarium* (Vespers) and the chanting of the Psalms of praise at dawn is called *matutinae laudes* (Lauds).

b. In Jerusalem and in Rome, the Saturday night vigil started to commemorate the resurrection of our Lord Jesus Christ—this later developed into the Hour of Matins.

c. Devout persons meet at the third, sixth, and ninth hours for private prayers, which later developed to be the Hours of Terce, Sext, and None.

---

[174] Read Vilma G. LITTLE, *The Sacrifice of Praise*, pp. 3-15.

    d. What could really be attributed to monastic customs and therefore of monastic origin is the morning reading of the Rule with a blessing for the day's work which later developed into the Hour of Prime and is today no longer in use even in monasteries. Another is the bedtime prayer which was given a fixed form by Saint Benedict and is known as the Hour of Compline.[175]

2. Another point worth noting is that in the very early beginning of Christianity, Christian prayer was exactly the way Saint Benedict stipulated it in his Rule centuries later; that prayer has to be *"brevis et pura"* (short and pure *RB* 20:4). Moreover, this point interestingly fulfils the elements which the Vatican Council later requires of the revised rites, namely, that they "should be distinguished by a noble simplicity. They should be short, clear, and unencumbered by useless repetition. They should be within the people's powers of comprehension, and normally should not require much explanation" (*Sacrosanctum Concilium*, 34).

---

[175] For a more elaborated scheme and sources of such developments, see Vilma G. LITTLE, *The Sacrifice of Praise*, pp. 3-22.

The Hours

The Church strives to conform its shaping of time and space to the life of Christ, the model of the relationship of man to God. The liturgical year and sacred space have evolved from Jewish and pagan roots according to the changing perception of this relationship of man to God. Through liturgy, the Church mediates the individual human experience of time and space. The liturgical year is proportioned with the Christian structure of time, neither linear nor cyclic, but spiralling towards union with God. Similarly, the Hours reflect the community's experience of the mysteries of Christ as it evolves in history.

Subsequently, with the knowledge of the development of the Liturgy of the Hours, one can understand the reason why among all the seven canonical hours, Matins, Lauds, and Vespers are called major hours (*legitimae orationes)* and the other hours, Prime, Terce, Sext, and None are called minor hours and their times are shorter because the day is meant for work. The minor hours are interwoven with the day's activities so that one can work and pray at the same time, *ora et labora.* So the Christian working is the Christian praying. The hours can best be appreciated by exploring them one by one, in an effort to determine what is the characteristic sentiment and theme of each, and as far as possible, how they reflect various mysteries of the history of salvation.

Once the mystery of every Hour is known, it becomes clear that apart from legislation, it is evident that an entire day's Office must not be said in one sitting. The benefit of the prayers increases to the degree that they are separated. The ideal is and remains: whenever possible, pray each hour separately. To this effect the General Instruction (no. 11) states: "that the day may be truly sanctified and the hours themselves recited with spiritual advantage, it is best that each of them be prayed at a time most closely corresponding to the true time of each canonical hour." The *LH* is supposed to make the day holy, be a companion along the day's journey, and a source of strength and healing at every station along the way. This goal can be realized only if it is prayed separately and at the proper time.

The clergy and religious persons who have the obligation to pray regularly the Liturgy of the Hours, may often end up feeling guilty when a particular Hour has not been prayed by them. Some, in fact, will then try to "catch up" what they have missed—even gluing a number of Hours together and praying them one after the other. This is very wrong. The Liturgy of the Hours is seen as the Prayer of the Church, and the spirituality that goes with this approach, flips this on its head. The Church as the Body of Christ, in that perspective, exists prior to individuals joining it, and individuals become Christians precisely through their incorporation into this community (primarily through baptism). The Liturgy of the Hours, as the Prayer of the Church and essentially the prayer of Christ, is ongoing, and we have the duty and joy of sharing in this prayer whenever possible. But when for any reason, one misses an Hour, one has to remember that the prayer goes on—we do not catch up with it, rather we pick it up again when we can. For those who want to incorporate this insight into their Rule of life, it is helpful to put time limits on when a particular Hour is prayed. If, for example, one's discipline is to pray the major Hours (Lauds—morning prayer, and Vespers—evening prayer) one might decide that one does not pray morning prayer after a certain time in the morning. If you miss it, you miss it[176]—and pick up the discipline when next again you can, i.e., pick up with the next Hour whose mystery ought to correspond to the time the person is ready to pray.

Emphasizing further the importance of this "ongoing-ness" of the Church's liturgical prayer, we will examine the Hours one by one, in an effort to determine the mystery and the spirituality of each one of them. One needs to bear in mind that any transcendent reality which is thought of or spoken about will be thought and spoken in terms of personification, embodiment, or projection of something in human experience. Any object of worship, when specifically identified and named, is already by that very fact an imperfect, limited idol, even when we call that object "He Who Is" or "Pure Act" or the "Ground of Being." The deficiency is not in the object of worship but in ourselves.[177] Thus the following images have been identified as an attempt to reproduce in a Biblical and spatiotemporal style the mystery of Christ's life and how they are re-enacted in the Liturgy of the Hours.

Furthermore, to show how wide the interpretation and the evolution of each Hour have gone, these depictions

---

[176] This point reminds me of an incident that happened some years ago. A group of student nuns were preparing for their examination and were not able to say their office for the feast of Saint Joseph. The day after, when they were through with their examinations, they sat down to say their prayers trying to "catch up," first with the preceding day's feast of Saint Joseph. This is a-liturgical. You do not catch up. Once the feast or the hour is gone, it is gone. One needs to move on with the next hour and next feast.

[177] Cf. Quentin QUESNELL, "The Search for Sophia," in *Continuum* 2, no. 2-3 (1993), pp. 6-26, here p. 25.

are to be employed as samples. Underpinning the concern for such illustrations or images lies the reality of the Scriptural allegorical meaning and the mystery behind each Hour. As we instinctively wrestle with the endless questions that make our lives human, we just as intuitively recognize that the ultimate answer to all possible questions does not reside in any human mind but in something or Someone. However, here is not the place to go into all the different stages of development and evolution of the different interpretations, theology, and spirituality of the Hours. That development and its accompanying theology have been extensively researched.[178] It is sufficient here to recall that, at some time in history, different imageries were used in trying to render comprehensible the mystery of Christ's life as celebrated in each liturgical Hour.

---

[178] For a coherent account of the extraordinary, complicated history and theology of the hours, see the book of Robert TAFT, *The Liturgy of the Hours in East and West: The Origins of the Divine Office and its Meaning for Today* (Collegeville, MN: The Liturgical Press, 1986). For the theology of the Liturgy of the Hours, see, for instance, pp. 331-373. Interesting also is the work of Stanislaus CAMPBELL, *From Breviary to Liturgy of the Hours: The Structural Reform of the Roma* Office, 1964-1971 (Collegeville, MN: 1995). The interest of this research is to find out how the Liturgy of the Hours help to deepen individual relationship with God.

Ad Matutinum (The Hour of Matins
or Vigil or Office of Readings)

This hour is also called Vigil or the Office of Readings.[179]
The hour of Matins is the hour of Parousia.[180] In early

---

[179] The word "Matins" is derived from the Latin word *Matuta*,
which was the Latin name for the Greek goddess of the dawn.
Its basic meaning is always connected with the early morning.
Initially, Matins referred to the dawn office (Lauds) which was
called *matutinae laudes*, meaning morning praise. The night
office (what we today call Matins) was at that time referred
to as the Vigils or Nocturns, or sometimes Tenebrae, all
these titles emphasising the thought of the night. The name
was later changed to Matins at a time when the Vigil Office
in the Roman basilicas was no longer said during the night
but very early in the morning and was followed immediately
with Lauds, making the two offices almost one, and the dawn
office was then shortened to Lauds to stress its characteristic
feature of praise. Read Vilma G. LITTLE, *The Sacrifice of Praise*,
pp. 8-9.

[180] Widespread yearning for the return of Christ in glory attests
to an intense *parousial* faith in the early Church. The great
Christian mysteries place the Second Coming (always an
essential truth of faith) side by side with the incarnation,
death, and resurrection of Christ (see the Apostolic, Athana-
sian, Nicene, and Nicene-Constantinopolitan creedal formu-
lations, in H. Denzinger, *Enchiridion symbolorum* 11, 30, 41,
76, 125-126, 150). The term "Parousia" is a transliteration of
the Greek word παρουσία. In classical Greek the word meant
"presence" or "arrival." The Greek word Parousia here cor-
responded to the Latin word *adventus*. Saint Paul used the
word to speak of his own presence among the Corinthians (2
Cor 10:10) and the Philippians (Phil 2:12), of the presence of
Stephanas, Fortunatus, and Achaicus among the Corinthians
(1 Cor 16:17), of his future arrival at Philippi (Phil 1:26), and
of the arrival of Titus at Corinth (2 Cor 7:6-7). In Hellenistic
Greek, *parousàa* acquired two technical meanings: (1) the
public arrival of officials, which was accompanied by appropriate ceremony; and (2) the presence of the gods, manifested
in acts of power, or assumed to be an invisible reality in the
cult. After the biblical period, the doctrine came to be known
as the Coming (*adventus*) or the Second Coming of Christ. The

Christianity, the idea of Parousia prevailed because of the strong longing for the coming of the Lord. Night was the symbol of earthly life while the dawn or the morning light was the image of the returning Christ, whose Parousia is realized in the Eucharist. Night is not just for sleep; night is also a time of prayer. The Church is like the virgins in the parable, waiting for the Bridegroom with burning lamps.

The mysteries which this hour celebrates are evident in the Gospels:

- At night, Christ was born, as *Light* in darkness. It was those shepherds who were keeping watch that got the message (Lk 2:6-14).
- It was at night also that Christ went through His agony (Mt 26:36-46). He begged His friends to keep watch with Him.
- Jesus rose from the dead before the dawn on the first day (Mt 28:1-8).
  a. Saint Luke tells us that the women went to the tomb at early dawn (Lk 24:1-8).
  b. Mark tells us it was very early on the first day of the week (Mk 16:1-2).
  c. John remarked that it was very early and still dark when Mary of Magdala came to the tomb and the Lord was already risen (Jn 20:1-8).

Today, Matins retains its proper theme only to a very slight degree. Matins is generally very loosely connected

---

word *parousàa* in the sense of the presence of the risen Christ at the conclusion of history is found in 1 Thes 2:19; 3:13; 4:15; 5:23; 2 Thes 2:1, 8; Jas 5:7-8; 2 Pt 1:16; 3:4, 12; 1 Jn 2:28. An exceptional usage occurs in 2 Thes 2:9, where *parousàa* refers to the presence of "the lawless one," the Pauline opponent of Christ at the end of history. Read S. J. DUFFY, "Parousia," in *New Catholic Encyclopaedia*, Second Edition, vol. 10, Mos-Pat (Washington, DC: Thomson Gale, 2003), pp. 894-902.

with the night hours and thus it can equally well be antic-
ipated, that is, prayed on the day before, without any
appreciable loss of devotion.[181]

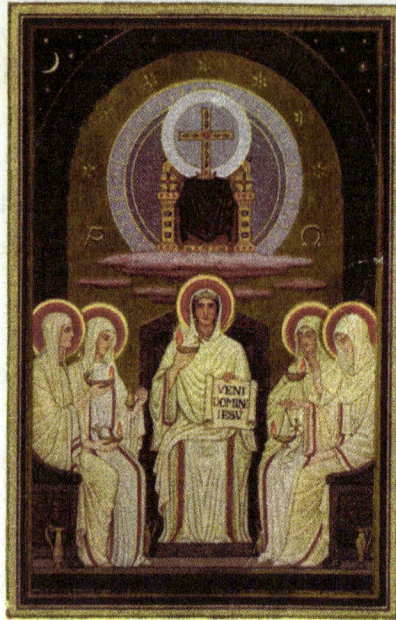

VLA 421 a

Ad Matutinum

The image above connects the parable of the wise
virgins with the hope of Parousia. One sees in the image
the five wise virgins who are seated in choir. At the centre
sits the Mother Church with a scroll on which is written,
"Come Lord Jesus." They are all carrying burning lamps in

---

[181] The following images and its explanations are from Volk-
sliturgisches Apostolat Klosterneuburg, and they have been
employed with copyright permission from the Direktor des
Pius-Parsch-Instituts Klosterneuburg, Prof. Dr. Andreas Red-
tenbacher CanReg.

the hand, praying and listening to the voice of the bride-groom ("At midnight there was a cry, 'The bridegroom is here! Go out and meet him'" [Mt 25:6]), all dressed in their wedding garments. Above them is the throne made ready for the Lord who comes again and is daily manifested in the Eucharist. Therefore, the hour of Matins is the hour of Parousia and a preparation for the next day.

Ad Laudes (The Hour of Lauds or Morning Prayer)

Sunrise and resurrection are the objectives of the hour of Lauds, the early morning praise. In this hour we celebrate triple resurrection:

- Resurrection of Christ, which is the background to the history of salvation
- Resurrection of nature; everything awakens from sleep and slumber
- Spiritual resurrection of humanity

These are what the hour of Lauds celebrates. The summit of Lauds is in the Benedictus, the song of Zacharias, wherein the Church greets Christ as the Gracious Rising Sun who comes from on high to dispel the darkness of the world (cf. Lk 1:67-79). Praise is the hour's central theme.

VLA 422 a

Ad Laudes

The image above presents to us the resurrection of the Lord, the empty rocky tomb and Christ the King who is dressed in white. He is enthroned on the clouds that gives radiance to the dawn. He has the triumphant cross on His right hand and a scroll on the left wherein is written "*Oriens ex alto*" (the rising sun from on high). This is to show that Christ is the Sun of the day of redemption, who visits us daily in the Eucharist. Different imageries are employed in the picture to show that all of creation acclaims Him; hence, the canticle of the three youths, who by the order of the king were thrown into the furnace; the mountains, hills, trees, seas, and oceans; even the legendary (fabled) phoenix,[182] which is the symbol of resurrection; and the cock, the heraldry of the day, are all present in the picture. Additionally, there is the presence of two deer that are drinking water, symbolising humanity's longing for God (cf. Ps 62).

Ad Primam (The Hour of Prime)

"May the Lord Almighty order our day and our work in his peace!" This is a typical blessing for the second Morning Prayer, the hour of Prime. While the hour of Lauds is full of the praise of God, the hour of Prime is engaged with man and his struggles and tussles and with his forthcoming day's work. So the hour of Prime is the hour for the

---

[182] A phoenix or phenix (Greek: φοῖνιξ phoinix) is a long-lived bird that is cyclically regenerated or reborn. Associated with the sun, a phoenix obtains new life by arising from the ashes of its predecessor. This unique bird, brilliant and beautiful, can live up to 500 years. The phoenix was subsequently adopted as a symbol in early Christianity for paradise and resurrection themes. The compiler of the Physiologus (original Greek c. AD 200) provided the phoenix story as allegory for John 10:18: "I have the power to lay down my life and take it up again," for "the phoenix is the symbol of our Saviour who came from heaven with both wings full of fragrant perfume, that is divine words." With time, commentaries acquired length and variety, and its attractive symbolism passed into frequent use in patristic and Medieval Latin and vernacular literature. In the historical record, the phoenix could symbolize renewal in general, as well as the sun, time, empire, consecration, resurrection. It was also used to symbolize life in the heavenly paradise, Christ, Mary, virginity, the exceptional man, and certain aspects of Christian life. M. F. MCDONALD, "Phoenix," in *New Catholic Encyclopaedia*, second edition, vol. 11, Pau-Red (Washington, DC: Thomson Gale, 2003), p. 309.

blessing of the day's work, equipping for the daily struggle and good opinion.[183]

VLA 423 a

Ad Primam

The image above brings to mind the parable of the workers in the vineyard (Mt 20:1ff). The vineyard is the

---

[183] According to John Cassian, this hour of Prime was introduced by the monks of Bethlehem towards the end of the fourth century as a way of keeping lazy monks from returning to bed after prayer at dawn and remaining there until the third hour. So, prime in fact was a duplication of morning office that is why it has no specific mystery attached to it. It persisted down to our time only because it had been adopted by the monastic lawgivers of Italy like Saint Benedict, Saint Caesarius, and Aurelian. However it is no longer prayed, except among the monks and nuns of Solesmes Congregation and some others.

Church, the Mystical Body of Christ. We are being hired every day by God. In the image above, the petitioner kneels with his symbolic tools before the Lord, to receive the day's blessing. Christ is wearing a robe of blue purple with a wide golden clavi,[184] sign of royal dignity. Blessing the petitioner, Christ says: "You go to my vineyard."

The vine interweaves itself upwards on a cross, the mark of Christ, thereby configuring Christ's life as the vine. Our daily work should be a participation in the redemptive work of Christ. A rainbow illuminates above the vine, and God's hand is reaching from the clouds, blessing the earth so as to consecrate the day and the work.

Ad Tertiam (The Hour of Terce)

At the third hour (9:00 a.m.), the Holy Spirit descended on the Apostles and on the whole Church. Quite appropriately, the Church recalls this mystery in the hour of Terce. Terce is thus the "first Confirmation," a strengthening for the conflicts of the day. The hour's theme is invocation of the Holy Spirit.

---

[184] In ancient Rome, a vertical stripe or band of purple worn on the tunic by senators and equites.

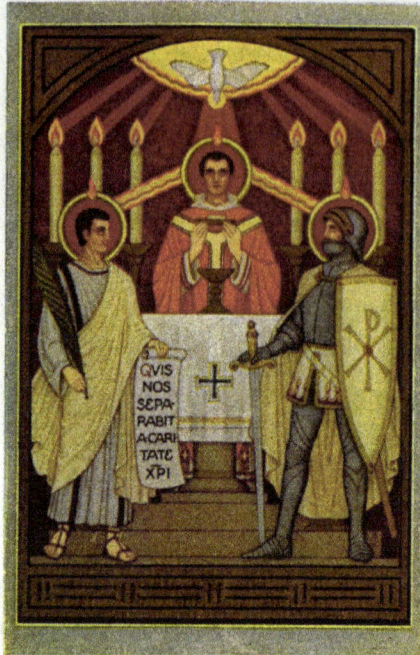

VLA 424 a

Ad Tertiam

The image above connects the descent of the Holy Spirit, Sacrament of Confirmation, and the Holy Mass. Confirmation is the consecration of Christians as priests, martyrs, and knights. This explains the presence of the three symbolic figures; priest, martyr, and knight upon whom the tongues of fire of the Holy Spirit is settled and radiated.

The message of the Holy Spirit accomplished itself in the Church by the power of the redemptive sacrifice and by priesthood.

The three-arm lamp is the symbol of the holy Church, hence an implicit reference to the Trinity. The knight's armour calls to mind the passage in Ephesians 6:11 where Saint Paul says: "Put God's armour on so as to be able to resist the devil's tactics." The martyr carries the victorious palm and the scroll as symbols of his having shed blood. On the scroll it is written: "Who can separate us from the love of Christ?" He made this word real through His death. On the other hand the priest brings the holy offering so that by the power of the Holy Spirit they may become the Body and Blood of Christ. Through the common priesthood of the faithful the Christians actively participate in this act.

Ad Sextam (The Hour of Sext or Midday Prayer)

At Sext or Midday hour, Christ hangs on the cross (noon-1:00 p.m.). This hour is the hottest hour of the day. The body is wearied with work, heat, and tiredness. The day's conflict is at its climax, the heat of passion is at its strongest, the powers of hell have greater influence over man, because man's lower nature seems to have gained mastery. The meditation of the hour is struggle with hell and the battle against sin, and therefore, the Church prays that she be not led into temptation. At this hour the sunlight and the burning sun is at its highest peak. Some of the hymns for the hour of Sext summarizes the good and the bad effects of the burning sun and gives them double symbolic meaning. The midday heat symbolises two evil conditions of human life: the heat of dispute and the fire of passion.

VLA 425 a

Ad Sextam

In the image, Christ is hanging on the throne of the cross as the High Priest and King. Just as the natural sun promotes growth, so does the Redeemer offer, through His cross, "Life in fullness." He has trampled on the head of the infernal serpent. The two sheep are peacefully drinking from the source of redemption. The sunflowers around are a symbol of Christians who are drawn by their exalted Lord. In a nut shell, the image portrays the healing power of the divine Sun.

Ad Nonam (The Hour of None)

At about the ninth hour (3:00 p.m.), Christ's sacrifice of the cross came to its fullness (cf. Lk 23:44-45). Blood and water gushed forth from the pierced heart of our Redeemer, symbol of the Church (in Baptism and the Eucharist). Just as Eve came from the side of Adam, so is the Church; the Bride came from the side of Jesus, the second Adam. The hour of None is the last hour which carries an eschatological bearing—the last things. This hour directs our thoughts to death and to the everlasting reward that follows a holy death. We pray for the grace of perseverance. This Hour is mentioned much in the Bible:

- At this hour of None, Peter and John went to the temple to pray (Acts 3:1-3).
- It is at this hour that the mystery of our salvation came to its fullest point (Lk 23:44-46).
- At this hour, also, we gaze at the foot of the cross to see Our Lady weeping. Is anyone's sorrow up to hers?
- It was at this hour that Cornelius found favour in the sight of the Lord.

VLA 426 a

Ad Nonam

In the above image, one sees the accomplished passion portrayed in the golden cross with a dark-red background and a symbolic palm of victory. The Church that was born from the side of Christ is presented as a young Bride in white garment. She is on a small boat which is sailing towards eternity. The boat is an old symbol of crossing over into the afterlife but also a symbol of the Church. In the hand of the Bride are also sheaves for the eternal sacrifice. So the Church returns home loaded to receive the everlasting reward which, as one can see in the picture, is represented in the Hand of God with a wreath of victory.

Ad Vesperas (The Hour of Vespers or the Evening Prayer)

Vespers is the evening praise of the Church, a special thanks and praise for redemption. In the history of salvation, this hour reminds us of the Last Supper united with the Eucharistic celebration understood as thanksgiving. As a matter of fact, a great number of the Vesper Psalms are Eucharistic songs or at least can easily be referred to the Eucharist. This is particularly true of the so-called *Hallel*[185] Psalms (Ps 112-117), which were sung at the Last Supper, and the Gradual[186] Psalms (Ps 119-131), which

---

[185] The Hebrew word *Hallel* (praise) is a Jewish prayer, a verbatim recitation of Psalms 113-118 (112-117), which is used for praise and thanksgiving during the evening prayers on the first night of Passover. In the Jewish liturgy, the Great *Hallel* (Psalm 136) is recited at the Passover meal after the Lesser *Hallel*. All through the refrain is a repeated reference to the Lord's steadfast love. This Psalm is a hymn that opens with a call to praise God because of God's great deeds in nature and His gracious historical actions in the history of Israel. It continues expressing God's mercy towards all and ends with another call to praise God. Although *Hallel* generally refers only to the aforementioned Psalms 113-118, the Talmud also refers to Psalm 136 as the "Great *Hallel*." Each verse of Psalm 136 concludes with the refrain, "for his mercy endures forever," and it contains mention of twenty-six acts of divine kindness and sustenance for the world. It is recited at the Passover meal after the standard *Hallel* is completed. There was also a difference between "full" and "half" *Hallel*. The "full" *Hallel* consists of Psalms 113-118, while the "half" *Hallel* consists of the "full" *Hallel*, excepting Psalms 115:1-11 and 116:1-11. The term "Great *Hallel*" refers only to Psalm 136. It is the daily Psalm on the last day of Passover.

[186] Gradual Psalms are also called Songs of Ascents, Songs of Degree, Songs of Steps, or Pilgrim Songs. These are titles given to fifteen Psalms, namely Psalms 119-133 or 120-134. They are Psalms recited when going up to the annual festivals in Jerusalem, hence their being called pilgrim songs. The days

were procession songs for pilgrimages to the Temple. The Last Supper is itself a symbol of the heavenly banquet. The peak of this hour is the *Magnificat,* the Church's thanksgiving prayer for the indwelling of Christ in Mary, in the Church, and in our individual souls.

VLA 427 a

Ad Vesperas

The image above shows the Last Supper, twelve unleavened loaves of bread, and in between the bread is a chalice with two handles. In the very middle we can see on the altar the Apocalyptic Lamb of God surrounded in sun-like

on which the Gradual Psalms were formerly recited are still indicated in the Roman Breviary, but the obligation of reciting them was removed by Saint Pius V.

aureole, and on one side a woman in a prayerful posture and an angel with incense on the other side. The woman is the Mother Church who sings the *Magnificat* for the grace of redemption won by the Lamb. The angel, through the incense, sends the evening prayer of the Church to heaven. The woman also represents Mary, the Mother of God, who sings daily with the Church the *Magnificat* at Vespers. The angel also represents Angel Gabriel who brought the message to Mary. The burning lamp signifies that the hour of Vespers is the hour of lighting of lamps, hence *lucernarium.*

Ad Completorium (The Hour of Compline or Night Prayer)

The thought here is on night rest and death. Night is the opposite of light and a symbol of the dark power of hell. Night is the mantel of the prince of this world. In the history of salvation, the background for this hour is the image of the agonizing Lord in the garden of olives and we pray for the "olives hours" of our lives. So the intentions are: for rest, for night protection, and trust in God.

Light and sun are favourite Scriptural and liturgical symbols of God, Christ, and the divine life. Christ is the divine Sun; the Christian is a child of the Sun. These thoughts are found frequently in the Hours. The opposite of light, night and darkness, are frequent liturgical symbols for the sinister power of the devil. The child of God, being a creature of light, is afraid of the night. How many sins does the night cover with her thick black veil! At night prayer, the Christian prays for protection from the powers of darkness.

Another reference to death occurs in the Canticle of Simeon—the *Nunc Dimittis* (Lk 2:29-32). He holds the child Jesus in his hands. His dearest longing has just been fulfilled, for he has seen the Redeemer and now he begs to be dismissed from his lifelong service of God. We are in a similar position. We bear the mystical Saviour in our hands and in our hearts—the saving graces of the day. Our eyes have seen "His salvation," the divine "light" has risen for us, Christ is our glory. Now we, too, can pray to be dismissed from service; it is the night of rest that follows the day's work. The antiphon to Simeon's canticle is also very rich and symbolic. Bodily and spiritual waking and sleeping intermingle: Save us, O Lord, while waking, then guard us while sleeping (at night), that awake we may watch with Christ (in life, through grace), and asleep we may rest in peace (by a happy death). Again and again, we cannot help noticing that Compline as a night prayer is a prayer for a happy death.

The Compline oration sums up all the day's prayer themes. It contains four points:

- Visitation: God is invited to dwell with us by the presence of His grace and His protection. Just as the God of the covenant once dwelt with His people in the midst of the desert, that is how we want God to visit us and live with us.
- God is also the guardian of the citadel of our soul. He must be begged to keep its portals closed against enemies.
- The angels, too, our guardian angels, are invited to dwell in this house. Here one can recall the dream of Jacob, the ladder to heaven and the angels going up and down upon it, carrying prayers and good works

to heaven, bringing grace and comfort down to us
(cf. Gen 28:10-22).

• Petitioning of God's paternal blessing upon us all for
the night. Thereupon as a parting adieu to our heavenly mother, Mary, one of the Marian hymns is sung.

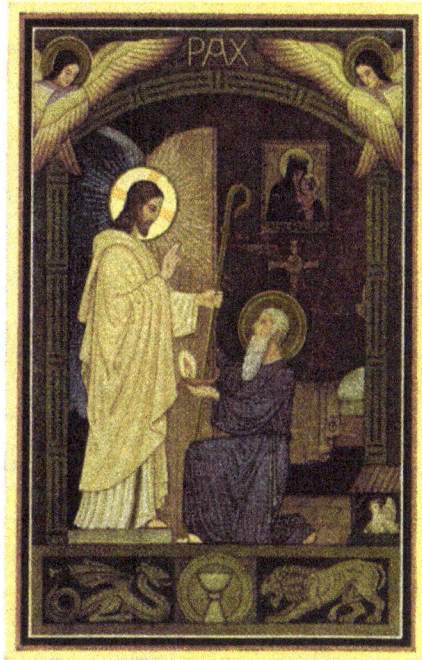

VLA 428 a

Ad Completorium

The general mood that envelops the image is the
watchful servant in the Gospel of Saint Luke (12:35f).
The night is associated with a time of watchfulness, like
the watchful servant, who with gilded loins and with a
burning lamp, opens the door to the Lord who comes to
him/her in death.

In the above picture, we can see lion and dragon as
signs of the power of hell and in-between them is a chalice.

Then above is found the angels whom we beg to watch over us, and Our Lady's picture because of the Marian hymn which we sing. In between the two angels is written *Pax*, which we earnestly need in order to have a good night's rest.

Christological and Soteriological Dimensions of the Liturgy of the Hours

It has been demonstrated so far that in the Christological dimension of the Liturgy of the Hours it is Christ who is the mystery celebrated and He is also the one who celebrates with, through, and in His Body the Church. He is the one who prays, through whom is prayed, and to whom prayers are directed. He is the Light that has come and comes daily in the liturgical celebrations to dispel the darkness in our lives and in the world.

Consequently, the major hours Matins (Vigils), Lauds, and Vespers celebrate three "hours": the hour of the night, the sunrise, and the sunset. During the night (Matins) with burning lamps the Christian keeps watch, prays, and waits for *Christ* the Light to come and dispel the darkness. Then comes the dawning light (Lauds), typifying *Christ* who has come through His resurrection. While the sun is setting, the hour of Vespers is dedicated to the evening lamps (*lucernarium*) that are then lighted, which also typifies *Christ*, the true star of evening that arose in the eventide of the world. Then throughout the day the minor hours Terce, Sext, and None recall the passing of the daylight (Terce), gathering of strength in the middle of the day's stress (Sext), which starts to diminish (None). Thus, the daily office is linked up with the symbolism of Christ as the Light: rising (Lauds), waxing (Sext), waning (None), and setting (Vespers)—Christ is the true Light. Light with all its associated benefits comes from the sun. That explains the reason why the sun is the starting point of the circle of divine praise. Even for the Jews the rising and setting of the sun mark the times of the day best suited for sacrifice and worship.[187] It is not surprising, then, that Christians prayed facing east, seeing in the rising sun a symbol of the Risen Christ, light of the world.[188] Then comes the hour of Compline; this is the hour that completes the circle of the day—it is a time of completion. It represents the peaceful transition into the silence of sleep. So, at night, Christ was born, a light in darkness; noonday turned to night when Christ suffered and died on the cross, but in the dawn of Easter morning Christ rose in victory from the grave. Christ the "Sun of righteousness," risen upon those who fear His name (Mal 4:2).

The Soteriological dimension of the Liturgy of the Hours stresses the salvation brought by Christ in time. Thus, the distribution of the Hours rests on the natural human experience of time, which is tightly knitted with the salvation brought by Christ in time. Hence, *Matins* consecrates the hours of the night, of silence and of darkness, the time of Christ's resting in the tomb and descent into Hades. *Lauds* consecrates the time of sunrise and celebrates the resurrection. *Terce* celebrates the descent of the Holy Spirit and the birth of the Church. *Sext* celebrates our Lord's crucifixion and hanging on the cross. *None* is the mystery of the death of Christ, a remembrance of our individual passing. *Vespers* is the time of sunset. This

---

[187] Cf. Vilma G. LITTLE, *The Sacrifice of Praise*, p. 28.

[188] Robert TAFT, *The Liturgy of the Hours in East and West: The Origins of the Divine Office and its Meaning for Today* (Collegeville, 1986), p. 351.

hour recalls, with the sun's setting, the true light, Christ, who never declines and the hour also celebrates the Last Supper. Lastly, *Compline,* after sunset, when we prepare for bed, invokes God's protection during the night. In this way the Christian, through the Liturgy of the Hours, sanctifies time[189] and brings it back to its source in the eternity of God. To sanctify time does not mean that Liturgy of the Hours renders secular time sacred, instead it proposes what the quality of all time should be. That is, the Liturgy of the Hours advocates an experience of time that is sacramental or revelatory of the mystery of Christ and a means of union with God and deep personal relationship with Him in Christ. The hours of Sext, None, and Lauds, for example, are meant to sanctify time by illuminating these three Hours of the day, revealing certain aspects of Christ's Paschal Mystery: crucifixion, death, and resurrection. This therefore encourages the Christian to see all moments of the day as sacramental expressions of that mystery. So the Liturgy of the Hours are celebrated making present at every moment the Paschal Mystery of Christ. This is also another way of encouraging ceaseless prayer which must be the concomitant of Christian life which is caught up in that mystery.

The various hours which constitute the Office have a basic structure which has been termed dialogical. This idea, however, does not really explain the real theological nature of the Liturgy of the Hours. In as much as it is the prayer of Christ and His Body the Church, it is more a duet than a dialogue, though some elements of the structure demand attentive listening to the Word of God through which God calls or teaches us. Other elements are

---

[189] General Instruction on the Liturgy of the Hours, nos. 10–11.

responsive in nature. Yet through them and in them, the Church in union with her Head—the Lord Jesus—responds to God's call in praise, thanksgiving, and petition.

The unity of the Christological and Soteriological dimensions of the Liturgy of the Hours is situated in the fact that, the Hours, as liturgy, are truly and fundamentally a celebration of the Paschal Mystery of Christ, of His dying and rising (Christology). This is not simply in the sense of action inaugurating salvation, but as a *present* salvific event actualized here and now (Soteriology) in the lives of His faithful people who constitute His Body, the Church. This fact is visibly accentuated in the celebration of feasts where the mysteries celebrated are brought to the present. Therefore, that which historically belongs to the past, the death of Christ, and that which historically belongs to the future, the Parousia, all become present when we celebrate the holy mysteries. This is the reason why in the liturgical prayer every feast is brought to the present as something happening here and now. God is present and for the Christian there is no past or future, only now: the divine "Today."[190] Salvation is taking place here and now in this celebration. At Christmas, for example, the Church sings:[191]

---

[190] Cf. O. CASEL, "Hodie," in MD 65 (1961), pp. 127-132, and here p. 127.

[191] *Antiphonale Monasticum* (Paris, 1934), p. 249.

Hodie+ *Christus natus est:*	*Today*+ Christ is born,
Hodie *Salvator apparuit:*	*Today* the Saviour has appeared;
Hodie *in terra canunt Angeli,*	*Today* the Angels are singing on earth,
Laetantur Archangeli:	Archangels are rejoicing;
Hodie *exsultant justi dicentes:*	*Today* the just are glad and are saying:
Gloria in excelsis Deo, alleluja.	Glory to God in the highest, alleluia.

The same spirit echoes in so many feasts of the liturgical year. Another example is in the celebration of Easter, which is the *sollemnitas sollemnitatum,* and the *festum summum,* the Christians' only festival in the complete sense of the word. The celebration of the Easter mysteries embraces, in the richest liturgical form, the complete redemptive work of Christ. On this day the whole Church sings at the responsorial: **Haec dies**, *quam fecit Dominus, alleluja. Exsultemus, et laetemur in ea, alleluja.*[192] (**This is the day** that the Lord has made, alleluia, let us be glad and rejoice therein, alleluia.)

So, it is in principle that the Hours make present the mysteries of Christ. They once were and must become again the living prayer of Christ realized in the here and now of the Church's existence. The Liturgy of the Hours is neither a novelty nor a mere legal obligation. Instead, its roots lie deep in the liturgical experience of Israel (temple, synagogue, and home), of our Lord Himself and of all the early churches that learned under the guidance of the Spirit to carry out His will. The observance of the Hours stands at the very centre of the Catholic tradition of prayer, and if it is obligatory as the General Instruction affirms it to be (GILH 28-32), it is because it is a vital

---

[192] *Antiphonale Monasticum*, p. 456.

instrument of the praying, interceding High Priest of our redemption. "It is the prayer of the Church with Christ and to Christ" (GILH 2). In being that, it is truly a duet with Jesus Christ who continues to pray *with*, *for*, *through*, and *in* His Church. The Paschal Mystery is itself a duet, personalized in Christ who is both the Word of God to humankind and the ultimate and absolutely faithful human response of praise, thanksgiving, self-offering, and petition to God.

Liturgy of the Hour as Nourishment of Personal Relationship with God

Saint Paul, in several of his letters, challenges the Christian community to "pray without ceasing" (1 Thes 5:16-18; Col 4:2; Eph 6:18). It is important to note that Saint Paul, by saying "pray without ceasing," was not talking to monks, nuns, priests nor to the religious men and women. He is addressing his letter to very ordinary Christians who live in the world. He knows very well that these people have a lot of other things to do, and yet he says, this is your vocation: to pray without ceasing! How is it possible to live our everyday lives in prayer or, as we often hear today, to live contemplatively in the midst of action? This is precisely the "art of prayer" that Saint John Paul II called Christians to embrace at the beginning of the new millennium.[193] But for prayer to happen at *all* times, it must happen at *some* time (cf. *CCC*, n. 2697). This is the reason why the Liturgy of the Hours is sometimes called the "Sacrament of Time," because it helps us to pray without ceasing and to keep Christ at the centre of our daily lives. By gathering in the morning to praise God and in the evening to give God thanks, the Christian prayer

---

[193] Saint John Paul II, *Novo Millennio Ineunte*, p. 32.

sanctifies all of creation. In that way, it helps deepen one's relationship with God and keeps the believer steadily in touch with the Paschal Mystery.

Some people think that prayer is just a part of our relationship with God, but it is not. It IS our relationship with God, a covenant relationship, a living relationship between God and us, individually, and like any relationship, it requires commitment. The Liturgy of the Hours is part of that commitment: through it we learn the heart of the Father and are constantly challenged by the Scripture to be transformed more fully into the image of Christ. The Psalms, the silence, and the other prayers help us deepen this relationship with Christ and the Church and continue to feed us so we can be true witnesses of the Gospel. Our relationship with God can only be enriched by our journeying towards Him hour by hour, day by day, month by month, year by year, hence the daily and yearly liturgical cycles.

As religious men and women and as Christians, prayer is essential to who we are. Given also the amount of ministry and work we do, the Christian and indeed every religious charism ought to be rooted in an experience of God through prayer. We could not do what we do, nor I suppose, could we find the motivation to even try, if we do not start with a relationship with God. Prayer is first, and foremost, about relationship, our relationship with God and our relationship with one another in the Body of Christ. These relationships fill our lives with meaning and purpose. Seen in this way, prayer, then, is not so much an exercise of piety as it is an exchange of love. The prayer of the Liturgy of the Hours is our common heartbeat, that rhythmic and unceasing exchange of receiving and giving that sustains our lives. To pray without ceasing (1 Thes

5:17) means approaching God at every moment through and in the middle of our ordinary daily life. Hence the Liturgy of the Hours punctuates the day with prayer at certain times: morning, noon, evening, and night.

The Liturgy of the Hours can be a "school of prayer"[194] wherein one learns to pray well and deepen one's relationship with God. This fact is attributable, among other things, to its objectivity and its symbolic quality. Hence, its objectivity lies in its universality with respect to the mystery it ritually symbolizes and not being restricted to particular subjective needs and concerns. Its symbolic quality is that of any sacramental activity of the Church, an activity which does not merely denote the mystery it symbolizes, but indicates its rich complexity, inviting participants to ever-deeper immersion in it. The Liturgy of the Hours, then, can be a framework in which the authentic dimensions of Christian prayer are apprehended, practised, and made one's own. Schooled in the common prayer of the Hours, one can enter more deeply into "private" prayer and, thus enriched, bring ever greater intensity and sensitivity to the Liturgy of the Hours with a gradual, deeper growth into the relationship with God.

Moreover, the Hours should be experienced as a communal prayer which is also personal. Authentic Christian life has both personal and communal or social dimensions which need to be present in all forms of prayer, public or private. The Liturgy of the Hours, as a public, communal form of prayer, would cease to express and to nourish a community's life of faith if it were not also a personal form of prayer for each one engaged in it.

---

194 Cf. Robert TAFT, *The Liturgy of the Hours in East and West: The Origins of the Divine Office and its Meaning for Today*, p. 367.

Through the Liturgy of the Hours and by means of the richness of the Psalms, we learn to address God, to communicate with Him, to speak to Him of ourselves with His own words, to find a language for the encounter with God. Then through those words, it will also be possible to know and to accept the criteria of His action, to draw closer to the mystery of His thoughts and ways (Is 55:8-9), so as to grow constantly in faith and in love. At times, this kind of prayer can seem to us to be stiff, formalized, not lively and spontaneous enough. Nevertheless, we can experience what great strength lies in praying as a community and not only alone in our rooms. There is power in the communal Liturgy of the Hours which in turn serves as a continuous empowerment in our individual bond with Christ. Thus, "by participating in the liturgy we make our own the language of Mother Church, we learn to speak in her and for her."[195] Praying with the Church, we are lifted up into a new understanding, into her true and full relationship to the living God. Pope Benedict XVI explained that this does not happen all at once. We must grow into the liturgy and its language. Thus he stated, "Of course...this happens gradually, little by little. I must immerse myself ever more deeply in the words of the Church with my prayer, with my life, with my suffering, with my joy, and with my thought. It is a process that transforms us."[196]

Private Prayer and Communal Liturgical Prayer

Prayer is a big paradox and a mystery of faith in the sense that there are no two identical prayers, because

---

[195] Pope Benedict VXI, General Audience, 3 October 2012.
[196] Ibid.

there are no two identical souls. Our Lord does not create us, nor does He save us, in series. His love for each of us is a personal one, a unique one, and our love for Him has this same character of intimacy. On the other hand, God does not save us separately; He makes of us a divine society, a body, the *Corpus Christi*. We are the Church and are in the Church: no one of us is the whole Church, but the whole mystery of the Church—which is the mystery of salvation—is given to each of us, even if each of us does not exercise all the acts of the Church's ministry. Therefore, our prayer is unavoidably a Church's prayer: a prayer in the Church, with the Church, and for the Church.

This is exactly where prayer becomes a mystery. Prayer is a mystery of faith: we believe in prayer like we believe that God is God, that grace is grace, that sin deprives us of grace, and so forth. If prayer is a mystery, it is because it is an activity of Jesus Christ in us. The only thing of importance is life in Christ. We live in Jesus and He lives in us, because of this, in spite of the indispensable role which private prayer plays in the deepening of our personal relationship with God in Jesus Christ, yet nothing supersedes the sacramental and mysterious role of the communal liturgical prayer of the Church. This is so because prayer in itself is not about the private project of making oneself holy and, in the words of O'Donohue, "turning yourself into a shining temple that blinds everyone else."[197] Prayer, on the contrary, has a deeper priority which is the sanctification of the world of which all are privileged inhabitants.

The doctrine which justifies this affirmation is that contained in the thesis of the superiority of liturgical prayer to private prayer, in virtue at least of the "action of

---

[197] John O'DONOHUE, *Eternal Echoes*, p. 224.

the Church," the *Opus Operantis Ecclesiae*. Pope Pius the XII in his Encyclical on the Sacred Liturgy, *Mediator Dei* (*MD*), has this to say about the worship of the Church:

> It should be clear to all, then...that the worship rendered to God by the Church in union with her divine Head is the most efficacious means of achieving sanctity. This efficacy, where there is question of the Eucharistic sacrifice and the sacraments, derives first of all and principally from the act itself (*ex opere operato*). But if one considers the part which the Immaculate Spouse of Jesus Christ takes in the action, embellishing the sacrifice and sacraments with prayer and sacred ceremonies, or if one refers to the "sacramentals" and the other rites instituted by the hierarchy of the Church, then its effectiveness is due rather to the action of the Church (*ex opere operantis Ecclesiae*), inasmuch as she is holy and acts always in closest union with her Head[198] (*MD* 26-27).

As regards the superiority of liturgical prayer to private prayer, the same encyclical states:

> Unquestionably, liturgical prayer, being the public supplication of the illustrious Spouse of Jesus Christ, is superior in excellence to private prayers. But this superior worth does not at all imply contrast or incompatibility between these two kinds of prayer. For both merge harmoniously in the single spirit which animates them,

---

[198] Encyclical of Pope Pius XII, *Mediator Dei*, On the Sacred Liturgy, in NCWC ed., nos. 26-7; AAS 36 (1947), 532.

"Christ is all in all." Both tend to the same objective: until Christ be formed in us[199] (*MD* 37).

The document in no way undermines the importance
of private prayer but is trying to check individualism in
prayer. Some people might think since in private prayer
one deepens one's relationship with God, What then is
the need for communal liturgical prayer? By doing so,
one forgets that our Lord Himself said where two or more
are gathered in His name he is there in their midst (Mt
18:20). Pointing out the mutual energy that is evident
in communal prayer, John O'Donohue remarks that "the
great thing about a community at prayer is that your
prayer helps mine—as mine helps yours."[200] Thus, both
private and communal liturgical prayers of the Church
admirably support each other. Private prayer prepares
for intra-liturgical prayer, and intra-liturgical prayer in its
turn is the abundant source from which private prayer can
overflow as its continuation even outside of the liturgical
action. When the special dignity and efficacy of liturgical
prayer is affirmed, it is not intended thereby to diminish
the value of purely private prayer. The intention is only to
safeguard in everything the hierarchy of values and the
correct mutual order.

The Christian community is a family of the one presence; this truth is the obscured belonging which communal prayer helps us to unveil. If one does not pray, if one
does not believe in prayer, then one is living off the prayers

---

[199] N. 37; *AAS* 39 (1947), 537. In his discourse of 22 September
1956, the same pontiff said that the Church not only toler-
ates but fully recognizes and recommends private forms of
worship "without prejudice, however, to the pre-eminence of
liturgical worship" (The Assisi Papers, 226-27).

[200] John O'DONOHUE, *Eternal Echoes*, p. 216.

of other people. It is so important that prayer happens in the world, every day and every night. In our precarious and darkening world, we would have destroyed everything long ago were it not for the light and shelter of prayer. Prayer is the presence that holds harmony in the midst of chaos. Every time that one prays, the person adds to the light and harmony of creation,[201] hence prayer both private and communal are all equally necessary for the synchronisation of creation.

Therefore, according to the different vocations received, each one must play his/her part in the building up of the Christian community. All the instruments enrich the symphony to which they contribute. But there is no confusion, and unity does not impair the individuality of those who make it up but rather perfects them through each other. Only liturgical prayer, properly understood, can give to personal prayer the necessary depth of the faith which underlies it. Every prayer, whether individual or collective, is always a contemplation of the coming of the Word into this world. It is made up of admiration and gratitude, dialogue and silence, wonder and self-abasement. Interior prayer fashions the "living stones" which build up the Kingdom of God. One can say truly with Edith Stein that every genuine prayer is a prayer of the Church: through every genuine prayer something happens in the Church, and it is the Church herself who prays in it, for it is the Holy Spirit living in her, who in every individual soul asks for us with unspeakable groaning.[202] The animating principle of this prayer in the Church is the Holy Spirit.

---

[201] Cf. Ibid., pp. 217-218.

[202] Cf. Hilda C. GRAEF, *The Scholar and the Cross* (London, 1955), p. 126.

The Spirit has a twofold task: He brings scattered humanity together into the unity of the one Church, and at the same time He inspires the Church to transcend its limits and to reach all men. The Spirit who prays within awakens in the Christian community, and in the individual Christian, a sense of the world's anguished aspiration towards salvation.

Chapter Six: The Eucharist: A Many-faceted Mystery

The Holy Eucharist, in the words of Fr. John Baldovin, is a "many-faceted Jewel,"[203] a precious jewel and a pearl of great price. One cannot appreciate it by looking at it from only one angle or in only one light. There is always the need to turn it now this way, now that, now in this light, and then in another in order to comprehend its true beauty[204] and to marvel at its wonder. This being the reality of the marvellous gift of the Holy Eucharist, this chapter will try to view an aspect of it for the interest of our investigation on prayer as a relationship.

Because of the enigma that surrounds the holy sacrifice of the cross which is re-enacted daily at the Altar of Sacrifice at Mass, it is difficult to give it a name or to define it. This complex nature of the Mass demands that it be called by so many names: Sacrifice, Mass, Eucharist, Thanksgiving, Last Supper, and so on.[205] Nevertheless, the main

---

[203] John BALDOVIN, S.J., "Eucharist: The Many-Faceted Jewel," in *The Church in the 21st Century Center*, C21 Resources (Boston College, 2011), pp. 2-3, here p. 2.

[204] Cf. Ibid., p. 2.

[205] Throughout in this work, the terms "Eucharist," "Eucharistic celebration," "Eucharistic Sacrifice," "The Holy Mass," and "Mass" are used interchangeably—and deliberately so. The motive is the wish to avoid the somewhat unfortunate division between the Eucharist-as-sacrifice and the Eucharist-as-sacrament which has been common in theological circles for some time. This dichotomy, however, does not have really ancient roots in the Church's past. The Eucharist is one: totally sacrificial and totally sacramental. Even when received

verb that governs what we do at Mass is "to give thanks." Appreciation for what God has done for us in making us (creation) and saving us (redemption) is constantly at the forefront in our worship. That is why we can give "Eucharist" even when we celebrate a funeral. For this reason, the document, *Sacrosanctum Concilium*, of the Second Vatican Council, gave some guidelines to the understanding of this mystery, the Eucharist. It is presented:

- as the visible sign of the Church (*SC* 2),
- as the event that shows the transforming presence of Christ in the world (*SC* 6),
- as a way of sharing the heavenly fulfilment of all the promises (*SC* 8), and
- as the encounter which is the summit or high point to which Christian activity is directed and from which the power of the community flows (*SC* 10).

The Mass is the action of Jesus because the main thing at Mass is what Christ does; He offers Himself in sacrifice for us. Thus the Church teaches that the Sacrifice of the Mass is the same as the sacrifice of the cross in an unbloodied manner. We should be present at Mass as if we were at the foot of the cross, like our Blessed Lady who was at the foot of the cross in loving contemplation of Christ who offers Himself lovingly for each one of us.

In order to participate well at Mass, we should identify ourselves with Christ in His sacrifice. Hence, the purposes of the Holy Sacrifice of the Mass are the same purposes of the cross. What purposes did Jesus have on the cross? His purposes can be summed up in four points: to give glory to God the Father, to thank Him, to make up for the sins of

---

outside of Mass, it is still always a partaking of the Victim of the sacrifice of Christ and of His Church.

men, and to ask Him for graces for us. Consequently, the Mass may not always be a deeply emotional experience, but it is always an experience of the Lord giving Himself to us in His word and His sacramental presence and calling forth our self-giving in return. It is where we experience sacramentally our destiny as members incorporated into the Body of Christ. It is also where we share in the fourfold purposes of the cross.

The Eucharist, therefore, is the central action and experience of Christian life. It constitutes the Church by bringing individual believers into relationship with one another in the Body of the Risen Christ. It is also the central icon of the Church and of Christ. More particularly, it is the symbol of our relationship to the transcendent God in and through Jesus Christ and with one another, and as such it has great depths of meaning, each successive layer building upon those that went before.

Christ's Presence in the Eucharistic Celebration Is Multifaceted

To celebrate the Paschal Mystery is to encounter the presence of a living person, Jesus Christ, sharing Himself with us. Just as the flourishing of human relationship requires multiple modes of symbolic communication, one person to the other, so also the risen Lord's sacramental presence to the faithful comes through a number of distinct yet interrelated modes. Thus, the Constitution on the Sacred Liturgy (*Sacrosanctum Concilium*) declares that Christ "accomplishes so great a work" by being present in the community assembled as they pray and sing, in the person of the presiding minister, in the proclamation of the word, and in the sacraments, "especially in the

Eucharistic species" (*SC* 7). In the years before and after the Second Vatican Council, the Church has taught about these multiple and unfolding presences of Christ at Mass (in the Liturgy).[206] While they differ, each of these presences is very real.

At Mass we identify ourselves with the sacrifice of Christ by first detecting those ways or areas where His presence is conspicuous, dynamic, and vibrant. Once we have done that then we ought to fix our attention on those areas. In his 2003 encyclical letter on the Eucharist, *Ecclesia de Eucharistia*, Pope Saint John Paul II recalled the program he suggested for the Church in his letter at the close of the Jubilee Year: "To contemplate the face of Christ, and to contemplate it with Mary, is the program which I have set before the Church at the dawn of the third millennium" (§6). "To contemplate Christ," the pope added, "involves being able to recognize him wherever he manifests himself, in his many forms of presence, but above all

---

[206] The following are some of the documents where the Church has taught of the multiple and unfolding presences of Christ in the Liturgy:

1943, Pius XII, *Mystici Corporis*.

1947, Pius XII, *Mediator Dei*.

1963, Vatican II, *Sacrosanctum Concilium*.

1965, Paul VI, *Mysterium Fidei*.

1967, Sacred Congregation (SC) of Rites, *Echaristicum Mysterium*.

1969, SC Divine Worship, General Instruction of the Roman Missal, chapter.

1973, SC Divine Worship, Holy Communion and Worship of the Eucharist outside of Mass, 6-21-73, General Introduction §6. See Michael G. W ITCZAK, "The Manifold Presence of Christ in the Liturgy," *Theological Studies* 59 (1998), pp. 680-702, here read pp. 681–690. The first section of this article provides a helpful comparison of the ordering of these modes in key documents.

in the living sacrament of his body and blood." Therefore, Jesus Christ is present at Mass in four[207] distinct ways:

- in the *community* gathered,
- in the *Word* proclaimed,
- in the *priest* who presides, and
- in the *Eucharist*.

In fact, Jesus is not only present through these means but He is indeed active and it is through these means that one is called to be "a full, conscious and active" participant at Mass. It is also through these four distinct ways that a deep personal relationship with God is established and deepened.

Jesus Christ Is Present in the *Community* Gathered

Entering the church when Mass is about to begin is not like entering into an ordinary empty space. At Mass we enter into that place on earth where heaven breaks in, where earth is drawn into heaven and time into eternity. The everlasting worship of angels and saints around the throne of God is breaking into time and space. Upon entering in some churches, one sees many statues, frescos, and paintings of angels and saints. These images are meant to remind us of those who are present with us. These angels and saints symbolically represented in those images are all part of the *community gathered*. At Mass, the covenant family of God that are in two different locations—heaven and earth—are joined together in the praise and worship

---

[207] In the real sense, the *Sacrosanctum Concilium* speaks of five modes of Christ's presence—the fifth being in the other sacraments—the focus of this chapter will be only on the four modes in the Eucharist.

of God: the angels, archangels, saints, virgins, martyrs, the honourable company of the prophets, the glorious company of the apostles, the Mother of God—"the great cloud of witnesses" (cf. Heb 12:22-24). All these joined with the Church on earth are "the community gathered" and Jesus is present in this community. The Church inhabits both heaven and earth. In the liturgical celebration, we are joined by saints in heaven and other heavenly hosts in rendering to God songs of everlasting praise. The liturgy gives us a vision of the Church that could only inspire confidence despite its present weaknesses and depressing failures.

The service begins with the "Gathering of the People." Often, of course, the people are gathered before the service begins. By means of singing the entrance hymn together, they form "the people" of God—the community gathered. Being the covenant family of God by virtue of our baptism, it is befitting that we start the Mass by saying: In the name of the Father, and of the Son and of the Holy Spirit. Amen! Once we have done this sign, three things should strike us:

- *The language of the Name:* We are identified by God's own name, i.e., God's family name. The name that points to the inner life, to the eternal communion of God, the Father, the Son, and the Holy Spirit. Everyone has a family/surname and each one is named according to his/her surname. We begin the Holy Mass by reminding ourselves that we all have a common surname because we are the children of God.
- *The implicit renewal of our baptismal vow:* It was by means of the Sacrament of Baptism that we were reborn, regenerated, and re-created. Baptism is the channel through which the divine life reached us.

We are adopted into the family of God by baptism.
So, by making the sign of the cross, we remind ourselves who we are: children of the most High God.
Everything we are going to do from now on will be
done in the name of the Father, and of the Son, and of
the Holy Spirit. The Sacrament of Baptism has been
renewed. It is like renewing an oath. That is why
in the Mass we are called to participate fully and
actively, we are not there to observe the priest, we
are offering with him.

- *The sign of the cross is the mystery of the Gospel in a
  moment:* It is our Christian faith summarised in one
  single gesture. It is the most profound gesture we
  have.

Very often, if not always, we start our daily activities
with the words, "In the name of the Father, and of the Son,
and of the Holy Spirit." Do we ever realize the responsibility heaped in hearing or speaking these words? To speak
in the name of the Son, Jesus Christ, means to speak from
within the Truth that Christ is. It is not to speak from
within some theoretical truth or from a particular point
of view, even if doctrinal. Instead, it means to speak from
a profound relationship with Jesus Christ, who is the
Truth, so that our words will convey not only their seman-
tic meaning but also become life to those who receive
them.[208] To speak in the name of the Holy Spirit means to
speak beyond one's own inspiration, speaking words that
are God's words committed to us; these words must be
fire, alive and active, setting hearts and minds aglow. Then
to speak in the name of the Father means to speak "from

---

[208] Cf. Anthony BLOOM, "The Life of Prayer," in *Theology Today*,
61 (2004), pp. 26-40, here p. 26.

within that unfathomable depth of serenity and silence that alone can bring forth a word adequate to the mystery of God and the serene silence of the divinity."[209] Nonetheless, these words—In the name of the Father, and of the Son, and of the Holy Spirit—have equal responsibility to one who hears them. We must learn, as we listen, to be deeply silent and completely open. We must listen with all our being in order that it should not be words only that we hear, but true communion with God. We should, therefore, try to reach true "encounter" through these words that are spoken. Then as a result we will learn to listen to one another, to be open to each other and beyond the imperfection of words and images, to reach out in faith, in worship and veneration to the Lord of truth in the Spirit of truth.

Moreover, the sign of the cross is first and foremost the sign of the cross, meaning: the Father sent His Son to save us and eventually give us the Spirit, and the way the Father did this was nothing less than the most agonising death, the greatest crime of human history—death on the cross. The greatest sin or rather the greatest evil ever perpetuated is precisely that which God transforms into the greatest act of merciful love.[210]

---

[209] Ibid., p. 27.

[210] For the earliest Christians, the sign of the cross was a symbol of victory of God over evil. From the last half of the second century, the sign of the cross was used: to sanctify each action in daily life; to acknowledge Christ at the beginning of every act and at the beginning of every day and the last sign at night; to strengthen believers facing trials and tribulations. It was also used as a sign of mutual recognition—Christians used it to identify themselves as brothers and sisters in the Catholic faith. With the sign of the cross we can proclaim the Gospel to everyone who sees us do it, and What is this gospel? That

After the sign of the cross at Mass, what follows immediately is the *penitential rite*. There are two reasons for this. In the first place, the Word of God, which we are about to encounter, and the Body and Blood of Christ, which we are about to receive, both pronounce sentence and both justify. Because of this, there is need for acknowledgement of faults before approaching them. Secondly, when we are in the presence of all-holy God, we immediately become aware that we are far from being holy and that we have sinned. Mass is a time when we come to the bright spotlight of God's holiness, and we instantly become aware of the darkness in our lives and of our sins.

This truth is comparable to Isaiah's experience of the presence of God which led him to confess that he was doomed, a sinful man (Is 6:4-7). Isaiah entered into a sacred space where a sacrifice was being offered to God. He was connected with that presence in a way he had never been before. Isaiah was a good man, he prayed, he kept the law, he did all the right things that he should do and yet when he perceived the presence of God, he knew himself to be unworthy of that presence. The description he made of himself was remarkable: "a man of unclean lips." An angel flew to him with a coal from the altar and touched his mouth with the words: "This has touched your lips, your sin is taken away." The parallel with the Mass is quite obvious. At Mass, we are not dealing with a coal from the altar, but the very Body and Blood of Christ, delivered to the congregation not by the hand of an angel, but by the priest who is the minister of the Word, and yet the gift is the same: forgiveness. We have the assurance of this fact

---

Jesus Christ paid a debt he did not owe because we owe the debt we could not pay.

from Saint John who said that it is the Blood of Jesus that forgives us and cleanses us (1 Jn 1:7). He is the sacrifice that takes our sins away. So the absolution that we get from our confession is already coming from the sacrifice of Calvary. It will be a pity for someone to just rattle the "I confess," without being conscious of what one is saying.

Then there is another point of great importance here, which is a clear indication that we acknowledge that the family of God is present at Mass, i.e., "the great cloud of witnesses." In the penitential rite we ask for prayers from both the brothers and sisters who are sitting with us at the pew and the unseen brothers and sisters (the saints) and the angels in heaven. A special mention is also made of the "Blessed Mary, ever virgin."

In addition to this, the word "confess" popularly means to acknowledge, to manifest or to express, *with others* or as a group, something that one has experienced in common with those others. The word "confess" etymologically originates, however, from a compound of two Latin words: a first word, "*con*," which means "with"; and a second word, "*fess*," which originates from an Indo-European root word that means "to speak."[211] As etymology suggests, the basic meaning in the popular usage of the word "confess" remains: reference to an act of speaking publicly with others *in one voice* about a shared experience, before or to others who may share, but do not necessarily share that confession. In this sense, the angels and saints, whom we beckon to share in listening to us and interceding for us,

---

[211] This point refers to the first meaning of the Indo-European root word, "*bha*," which yields the Latin word, "*fari*," and means "to speak." See Joseph T. SHIPLEY, *The Origins of English Words: A Discursive Dictionary of Indo-European Roots* (Baltimore: Johns Hopkins University Press, 1984), p. 25-26.

are not confessing any sin with us. The etymological background of the word "confess," nevertheless, also suggests another and even more basic meaning of the word "confess": to speak with, as in speaking, conversing or dialoguing with another person. For example, and most basically, this could mean to disclose to another person something intimate, something deep within oneself about one's relationship to, or one's feelings for, that other person. There is also another sense of confession being an affirmation of a formal, written, and communally adopted doctrinal statement, like a confession of faith, or creed.

So Christ's presence in the community at Mass extends far beyond the community of those on earth to the angels and saints in heaven who are also present. These are all those present in the Church; they are the *community* gathered and each one of us is asking all of us, the visible and the invisible members of Christ's family, who form the "community gathered," to pray for him/her.

Also, when we sing the *Gloria in Excelsis,* we are confessing our sins by acknowledging God's glory. In acknowledging the truth of grace, one must acknowledge that he/she is in the wrong. In confessing grace (*confiteri Domino),* man must of necessity go on to confess his/her guilt (*confiteri peccatum*). This is all, perhaps, so hidden and so simple that it can scarcely be put into words: "Your light, my darkness! Your sweetness, my bitterness!"[212] The contrast between the holiness of God and our sinfulness

---

[212] Jean LECLERCQ, "Confession and Praise of God," in *Worship,* 42 (1968), pp. 169-176, here p. 172. Saint Augustine, with his own particular intensity, expresses the same ideas about the Psalms: "You praise God by accusing yourself, for his mercy consists in forgiving your sins. Thus, when you confess your sins, is it not part of the praise of God? For the doctor deserves

is always defined and conspicuous. Consequently at Mass, we are reminded that as we are community gathered together in Jesus' name, we are not there as individuals doing our own thing and experiencing God. Rather, we are the *qahal*,[213] the gathering of God's people responding to God's call.

The song of adoration to God, so well epitomized in the *Gloria in Excelsis*, objectively declares who God is. It is the song of the whole people of God. To God the Father we sing, "*We* worship you, *we* give you thanks, and *we* praise you for your glory." To Jesus Christ *we* pray, "You take away the sins of the world, have mercy on *us*... You are seated at the right hand of the Father, receive *our* prayer...." Similarly, most liturgical prayers are in the plural, seldom in the singular. The rare exceptions are the prayer of confession at the penitential rite and the prayer of humble access before communion in the new Roman Missal. The latter has: "Lord, *I* am not worthy to receive you, but only say the word, and *I* shall be healed." By this point, the people are penitent, more in awe than in remorse or regret, struck by the enormous gulf between God and man and by the fact that through the grace of the Sacrament it can nevertheless be bridged. So before the awesome Mystery of the Body and Blood of Christ, each person kneels as a responsible member of His Body, engaged at the highest level of "active participation."

---

all the more credit if he cures a patient for whom we had lost hope" (In Ps 94:4; cf. also Sermo. 67, 2-4; In Ps 99:16). By confessing our sins to God we glorify Him. Praise and avowal are both a part of the Christian life. The praise occasioned by evil is avowal, by good, thanksgiving.

[213] *Qahal* is a Hebrew word meaning, assembly, convocation, or congregation.

It is not surprising at this point that in singing the *sanctus,* the visible *community gathered* join their voices with the invisible members of the same community to sing holy, holy, holy. Alongside this emphasis on the unity of the visible and invisible members of the family of God is the combination of this prayer, which originates from two places: heaven and earth. The first part of it comes from the vision of Isaiah (Is 6:1-3). This signifies that our prayer at Mass draws up to the worship of God in heaven. Therefore, the priest introduces this by inviting the assembled community to join voices with those of the angels, archangels, and the whole company of heaven. The second part of this *sanctus* comes from Jesus' triumphal entry into Jerusalem on Palm Sunday: "Blessed is he who comes in the name of the Lord." This is so because Jesus indeed is about to enter his holy place in all humility, in the form of bread and wine, just as he entered the city of Jerusalem in a humble way, riding on a donkey (cf. Jn 12:13-14).[214] So at Mass we are gathered as a community that extends from earth to heaven and Jesus Christ is present.

Jesus Christ Is Present in the *Word* Proclaimed

With the proclamation of the Word we enter into the first primary part of the Mass. The Mass is divided into two primary parts: the Liturgy of the Word and the Liturgy of the Eucharist. The first part, the Liturgy of the Word is in turn divided into two sections: the introductory rite and the proclamation of the Word. One would have no

---

[214] This wonderful comparison was made and explained by Tom CURRAN, *The Mass: Four Encounters with Jesus that will Change Your Life* (MCF Press, 2008), pp. 83-85.

doubt to acknowledge the presence of Christ in the Liturgy of the Word, because He is the Word of the Father and it is He that is being proclaimed to the community gathered. So Jesus is certainly present in His words.

Having thus been disposed by the introductory rites, wherein the faithful were able to acknowledge their misdeeds and shortcomings, they are now ready to listen to the proclamation of the Word.[215] This Word is the very Word that the Letter to the Hebrews (4:12) said is "living and active, sharper than any two-edged sword, piercing to the division of soul and spirit, of joints and marrow, and discerning the thoughts and intentions of the heart." Given the dynamic characteristics which the Word of God possesses, one needs to be prepared before encountering it, hence, the need for the penitential rite which precedes it. Here Jesus wants each individual present at Mass to encounter Him as Word and as One who has a message for each one personally.

In the Liturgy of the Word, God and His people engage in a dialogue in which the great deeds of salvation are proclaimed and the demands of the covenant are continually restated.[216] God speaks and expects a response. The dynamic progression taken by the proclamation, meditation, explanation, and assimilation of the Word is intended to make out of the assembled community "doers of the Word and not hearers only" (Jas 1:22), heralds and

---

[215] Cf. General Introduction to the Lectionary for Mass, 2nd ed., 21 January 1981, nos. 6, 7.

[216] Read Pope Francis, Apostolic Exhortation *Evangelii Gaudium* (EG) on the Proclamation of the Gospel in Today's World, 24 November 2013, 110; Paul VI, Apostolic Exhortation *Evangelii Nuntiandi* (EN), 22.

not only recipients of divine revelation.[217] For the Word of God has the power to illumine human existence, compelling its hearers to taking an inward and outward look at themselves and into the world, and stirring an irresistible impulse to engage oneself in the world towards the realization of justice, reconciliation, and peace. Special help in this regard is expected from the priest who ought to give the faithful a well-prepared homily through which God seeks to reach out to his people. Delivered by a pastor who truly knows his people and who communicates well, "The homily can actually be an intense and happy experience of the Spirit, a consoling encounter with God's word, a constant source of renewal and growth."[218]

The Holy Spirit who causes the Word of God to be proclaimed also empowers the faithful to hear, understand, and carry it out in their lives. Having received the Holy Spirit at Baptism and Confirmation, they are called to conform their way of life to what they celebrate in the liturgy. By the witness of their lives, the faithful are sent out to be the bearers of the same Word they heard so that they may be the presence of Christ in the world, who Himself is the Word. Indeed, the words of eternal life that we receive in our encounter with the Lord in the Mass are meant for everyone individually and collectively.

---

[217] General Introduction to the Lectionary for Mass, 2nd ed., 21 January 1981, n. 6.

[218] Pope Francis, *Evangelii Gaudium* (EG), The Joy of the Gospel, 135.

Jesus Christ Is Present in the *Priest* who Presides

Recognizing Christ in the priest would be much easier if we put the priest on a pedestal and thought of him as not quite human. If we imagine a person as perfect or intrinsically holy, it is easy to think of that person as "another Christ." But it is very important and essential to understand that priests are human, with their clay feet, which means that they are sometimes sinful, just like the rest of us. It is a central principle of our faith that God comes to us through human nature. As God became human in Jesus, He continues to meet us through human beings. Indeed, if we are able to recognize Jesus in the flawed human beings who are priests, we will find it easier to recognize Him in all other people and in ourselves as well. We do not have to be perfect for Christ to work through us or dwell in us. We just have to be human, but open to the gift of His loving presence.

The presence of Christ in the priest becomes conspicuous in the second primary part of the Mass: the Liturgy of the Eucharist, which is divided into four parts:

- the Offertory
- the Eucharistic prayer
- the Communion Rite
- the Concluding Rite: greeting, blessing, and dismissal

With the offertory procession starts one of the most dramatic parts of the Mass. Here the assembly gathered participates actively to this drama by walking up to the altar and handing over the bread and wine to the priest. Others take to the altar their gifts as well. This gesture signifies the handing over of ourselves and our lives to God. All these different gifts represent our lives, past, present and future, our hopes and dreams, families and friends, loves and hates. All that you are is freely given to God through the hands of the priest. You are no longer your own (cf. 1 Cor 6:19-20), now you are God's possession. The meaning of this gesture of Presentation of Gifts is that the bread and wine offered *will* become Jesus Christ but at this point of presentation they represent ourselves given over to God through the hands of the priest as a spiritual sacrifice. That is why the bread and wine are brought from the midst of the community and by the members of the community.

We are not offering ourselves because we are special but because we are convinced that God can take the ordinary and make it extraordinary. The Lord can take what is natural and make it supernatural. He can take what is earthly and make it heavenly. He takes what is human and makes it divine and we become partakers of the divine nature. In presenting ourselves we are asked to hold nothing back, no situation, no relationship, and no part of our life. All that we have and all that we are, are completely handed over to God for transformation. If you do not bring anything to the Altar of Sacrifice, do not expect any transformation.[219] After placing all these gifts (you and I) on the altar, then the priest offers them up to God and our response is "Blessed be God forever!" At this point the passage of Romans (12:1) is being fulfilled: we are thereby offering our body as a living sacrifice holy and acceptable to God, our spiritual worship.

---

[219] Here we are not talking of "bringing something to the altar" in terms of bringing only material things, but what those material things symbolise: bringing our worries, troubles, sorrows, preoccupations; in a word, bringing our whole lives, past, present, and future for transformation.

In the preparation and Prayer over the Gifts there is a mingling of water with wine. This act is not only to show the union of our life with Christ, but also to show the co-mingling of the divine and the human. Hence the priest murmurs a prayer: "By the mystery of this water and wine may we come to share in the divinity of Christ, who humbled Himself to share in our humanity." This means that our self-offering is now immersed into Christ's and we become sharers in the divine nature (2 Pt 1:4).

We now are ready to enter into the climax and the central part of the Mass which is the Eucharistic prayer. The priest says: "Lift up your hearts," to which we reply, "We lift them up to the Lord." Why should we lift up our hearts? Because we are no longer going to work by sight but by faith. We are going to look at the reality now through the eyes of faith and see how the Lord has conspired with the Church who assembled. From now on, we should be more aware that Jesus the Lamb of God is present with His angels and saints. Heaven and earth are at this juncture joined together. Do we really believe this? That is the mystery of faith.

The core role of the priest at Mass comes from the Eucharistic prayer or what is also called the Canon of the Mass. At this point Christ's presence in the priest becomes most profoundly expressed. This is the very high point of Mass, what the ritual calls *Epiclesis* and the Prayer of Consecration, sometimes called Narration. At *Epiclesis,* the priest puts his hands over the bread and wine and calls down the Holy Spirit so that they will be transformed into the Body and Blood of Jesus Christ. At the Prayer of Consecration, or the Narration, the priest repeats the words of Jesus at the Last Supper: "Take this, all of you, and eat of it, this is my Body...."

It is important at this point to observe the sequence in the Prayer of Consecration; the priest must call down the Holy Spirit (*Epiclesis*) before he (the priest) takes part of Jesus Christ (Narration). That is to say that the priest is totally dependent on the Holy Spirit to bring about this transformation.[220] On the other hand, God wills to bring about this transformation through his priest and not directly. There is a radical mutual interdependence between the Holy Spirit and the priest.[221] God chose to give us the Eucharist through His priest who at that moment is acting in *persona Christ*. Therefore, in the Prayer of Consecration the priest does not say "this is his body, nor this is your body," but we hear him say: "This is my Body... This is the chalice of my Blood..." The priest is a minister, and through his ministry God Himself is at work. He, the priest, has entered into a kind of covenant with the High Priest by which his vocal chords are consecrated, by which the tongue is dedicated. So it is Jesus speaking more than the priest. There is a shift here from Narration to Quotation. The priest shifts from telling the story in the third person to quoting in the first person, "Take this, all of you, and eat of it, this is my Body."

The presence of Christ at Mass to which we are privileged to participate is a presence which transforms and renders the participants whole. In this presence, through this presence, and with this presence we are able to connect with one another in a way that reminds us of our bonds in Christ, which expresses the love of Christ that

---

[220] Cf. Tom CURRAN was wonderful in his presentation of the presence of Christ in the priest. Read Tom CURRAN, *The Mass: Four Encounters with Jesus that will Change Your Life* (MCF Press, 2008), pp. 71-97.

[221] Cf. Ibid., pp. 85-87.

unites us. This presence also deepens and tightens our individual relationship with God in His Son, Jesus Christ. Therefore, Tom Curran, summing up the three presences that we have already dealt with, said:

> Christ is present in the community, drawing us up into the very worship of heaven. Christ is present in the Word, unveiling his heart for us and exposing our hearts to Him, causing us to take up our place in the drama of dramas. Having been welcomed into the praise and worship of God, having heard that Word unveiled, and having been unveiled by God to it, we encounter Christ the High Priest through the ministry of the earthly priest, most profoundly in the conse- cration of the Eucharist.[222]

In worship, we become present to the God who is present to us. The operating biblical metaphor regarding worship is sacrifice. We bring ourselves to the altar and let God do to us what He wills. We bring ourselves to the Eucharistic table, entering into that magnificent fourfold shape of the liturgy that shapes us: *taking, blessing, break- ing, giving*—the life of Jesus taken and blessed, broken and distributed. That Eucharistic life now shapes our lives as we give ourselves, Christ in us, to be taken, blessed, broken and distributed in lives of witness and service, justice and healing.

Jesus Christ Is Present in the *Eucharist*

The presence of Christ in the Eucharist unveils itself gradually with the Eucharistic prayer. This is the key,

---

222 Ibid., pp. 96-97.

the sacrificial climax of the Eucharist. It is divided into eight sections:

- *Thanksgiving*
- *Acclamation:* Holy, Holy, Holy Lord of Hosts. Our joining the angels and saints singing around the throne of God.
- *Epiclesis:*[223] Calling down of the Holy Spirit on the gifts.
- *Narration:* Also called words of the Institution.[224] Narration and *Anamnesis* are the climax of Mass.

---

[223] The word *epiclesis* is a Greek noun, which derives from the verb *epikaleo* (to call, invoke). In the technical sense, it means an invocation to God the Father or to God the Holy Spirit, but in the exposition that follows our interest, it is the action of the Holy Spirit.

[224] One mark of controversy between West (Catholics) and East is whether it is the words of Institution (*Narration*) or the prayer that calls down the Holy Spirit (*Epiclesis*) that changes the elements of bread and wine into the Body and Blood of Christ. The West holds that this is accomplished by the Institution Narrative and the East believes it is accomplished by the Epiclesis. The *Epiclesis* was originally a prayer calling on the Spirit to unify the Church, which later developed to become the explicit invocation of the Spirit to consecrate the elements. This is seen in the ancient Eucharistic prayers of Saint Basil and Saint John Chrysostom where the *Epiclesis* comes after the words of Consecration. The West, however, focused on Christ's words as quoted by Saint Justin Martyr and Saint Ambrose, both of whom quite explicitly taught that Christ acts through the words of the Consecration. The belief in the change (transubstantiation) is demonstrated by adoring the Body (host) and the Blood (chalice) as they are held up by the priest immediately afterwards. After AD 1054, the hardening of the schism between East and West saw the East saying that it was only through the *Epiclesis* that the elements changed and the West stressing only the Narration. Pope Benedict XVI in *Sacramentum Caritatis* 13 restates that transubstantiation is the action of the Holy Spirit working through the words of Christ in the Institution Narrative and in the *Epiclesis*, or

- *Anamnesis:*[225] The word anamnesis is the Greek word for remembrance. "Do this as an *anamnesis* of me," translated as "memorial" or "remembrance."
- *The Offering*: The greatest Gift of God is Christ Himself, who has come down on earth and through the priest we offer Him back to our Father and His Father. We do this while acknowledging that the bread and wine were only a token that God can transubstantiate into His Son.
- *Intercession*: At this point, with the communion of the saints, we go over to the intercessions.
- *Final Doxology*: The great *Amen* follows the final doxology. This Amen is more than "so be it." It means, "I swear that it is so."

"Do this in my *anamnesis*," primarily means that we do this *prayer-action* in order that Jesus Christ is remembered and named as the focus of the act for which God is praised and as the basis of the thanksgiving, as source of the knowledge, and as centre of the supplication of the community. Interesting to note is that Christ never said: "Write this in remembrance of Me." He commanded: "*Do*

---

invocation of the Spirit. He points out that the change of the elements is oriented towards individual transformation as the Body of Christ. In receiving the sacramental Body of Christ, one becomes more the Mystical Body of Christ, the Church. See Giles DIMOCK, O.P., *The Eucharist: Sacrament and Sacrifice* (New York, 2009), pp. 16-17.

[225] *Anamnesis* is a Greek word, which means remembrance. From the same root we derive our words amnesia, mnemonics. It is applied traditionally to that part of the Eucharist which consists in the recalling to the memory, remembering. In a technical sense we could distinguish and oppose *anamnesis* and *epiclesis*, as a text in which we narrate and a text in which we invoke.

this in remembrance of me."[226] It is in the "*doing*" that we are obeying the commands of our Lord Jesus Christ. Therefore, the Eucharist is the New and everlasting Covenant, which we *do* in remembrance of Him, who gave us the New Testament in His Blood. Again we must ask ourselves: What is this "this" that Jesus has just done and commanded that we do in His *anamnesis*? He had taken Himself, His very life in His hands and given it up, a self, poured out in reality, though in anticipation. This prediction or anticipation brought His dying and His undergoing death fully present. It was so present that nothing else was left but love. So if Jesus told His disciples to do "*this*," He meant

---

[226] Quite often we tend to forget how important the "memory" is. We forget that without the memory one cannot even complete a sentence, and yet we take it for granted. The memory is correlative to our being in time. It allows us to make present facts and data, which are far away in space and time. Memory is more than recalling the past events and experiences of our lives, memory is also the way in which the soul has access to reality. Saint Augustine describes the soul as having three faculties: memory, and intellect, and the will reflecting the Trinity—Father, Son, and Holy Spirit. He said that the memory is the father in the trinity of the soul. Memory he said is the storehouse of the being for the soul. In *Anamnesis* we have the act of remembrance par excellence. Remembrance is very important, hence in Genesis 9 we read: "God remembers His covenant." The question would be: What happened before? Has God forgotten it? God never forgets anything, as He is Omniscience. Why does the Bible say that God remembers His covenant? The answer could be: in the same way I would say I remember my anniversary. It does not mean that within the 364 days in a year I forget that I am a sister. No! It is only that it is on a very specific day that I celebrate my consecration. When we celebrate birthdays we do not forget the birth of all those people all other days, but we just set a day aside to remember or to commemorate their births and thereby to celebrate it. On that day we experience time and that is the way we experience God.

that they should give their lives up as He had just done in anticipation. To do "this," therefore, implies that we, like Jesus and as Jesus, must die the kind of death He was about to die, a dying in love and for love of others. Only in doing "this" could the meaning of the Eucharist as a sacrament of love and as the Blood and Body of Christ begin to come true.[227] As is well known, the account of the Last Supper in the Gospel of Saint John does not contain narrative of the institution of the Eucharist, as the other Gospels do. In its place we find, instead, Jesus washing the feet of His disciples and instructing them: "I have given you an example: as I have done to you, you also must do" (13:15). Therefore, the injunction of Christ, "do *this* in memory of me," repeated at every celebration of the Eucharist, embraces both the breaking of the bread (letting our lives be broken for others) and the ongoing service of others (washing the feet of others). These Eucharistic actions are both performed for the life of the world, for the fuller realization of Christ's presence in all. Therefore, in the *Anamnesis* we recall what happened in the upper room, what happened on the cross, what happened in the tomb when He was buried, and His resurrection. For the Jews, remembrance means re-enactment, re-presentation. Christ's sacrifice is being re-presented on the altar and that is the essence of what it means when we speak of covenant renewal. The covenant being renewed is the covenant being celebrated and being re-enacted. The covenant is now Jesus Himself. This is the climax of the climaxes.

It is in the Eucharist that we have the most profound encounter with Jesus Christ because that is the place He is

---

[227] Cf. Read Rosemary HAUGHTON, *The Passionate God* (London: Darton, Longman & Todd, 1981), pp. 202-203.

accessible to the point of being consumable. His power to transform us is at its highest peak in the Eucharist. Besides, it is precisely in the Eucharist itself that Christ's multifaceted real presence is recognised. The four-fold presence is not a movement from Eucharist to Word, to the priest and to the congregation or even world, through some kind of transference in which the original Eucharistic actions are dissolved, but, rather, it is a *movement towards* a Eucharistic worldview which incorporates Word, congregation (or other Christians) and, indeed, the world. It remains, therefore, the principal lens through which Christ's real presence is perceived.

The various modes of Christ's presence in the Eucharist are not in competition with one another. All are real. All are unique. All support each other. However, the Eucharist is the symbol of our unity with God and one another. Through it we make known that we are the Body of Christ, a communion of persons—radically, socially—in the image of God. Again through all of these we claim that Christ is truly, fully, really present. The Eucharist, then, offers us varied ways to experience Christ's continuing presence and to fill us with His love. It teaches us how to recognize Him and where to look for Him. If we grow in our ability to recognize Him when we gather to celebrate the Mass, we will also find it easier to see His face around us all through the week. What a wonderful Sacrament Christ has given us!

The Intrinsic Unity Between
Christ's Presence in the *Community*
Gathered and in the *Eucharist*

The link between the sacramental Body of Christ and His Mystical Body, the Church, lies at the core of the meaning of Communion. This is not simply a private moment between Jesus and me, but rather an intensely *personal and communal moment,* a moment when we are deeply united to all those who share this sacred meal. Reverence requires that we recognize the corporeal Presence of Christ in what appears to be mere bread and wine as well as recognizing His spiritual Presence in all those who eat and drink with us. It is the same Christ in both forms.

Originally, the disciples experienced their personal relationship with Jesus by sharing table fellowship with Him. After the resurrection, the Eucharistic meal became an experience of their personal relationship with the resurrected Christ. More specifically, the liturgical words over the bread and wine

> expressed what the personal relationship—the community at table—with Jesus meant to the primitive Church and continued to mean after his departure—namely, his real presence in the assembled community. Jesus had died, but his followers had the visible experience of his continued life and active presence among them, because they, the believers, formed one community by virtue of his death "for our sins" and his resurrection.[228]

---

[228] Edward SCHILLEBEECKX, *The Eucharist* (London: Sheed and Ward, 1968), p. 123.

In this way, the sharing of the Eucharist after the Ascension became the occasion for recognizing, once again, His continued presence among them. This is quite different from the eventual shift to perceiving the presence of Christ almost solely in the sacred species, quite distinct from the community's gathering to celebrate the Eucharist.

Christ did not give us the Eucharist only to transform bread and wine into His Body and Blood, but also He gave us this Sacrament to transform us into His Body. That is the goal of the Eucharist and the meaning of Communion. As Saint Augustine teaches, the mystery of the intimate union of our lives with Christ's, of ourselves as members of His Body now in the world, is proclaimed so as to elicit our life committing response:

> Thus, if you wish to understand the body of Christ, listen to the Apostle, who says to the believers: You are the body of Christ and His members (1 Cor 12:27). And thus, if you are the body of Christ and His members, it is your mystery that has been placed on the altar of the Lord; you receive your own mystery. You answer "Amen" to what you are, and in answering, you accept it. For you hear, "The body of Christ" and you answer "Amen." Be a member of Christ's body, so that your Amen may be true.[229]

Thus the fourth mode of Christ's presence in His Body and Blood brings us back to the first mode in the assembly. The sacramental Body exists for the sake of the Mystical Body. In the first thousand years of the Church's history,

---

[229] Augustine, Sermon 272, *Patrologiae Latina*, trans. J.P. Migne, cited in Joseph M. Powers, *Eucharistic Theology* (New York: Seabury Press, 1967), p. 20.

Christians spoke of the Church as the real Body of Christ and the sacrament as the Mystical Body. In the last thousand years we have reversed the terms, calling the sacrament the Real Presence and calling the Church the Mystical Body of Christ. The key is that these two are intimately linked. The core of the mystery of the Eucharist can be found in this link. The body of Christ shares the Body and Blood of Christ to become more fully the Body of Christ.

That is to say that, a sense of Church is a prerequisite for a sense of presence—Christ's presence to us, our presence to Christ and to one another. The ritual action of gathering, with all its symbolic interplay, is one of those interpersonal dynamics that can provide a sense of community, a sense of belonging, and a sense of hospitality. A logical first place, then, for examining the possibility of the experience of community that might enable a sense of Church, and ultimately a sense of Christ's presence in the assembly, is the gathering rite.[230] Its purpose is to provide the possibility for individuals to experience a sense of belonging to the group gathered in a significant way, one that includes not only feeling welcomed, but also belonging as an integral participant. There is also an awareness of the presence of the invisible members of that same community. What is at stake here is the negotiating of identity and the mediating of relationships. These are achieved through the symbolic

---

[230] The gathering rite consists first of all in one's preparations at home before coming to church, then one's being at the church before Mass, followed by the opening hymn, the sign of the cross, the greeting, the penitential rite, the Gloria, and the opening prayer.

activity that constitutes the Eucharistic rite. The gathering rite is the entrée into that symbolic activity.[231]

To speak of Christ's presence in four ways, however, is not to assert four identical modalities of presence within the Eucharistic celebration. These presences are differently expressed but nevertheless form a unity.[232] So, according to Schillebeeckx, "the Eucharistic presence is thus no longer isolated. We no long say, 'Christ is there,' without asking for whom he is present."[233] This fundamentally means that Christ's presence in the Eucharist is a "presence for," that is, centred upon relationships within the *gathered Body of Christ*. Frank O'Loughlin sums this up nicely when he suggests that "we need to see each mode of presence within the context of Christ's relationship to his disciples being gathered into the communion of his Church which is becoming his Body."[234]

In singing the *Agnus Dei*, for example, the community gathered communally confesses the real presence of Christ. This is evident in the fact that the Church does not merely sing "about" Christ; rather, because He is present among them with His Body and Blood, the Church speaks

---

[231] Cf. Judith Marie KUBICKI, "Recognizing the Presence of Christ in the Liturgical Assembly," in *Theological Studies* 65 (2004), pp. 817-837, here p. 826.

[232] It should be noted that certain questions regarding the way these modes of Christ's presence in the Eucharist and the liturgy are related and understood have been the cause of some ongoing research and investigation among sacramental theologians. See Michael G. WITCZAK, "The Manifold Presence of Christ in the Liturgy," pp. 696-697.

[233] Edward SCHILLEBEECKX, *The Eucharist* (London: Sheed and Ward, 1968), p. 104.

[234] Frank O'LOUGHLIN, *Christ Present in the Eucharist* (Strathfield, NSW: St. Paul's Publications, 2000), p. 51.

directly to Him saying: "Lamb of God, *You* take away the sins of the world; have mercy on us...grant us peace."

The real presence of Christ is not a "thing" but, rather, an experiential reality which calls us to be the Body of Christ in the world. The theology of the real presence draws out the interconnectedness of liturgy and life. This means that Christ's presence must flow from the liturgy out into the world through the "members" of His Body. This is fundamental, if liturgy is to be authentic, if Christ's presence within the gathered assembly is to be "real," then it must be grounded in the recognised realities of a world which is both beautiful and terrible, a world of joys and sufferings, a world of hope but also of pain, confusion, and disillusionment. Christ's presence in the Eucharistic liturgy is only "real" to the extent that our liturgical actions are anchored in the "real world." Drawing upon Karl Rahner's notion of the "liturgy of the world," Nathan Mitchell asserts "the primary liturgy through which Christians experience the Real Presence of God in Christ is nothing more or less than 'the liturgy of the world'. It is to this liturgy, 'smelling of death and sacrifice', that all the Church's ritual actions return... We arrive at Mystery, at Real Presence, at God, only by embracing the human with all its poignancy and terror."[235]

In the celebration of the Eucharist, not only is the congregation made one in and through Jesus, it also binds together the Church of all times and places. It even binds together earth and heaven. This fact is evident in the *Gloria* and the *Sanctus* that we pray during the Mass: "Glory to God in the highest," sang the heavenly host at the birth of

---

[235] Nathan Mitchell, "Who Is at the Table? Reclaiming Real Presence," in *Commonweal* 122, no. 2, 27 January 1995, p. 15.

the Saviour (Lk 2:14). "Holy, holy, holy...the whole earth is full of his glory," cried the angels in the prophet Isaiah's vision of God (Is 6:3). In the prayers of the Mass, in which we take up the same words, the praying Church unites itself to the praise of the angels in heaven. The earthly liturgy is always our participation in the eternal praise of heaven. We call the Eucharist the "pledge of future glory" (cf. *CCC*, n. 1402) because it is—already now—an anticipation of heavenly life.

Spatial-Temporality of the Eucharistic Sacrifice of the Mass

The Eucharist is the transubstantiation of the human into union with the divine. Christ's presence in the breaking of bread transforms not only the Eucharistic elements or signs, but all creation. Therefore, the liturgy expresses a new configuration of *time* and *space*, a different world, one that shapes and forms the believer into a new creature. There is a kind of cosmic dimension to every celebration in which the realities of our world (bread, wine, men, and women) are all transformed into the Body and Blood of Christ. The world with all of its needs, worries, joys, and struggles are present every time we celebrate the Eucharist together, and our consciousness of the world helps to make the Mass the experience of Christian life in a concentrated and concretized way.

In the same vein, the four presences of Christ at Mass stretches in every direction: past, present, and future. Thus the presence of Christ in the *community* draws us upwards from life today into the heavenly realm of eternity. With the presence of the saints and the angelic hosts of heaven, it binds earth and heaven together. His presence in the

Word opens us to what comes down like lightening from heaven, striking our lives, judging the secret thoughts and purposes of the heart, here and now. His presence in the *priest* draws two thousand year-old events from the past into the present. In the "community" and the "Word" there are movements from earth to heaven and heaven to earth, from time to eternity and eternity to time. In the "priest," we have the past being brought into the present. Then the fourth way of Christ's presence, the *Eucharist,* draws the dimension of the future into our present moment. Receiving communion is a foretaste of the heavenly banquet that awaits us in the future.[236]

Therefore, the Christian learns to experience God by acknowledging His operative work in time. The way to see God is to look back on those moments in our experience, both as individuals and as a people, in which the mercy and compassion of God resonated in a particularly compelling way. In remembering, reflecting upon, and celebrating that experience, we learn to see what God is doing in our present situation and to reach forward in hope towards the yet unfulfilled promises implicit in the past event. In this way, the liturgical experience increases the presence of mystery in the life of the faithful as he/she celebrates. This mystery is made perceptible by the liturgical modalities of memorial (*anámnesis*), of participation (*méthexis*), of the presence of the Spirit that has been invoked (*epíklesis*), and of its action (*paráklesis*), looking forward to its return to the Father (*anáklesis*).[237]

---

[236] Cf. Tom CURRAN, *The Mass: Four Encounters with Jesus that will Change Your Life* (MCF Press, 2008), pp. 104-105.

[237] Cf. A. TRIACCA, "Il rinnovamento liturgico fermento della riforma liturgica," in *Ephemerides Liturgicae* 113 (1999), pp. 347-365, here p. 357.

The Holy Mass as Covenantal
Relationship with God in Jesus

To understand the effectiveness of this sacrament in furthering one's personal relationship with Christ, it is advisable to appreciate this passage from Hans Urs von Balthasar:

> No relationship is closer...than that between the man in grace and the Lord who gives grace, between the Head and the body, between the vine and the branch. But this relationship can only have full play if it prevails, too, in the realm of the spirit, that is, if the freedom of the Word is answered by a corresponding readiness on the part of man to hear, to follow, and to comply.[238]

A clearer understanding of the Eucharist opens us to a deeper, personal relationship with Jesus who gives Himself to us in this sacrament. This relationship is a covenant *with all of us* in His Blood, and *with each one* of us *in a personal and intimate way*. The whole point of the Eucharist is to nurture a movement from fragmentation to integration: The broken bread becomes the salvific means for the gathering in of the many; the blood outpoured achieves the at-one-ness of the world. What is de-centred finds its centre in the Eucharist. Those who despair of meaning can find here God's meaning and purpose. In this way, Christ in the Eucharist brought a radical newness. This is a point upon which the Holy Father Pope Benedict XVI, in his Apostolic Exhortation *Sacramentum Caritatis* (71) lays great emphasis. This newness, "is that the worship of

---

[238] Hans Urs von BALTHASAR, cited by Tom CURRAN, *The Mass: Four Encounters with Jesus that will Change Your Life* (MCF Press, 2008), p. 47.

God in our lives cannot be relegated to something private and individual, but tends by its nature to permeate every aspect of our existence. Worship pleasing to God thus becomes a new way of living our whole life, each particular moment of which is lifted up, since it is lived as part of a relationship with Christ and as an offering to God." Therefore by its very nature the Eucharist commits us to a whole way of life. It pledges us to making our whole lives a sacrificial life and a self-offering to God.

The focus of the Eucharist as the invitation and presence to us of Christ crucified and risen, adds a new dimension to its understanding. Jesus presents Himself as a host at a banquet, but the content of His hospitality is His own person. This highlights a truth about human relationships that is pervasive in community life, family life, in work, in friendship, and in public service. What we have to give to others is in the first place ourselves, in terms of our talents, time, energy, and service. Moreover, in nourishing the bodies and minds and hopes and spirits of others, we are in some sense consumed. We are called by our interdependence in the plan of creation to become nourishment for others in a great many ways, and this is sacrificial not only in the sense of demanding renunciations of self-interest, but also in the basic sense of constituting a dedication, a making holy or sacred to God according to the purpose of God. This focus on being nourishment for others might have been expressed in Eucharistic form by a commemoration and re-enactment of Jesus in His public ministry of teaching, preaching, healing, and exorcizing. In the Eucharist, Jesus is necessarily identified with the cross. To be invited to table fellowship in the Eucharist is to be invited to share redemptive self-giving in a hostile world for the nourishment of others who are struggling in that world.

A meal, especially one with family and friends, and particularly on an occasion of celebration, is an opportunity to deepen closeness, bonding, communion, and even union. It is an intimate occasion. Think by contrast of meals taken alone or with strangers or when there is tension and resentment, and how the meal then is somehow lacking in harmony. Jesus gave us the Eucharist at the Last Supper. But in this case, we not only eat with the host of the meal, we also eat and drink the consecrated host and wine and thereby eat the giver of the gift, becoming one with each other as we become one in Jesus Christ. Lovers often express a "consuming" desire to be united to each other. This consuming desire for Him is satisfied when we receive the Eucharist. The Last Supper of Jesus was a celebration of the Pasch, the Passover meal in which the Israelites were incorporated into God's chosen people as they ate the Paschal Lamb before their exodus from Egypt to the Promised Land. This sacrificial meal grounded a special relationship with the Lord; it gave them an identity as His people and strengthened their covenant with Him. Jesus established a new covenant, a new relationship with us, through offering not a lamb but Himself, the Lamb of God who takes away the sins of the world. When we do this in memory of Him, we do it at a meal, the new Paschal Meal participating in the Paschal Mystery of the death and resurrection of Jesus Christ. We eat His Body and drink His Blood. In the Eucharist we do not learn about Christ, but from Him.

The Mass and Religious Consecration: Self-Emptying for Love

The religious is called to follow Christ and become part of Christ's Body. This vocation finds its kernel and its fastening knots in the Eucharistic celebration of the Mass, wherein this covenantal bond is tightly sealed. Thus, in the Eucharist, the act of consumption is reversed and becomes an act of *kenosis,* or self-emptying. Becoming part of Christ's Body is to descend with Christ into the broken human condition, to empty oneself taking the "form of a slave" (Phil 2:7). The great capacity for self-sacrifice that characterizes the religious consecration will not have much significance unless it is coupled with the readiness to share one's life, through sharing of one's time, talents, and service. One's self-emptying finds significance only when by it, another person is made full. Christ emptied Himself so that we may be filled with His life, and that we may have it abundantly (cf. Jn 10:10).

Jesus taught on many occasions that, in order to find our lives, we must first lose them (Mt 10:39). Paul, as well, teaches that it is only to the degree that we have died to ourselves that Christ's resurrection can become the source of our new life (Rom 6:4). Presenting himself as an example of this new creation, he proclaims that, "the life I live is not my own, it is Christ who lives in me" (Gal 2:20). He has exchanged the old man for the new (Col. 3:9-10). Through the reception of the Holy Eucharist, the religious is taken up in the oblation, in the *kenosis* of Jesus Christ. This dynamism becomes the animating principle of his/her life of consecration. In imitation of Jesus, religious empty themselves in order to give themselves in love in a variety of ways, mindful that self-giving and sacrificial love are the means to their joy and fulfilment, for we are all created in the image and likeness of God whose Trinitarian life is self-surrender and love. The religious is therefore called to this self-surrender, which without any doubt brings joy that is contagious which makes people who see us "want to believe in the same Christ that we worship and want to give themselves to His service too. Our witness, then, will be as effective as we testify by the joy that is ours, that the only way to happiness in life—even this life—is in self-surrender to the loving although demanding will of God."[239]

Religious consecration, and the religious life in general, are comparable to all the sacrificial elements of the altar. For example, let us see how the consecration of a religious can be likened to the chalice of the altar. This comparison can be seen in so many ways.

In the first place, the most precious part of the chalice is not the part that is made of precious materials of gold, silver and jewels, but the part that is not there: the emptiness of the cup.[240] For the chalice can be filled with Christ only in the measure in which it is empty. In the same way, religious through their lives of self-emptying, which is established by their vows of poverty, chastity and

---

[239] Lucius Iwejuru UGORJI, "The Religious and the Apostolate," a paper delivered to the DDL Sisters Silver Jubilarians, DRAC (Enugu, 2015).

[240] Some years ago during my retreat sessions with some religious men and women, I severally employed this comparison but with the image of an empty glass cup, which served the same purpose in so many ways. But recently, I came in contact with the article of Bernard MULLAHY and saw that his comparison with the sacred vessels of the altar is a wonderful idea. So thanks to him. See Bernard I. MULLAHY, "The Religious Life and the Mass," in *Orate Fratres*, XXIII (1949), pp. 337-344.

obedience, *try* to be empty chalices so that Christ may be poured into them. In this way, they will be able to enfold Him lovingly within the depths of their being.

Secondly, like cups in general, chalices are curved vessels. Viewed from the outside they are convex—they are turning away from things. But viewed from the inside they are concave—they are turning towards something, embracing and enfolding something.[241] The "world" sees these beautiful chalices only from the outside. It sees them turning away from the world, from its vanities, its pleasures, its attractions and so on, but always turning away. This is why the world can never comprehend nor appreciate the sense, essence, and meaning of such a life of continuous "turning away from...pleasures, vanities, and worldly glories." The consecrated men and women understand, because they see it all from the inside, realize that what makes their life of detachment and self-emptying meaningful is not that it turns away from things, but that it turns towards something, or rather towards Someone— Someone whom they want to possess, to enfold, to embrace, and to cherish—hence, they are turning towards Jesus Christ who will eventually fill their emptiness.

It is the primacy of God as love that the consecrated is emphasizing by their life of self-emptying. But a possible debilitation of such a life would be an emptiness of self-emptying. To understand this point, one could juxtapose it with what Carlo Carretto, writing about Saint Francis of Assisi on the virtue of poverty, said: "Never forget that love is God himself, while poverty is just the dress. So do not rely on the dress if you are not capable

---

[241] Cf. Bernard I. MULLAHY, "The Religious Life and the Mass," in *Orate Fratres*, XXIII (1949), pp. 337-344.

of seeing, bearing and loving the person who wears it."[242] Consequently, poverty or self-emptying is only the dress that love wears. Any attempt to live in poverty should equal the learning or the possession of love. The self-emptying, the turning away from pleasures, vanities, etc., of the consecrated religious is meaningless if it is not geared towards a loving relationship with God in prayer.

Thirdly, the chalice which embraces the all-holy God cannot be an ordinary cup. It cannot be used to contain ordinary things. It must be a sacred vessel, set aside and made holy. It must be consecrated to possess Him alone. This consecration of the chalice symbolizes the religious consecration (and the vow of chastity in particular) by which religious make themselves consecrated vessels, thereby setting themselves aside from the ordinary ways of the world in order to possess Him alone. Renouncing the ordinary love of an equal, they cry out with their whole life and all their earthly passions for a God to love, to adore, and to enfold.

Fourthly, not all materials can be fashioned into a sacred chalice to enfold Jesus, the Innocent Lamb. They must be malleable and pliant. They must be materials which will not resist the workings of the artist. Consecrated persons understand this, and they make it clear through their vow of obedience. Obedience will make them flexible and bendable in the hands of the Divine Artist, so that He can realize in them His wonderful design. He can continuously

---

[242] "Vergesst nie, die Liebe ist Gott selbst, während die Armut nur das Kleid ist. Hängt euch also nicht an das Kleid, wenn ihr nicht fähig seid, den Menschen, der es trägt, zu sehen, zu ertragen, zu lieben." Carlo CARRETTO, *Was Franziskus uns heute sagt* (Freiburg i.Br., 1981), p. 90.

mould and remould them into living chalices which will possess Him and never let Him go.[243]

Christ's immolation on Calvary was one simple act, but it is constantly renewed each day on our altars. So it is with religious consecration, which once made, the sacrifice needs to be each day embraced anew in the daily living of religious obligations. As each day dawns with its own particular sacrifices to be embraced, the religious will draw energy and strength from the sacrifice of Christ at Mass. Every time they celebrate in faith they are bonded more truly with Christ in His Paschal Mystery. Each day at the offertory, religious place themselves as hosts on the paten with the hosts of the Mass. When the words of consecration transform the hosts of the Mass, they, too, are transformed into Christ more and more each day. This fact is also true for every Christian, because the life to which consecrated persons are called to embrace is not something apart from Christian life. It is not even something added on to the Christian life. It is simply the Christian life itself. If, therefore, Christian life is essentially a sacrificial life, then the whole purpose of religious life is to bring this sacrificial life to its fullness.

Using the chalice and the hosts as examples of how the life of the consecrated can be associated to Christ's sacrifice of the altar is only a mere illustration. The concrete ways in which religious experience God entering and shaping their lives in Christ is by living in Him. To so live in Christ they need to know Him and not merely to know about Him or His teaching, but to truly know Him intimately in a deep bond of friendship (Jn 15:15). To know

---

[243] Cf. Bernard I. MULLAHY, "The Religious Life and the Mass," in *Orate Fratres*, XXIII (1949), p. 339.

Him is to "have the words of eternal life" (Jn 6:68). It has been shown in Chapter Two how the Scriptures are an excellent means for this purpose. Therefore, the altar with its two great treasures, the Word of God and the Eucharist, must become the focal point of their existence. Once one believes that Christ is really present in the Holy Eucharist, it is only logical to conclude that the person should worship Him. The last thing we human beings want from another human being is to be ignored. The same is true with Christ present in the Eucharist. So His real presence in the Eucharist offers the consecrated religious an opportunity for heart-to-heart conversation with Him. This underlines the need for Adoration which is recommended by the Canon of the Church (663 §2) as one of the available means for expressing devotion and growing in this union with God.

Adoration of Jesus Present in the Blessed Sacrament

In his homily at World Youth Day in Cologne, Germany, in 2005, Pope Benedict XVI, speaking of the importance of adoring Jesus present in the Blessed Sacrament, clarified the two essential dimensions of Eucharistic Adoration. In doing this he used the two roots of the word "adoration" from Greek and Latin. The word for "adoration" in Greek is *proskynesis*, which literally means "falling down" before God, reverencing and acknowledging Him in His greatness as God. Then the Latin word *adoratio* means "mouth to mouth contact, a kiss, an embrace, and hence, ultimately love."[244]

---

[244] Benedict XVI, "Homily of His Holiness Pope Benedict XVI," On the Occasion of the XX World Youth Day, Eucharistic

Etymologically, the Latin word *adorare* is derived from *ad*, "to," and *os, oris*, "the mouth," and thus the most primitive act of adoration was by the application of the fingers to the mouth: to bring the hand to the mouth and kiss it, *manum ad os admovere.* Such was the way in which the pagans honoured their gods. This is also the background to the passage in the Book of Job (31:26-28) where it says: "If I beheld the sun when it shined, or the moon walking in brightness, and my heart hath been secretly enticed, or *my mouth hath kissed my hand*, this also were iniquities to be punished by the Judges; for I should have denied the God that is above." Here the mouth kissing the hand is equal in meaning and force to *adoration*, as if he had said, "If I had adored the sun or the moon." To adore, the pagans bring the right hand to the mouth and kiss it. By carrying the hand to the mouth, man pays the homage of his person to the divinity.[245]

The question that spontaneously comes to mind is this: Why did this gesture express the sovereign worship? One would believe that it is probably because man is the image of God. God is entire in His Word; by Him He does all things. Like God, man is also "somehow" entire in his word; it is by it that he does everything. So to carry the hand to the mouth is to repress the word; it is, in some sort, to be annihilated. As a result, to do this, to adore, to render sovereign homage to God as the pagans did to their monarchs and later to their gods, is to declare ourselves vassals, subjects, and slaves of God.[246]

Celebration, Cologne, 21 August 2005.

[245] See Jean Joseph GAUME, *The Sign of the Cross in the Nineteenth Century* (Aeterna Press, 2015), pp. 41-42.

[246] This mode of adoration is said to have originated among the Persians, who, as worshippers of the sun, always turned their

With the Greek and Latin etymological background, it becomes clear that Eucharistic Adoration leads us to a direct encounter with God. To adore Jesus present in the Eucharist is to reverence and to bow profoundly before the greatness and majesty of God. Adoration is a kind of continuation with receiving Christ in Holy Communion, which manifests the most profound communion of love

---

faces to the east and kissed their hands to that luminary. The gesture was first used as a token of respect to their monarchs, and was easily transferred to objects of worship. Other additional forms of adoration were used in various countries, but in all of them this reference to kissing was in some degree preserved. It is yet a practise of quite common usage for Orientals to kiss what they deem sacred or that which they wish to adore as, for example, the Wailing Place of the Jews at Jerusalem, the nearest wall to the Temple where they were permitted by the Mahommedans to approach and on which their tears and kisses were affectionately bestowed before the British General Allenby took possession of the city in the World War and equalised the rights of the inhabitants. The marble toes of the statue of Saint Peter in the Cathedral of Saint Peter's at Rome have been quite worn away by the kissings of Roman Catholics and have been replaced by bronze. Among the ancient Romans, the act of adoration was thus performed: The worshiper, having his head covered, applied his right hand to his lips, thumb erect, and the forefinger resting on it, and then, bowing his head, he turned round from right to left. Hence, Lucius Apuleius, a Roman author, born in the first century, in his *Apologia sive oratio de magia*, a defense against the charge of witchcraft, uses the expression to apply the hand to the lips, *manum labris admovere*, to express the act of adoration. The Grecian mode of adoration differed from the Roman in having had the head uncovered, which practise was adopted by the Christians. The Oriental nations also express the act of adoration by prostrating themselves on their faces and applying their foreheads to the ground. The ancient Jews adored by kneeling, sometimes by prostration of the whole body, and by kissing the hand. See online Albert G. Mackey, *Revised Encyclopaedia of Freemasonry and Kindred Sciences.*

that is possible on this earth.[247] For this reason, both Saint John Paul II and Pope Benedict XVI had continually invited people to this deepest of all forms of personal prayer.

It is not surprising that even before he became pope, the then Joseph Ratzinger, in a homily at the Cathedral of Our Lady in Munich, delivered a distinctive teaching on the Eucharist as meaning "God has answered." Describing what he meant, he explained that before the Eucharist we pray in a space in which we are lifted up, for we pray in the space of the Lord's death and resurrection. We pray there, where the real plea for all our requests has been answered: the plea for death to be overcome, the plea for a love that is stronger than death. In this prayer, he observed, we no longer stand before a God we have thought up ourselves. Rather, we stand before the God who has truly given Himself to us, who became communion for us and so freed us from our limitations, for communion—the God who leads us to the resurrection. We must seek this kind of prayer anew.[248] It is before this God that Saint Matthew wrote; "Going into the house, they saw the child with Mary his mother, and they fell down and worshipped him" (Mt 2:11). Other examples are the Adoration of the Shepherds (Lk 2:15–16), and the Adoration of the Lamb (Rev 5). These are Scriptural sources of popular devotion. Moreover, here in the Sacred Host the same Jesus whom the Magi and the shepherds adored is present before us and in our midst, so let us fall down and worship Him. As at that time, so now He is mysteriously veiled in a sacred silence. As at that time, it is here that the true face of God

---

[247] In the late Middle Ages, devout Catholics developed a theology of Eucharistic adoration that they called "ocular Communion."

[248] Joseph Ratzinger, Homily in the Cathedral of Our Lady, Munich, Germany, 1978.

is revealed. For us He became a grain of wheat that falls on the ground and dies and bears fruit until the end of the world (cf. Jn 12:24). He is present now as He was then in Bethlehem. He invites us to that inner pilgrimage which is called adoration.[249]

In his 2005 Christmas Address to the Roman Curia, Pope Benedict XVI said among other things,

> It is moving for me to see how everywhere in the Church the joy of Eucharistic Adoration is reawakening and being fruitful. In the period of liturgical reform, Mass and Adoration outside it were often seen as in opposition to one another: It was thought that the Eucharistic Bread had not been given to us to be contemplated, but to be eaten, as a widespread objection claimed at that time.

The pope went on to say that such an opposition between Mass and Adoration by certain liturgical scholars is "nonsensical," especially in the case of the Eucharist. To this effect the pope cited Saint Augustine's *Enarrationes in psalmos*: "No one should eat this flesh without first adoring it...we should sin were we not to adore it." So receiving the Eucharist means adoring the One whom we receive. Precisely in this way, and only in this way can we become one with Him. In conclusion, the pope noted that Adoration is therefore "the most consistent consequence of the Eucharistic mystery itself." Besides being doctrinally

---

[249] Pope Benedict XVI, "Homily of His Holiness Pope Benedict XVI," On the Occasion of the XX World Youth Day, Youth Vigil, Cologne, Germany, 20 August 2005.

sound, however, the pope sees it as speaking powerfully to the youth.[250]

Eucharistic Adoration: A Surrender to the Divine Radiation of Love

The modern evangelical writer Darrell Johnson has said it well in his book, *Experiencing the Trinity*: "At the center of the universe there is a relationship... It is *out* of that relationship that we were created and redeemed, and it is *for* that relationship we were created and redeemed."[251] In every authentic love relationship there is always a surrender of will, likes, etc., but at the core of it all is the surrender of the heart. Hans Urs von Balthasar cheered in agreement to this fact. Consequently he presented what I would call the "Theology of the Adoration of Jesus in the Blessed Sacrament." Although the contexts were on a different note, but it is pertinent and inevitably applies to the Adoration of Jesus in the Sacrament. It is a powerful summary of the penetrating and piercing effect of gazing at the Lord who gazes at us. Thus he writes:

> Holiness consists in enduring God's glance. It may appear mere passivity to withstand the look of an eye; but everyone knows how much exertion is required when this occurs in an essential encounter. Our glances mostly brush past each other indirectly, or they turn quickly away, or they give themselves not personally, but

---

[250] "Address of His Holiness Benedict XVI to the Roman Curia Offering Them His Christmas Greetings," Thursday, 22 December 2005.

[251] Johnson DARRELL, *Experiencing the Trinity* (Canada: Regent College Publishing, 2002).

only socially. So too do we constantly flee from God into a distance that is theoretical, rhetorical, sentimental, aesthetic, or most frequently pious. Or we flee from Him to external works. And yet, the best thing would be to surrender one's naked heart to the fire of this all-penetrating glance. The heart would then itself have to catch fire if it were not always artificially dispersing the rays that come to it as through a magnifying glass. Such enduring would be the opposite of a Stoic's hardening his face: it would be yielding, declaring oneself beaten, capitulating, entrusting oneself, casting oneself into him. It would be child-like loving, since for children the glance of the Father: with open wide eyes they look into his... Augustine's magnificent formula on the essence of eternity: *videntem videre*—"to look at him who is looking at you."[252]

In other words, Balthasar is saying that holiness resides in one's capacity for endurance before the all-penetrating glance of God. It might appear to be a mere passivity but it is not. Instead it is the exertion of being there, enduring, indeed welcoming the inexorable pressure of God's transforming glance. It means enduring the burning glance of the holy, especially where that glance falls on imperfection, hardness, and sin. Instead of fleeing from God into a distance that is theoretical, sentimental and pious, or into activism, under the pretence of "working for God," "the best thing would be to surrender one's naked heart to the fire of this all-penetrating glance." It is in surrendering

---

[252] Hans Urs von BALTHASAR, *The Grain of Wheat* (San Francisco, CA: Ignatius Press, 1995), pp. 3-4.

one's naked heart that one is freed from all the shackles. Adoring Jesus present in the Sacrament is learning to be still before Him, casting oneself into Him and letting Him take control.

The best thing before the Lord "would be to surrender one's naked heart to the fire of this all-penetrating glance." Surrendering one's naked heart is an acknowledgement of the absolute presence of God before whom one bows in silence. It is a surrender that is also a helpless gazing at Jesus, a confession of meekness, littleness, and forlornness. It is likewise a declaration of one's trust that God will, in His own time, come to one's help—the quiet resting in Him alone.

Balthasar is in another way saying that enduring God's glance "would be yielding, declaring oneself beaten, capitulating, entrusting oneself, and casting oneself into him." This is one of the most beautiful aspects of this enduring of God's glance. It is so because it indicates one's desire to sink into one's nothingness and to let Him work and reveal Himself. Do gaze on God and allow Him to gaze on you, wait quietly. In daily life, let there be in a person that is waiting for the great God to do His wondrous work, a quiet reverence, an abiding watching against too deep engrossment with the world, with worry and hurry (Rom 9:16). Then, the whole character will come to bear the beautiful stamp—quietly waiting for the salvation of God.

Alongside the emphasis on the exertion caused by the glance of God, the tender effect of such surrender conveys a tremendous love relationship. Thus Balthasar goes on to say: "The heart would then itself have to catch fire. It would be child-like loving, since for children the glance of the Father: with open wide eyes they look into his." The fire that the heart catches will eventually warm it. A wonderful aspect of this warmth is allowing Him to truly see us, love us, and be close to us, igniting the relationship between Himself and ourselves, which in turn nourishes us and fills us with His mercy. If this warmth of God's love is not in our heart, we are unable to warm the hearts of others. Consequently it follows that if we do not surrender ourselves to God's merciful gaze, we cannot extend mercy to others or love to others.[253]

Re-emphasizing the importance of "being still" in the Eucharistic adoration, Tom Curran made a wonderful comparison with the raising of Lazarus from the dead (Jn 11:14). He noted that the last thing that Jesus said about Lazarus' situation was "unbind him and let him go." While the people were unbinding him "the best thing he could do to support this action of being set free was *to stand there and be still.* Similarly, we are invited to sit and be still in the presence of the Lord in Eucharistic adoration. Like Lazarus we give the Lord a chance to unbind us and let us go free."[254] So in Adoration, God sets us free with His light and love, removing one band at a time. The loving gaze of the Lord and the warmth of His presence gradually sets us free. This experience of unshackling and releasing, coming from the piercing gaze of Jesus present in the Sacrament, is a frequently recounted testimony of many adorers. Aaron Pidel narrated his experience, explaining that his vocation to the priesthood came as a result of the "re-enchantment" of the Eucharist: "The weekly commitment of an hour helped me to persevere in dryness and

---

[253] Read Pope Francis, *The Church of Mercy*, ed. Giuliano Vigini (London: Darton, Longman and Todd, 2014).

[254] Tom CURRAN, *The Mass: Four Encounters with Jesus that will Change Your Life* (MCF Press, 2008), p. 127. The emphasis is mine.

discouragement. The sense of Presence radiating from the monstrance encouraged a conversational prayer style and helped correct some of my natural tendencies to intro-spection and self-absorption."[255] It is because of this expe-rience that he said that the very structure of Eucharistic Adoration provides a sound pedagogy of prayer, or what *Sacramentum Caritatis* would call a "mystagogy."[256]

Andreas Knapp, in his usual thought-provoking med-itation, noted that Adoration of the Blessed Sacrament could be a way of getting out of one's egoistic cycle of I-me-myself-and-mine so as to lend presence to the Lord, listen to Him, and be transformed by His presence. It is a moment to remind myself that I do not have the last word, instead, before the Absolute I bow in silence and allow myself to be looked at from that silent Mystery. [257] Exposing oneself to the gaze and the "divine radiation" of the Host, indeed demands endurance and perseverance because one does not have the satisfying feeling of having done something useful, but its fruits are enormous. Ulti-mately one carries with him/her the graces of love and mercy wherever he/she goes, in whatever he/she does, and extends a bond of loving attention among neighbours as if he/she is creating a chain of uninterrupted love relationships.

In Eucharistic Adoration, we gaze at this great gift of His love. We know in faith that He looks at us with the same

---

[255] Aaron PIDEL, "An Experience of Adoration," in *The Church in the 21st Century, C 21 Resources* (Boston College, Fall 2011), pp. 29-30.

[256] Ibid.

[257] Andreas KNAPP, *Lebensspuren im Sand: Spirituelles Tagebuch aus der Wüste* (Verlag Herder GmbH, Freiburg im Breisgau, 2015), p. 153.

love with which He once spoke to His disciples: "This is my body which is given for you" (Lk 22:19). So Eucharistic Adoration consists essentially in "knowing and believing the love God has for us (cf. 1 Jn 4:16), allowing ourselves to be loved by God, and gratefully returning love for love. It is a profound, wordless, personal encounter with God: "I look at Him and he looks at me," said Saint John Vianney.[258] Just like two persons gazing into one another's eyes for a long time, this is a very personal encounter. It is simply being and resting in the personal love of God, who is present and who gives us His love.

In his encyclical letter on the Eucharist, *Ecclesia de Eucharistia*, Saint John Paul II described very personally how Eucharistic Adoration was for him a resting on Jesus' heart, just as the Apostle John was permitted to rest at Jesus' side. "It is pleasant to spend time with him, to lie close to his breast like the Beloved Disciple (Jn 13:25) and to feel the infinite love present in his heart…. How often, dear brothers and sisters, have I experienced this, and drawn from it strength, consolation and support!"[259]

Eucharistic Adoration: A Prolonged, Prayerful Love Relationship with Jesus Christ

As soon as we start to like someone, we want to get to know him/her better in order to develop a relationship. We do this by seeking opportunities for being with, talking to, and observing the person. In the Eucharist, we encounter Jesus in person. The mystery of the Eucharist is the mystery of the Church. Therefore gazing

---

[258] Quoted in *CCC*, n. 2715.

[259] John Paul II, Encyclical Letter on the Eucharist in Its Relationship to the Church, *Ecclesia de Eucharistia (EE)*, 25.

at the consecrated host or praying before the tabernacle is not gazing at an object or at a thing. It is important to remember and re-emphasize that the Eucharist is not an object to be stared or gazed at, not an idol, but a person, a relationship.

As we receive the Eucharist or adore in silent prayer, we can relate to the Eucharist as Jesus present, actively offering Himself to us. This relationship, like all relationships, requires faith, but a faith that bears fruit. The Adoration of our Lord in the Blessed Sacrament allows the fruits of our reception of Him to ripen and deepen into communion and into a fullness of love flowing forth into our daily lives.

Adoration of the Blessed Sacrament is an answer to people craving the quiet of a more personal relationship with the Lord. Some people look for a relationship sustained over a time outside the Eucharistic celebration when they have the opportunity for a more extended period of quiet prayer and Adoration. This devotion supplements and extends the celebration and reception of the Eucharist at Mass and flows from it. The Church has always taught that Jesus Christ remains truly present in the Eucharist even after the celebration of Mass, and hence in the Eucharist reserved in the tabernacle. Jesus Himself shows this need for a more contemplative, prolonged loving union in prayer to His beloved Father, and Scripture often shows Him continuing His prayer through the whole night.

In the Eucharist, Adoration becomes union. We all eat the one bread, and this means that we ourselves become one. In this way, Adoration becomes union. God no longer simply stands before us as the One who is totally *Other*. He is within us, and we are in Him. His dynamics enters into us and then seeks to spread outwards to others until it fills the world, so that His love can truly become the dominant measure of the world.

There are different nuances of the word "adoration" in Greek and in Latin. The Greek word *proskynesis*, refers to the gesture of submission, the recognition of God as our true measure, supplying the norm that we choose to follow. It means that freedom is not simply about enjoying life in total autonomy, but rather about living by the measure of truth and goodness, so that we ourselves can become true and good. Therefore, we submit to God through loving obedience to His commands. The Latin word for adoration is *ad-oratio*—mouth-to-mouth contact, a kiss, an embrace, and hence, ultimately love. Submission becomes union, because He to whom we submit is Love. In this way, submission acquires a meaning, because it does not impose anything on us from the outside, but liberates us deep within.[260] In his Post-Synodal Apostolic Exhortation *Sacramentum Caritatis,* Pope Benedict XVI, pointed out the intrinsic relationship between Eucharistic celebration and Adoration:

> As Saint Augustine put it: *"nemo autem illam carnem manducat, nisi prius adoraverit; peccemus non adorando*—no one eats that flesh without first adoring it; we should sin were we not to adore it."[261] In the Eucharist, the Son of

---

[260] Cf. Pope Benedict XVI, "We Have Come to Adore Him": Homily at World Youth Day (Cologne, 2005), in Andreas SCHMIDT, *We Have Come to Adore Him: An Introduction to Prayer at the School of Benedict XVI,* #5, The New Evangelization Series (Washington: Knights of Columbus, 2013), p. 33.

[261] *Enarrationes in Psalmos* 98:9, CCL XXXIX, 1385; cf. Benedict XVI, Address to the Roman Curia (22 December 2005): AAS 98, 2006, pp. 44-45.

God comes to meet us and desires to become one with us; Eucharistic adoration is simply the natural consequence of the Eucharistic celebration, which is itself the Church's supreme act of adoration. Receiving the Eucharist means adoring him whom we receive. Only in this way do we become one with him, and are given, as it were, a foretaste of the beauty of the heavenly liturgy. The act of adoration outside Mass prolongs and intensifies all that takes place during the liturgical celebration itself. Indeed, "only in adoration can a profound and genuine reception mature" (*SC* 66).

One who wants to go to Mass and be transformed should learn to take time to be with the Lord outside of Mass. Adoration is an extension of the Mass you have attended and a preparation for the next. It makes one's whole day be an act of worship that overflows in aspirations and the offering up of one's daily activities. Adoration and contemplation go hand in hand since what is demanded in them is active presence and willingness to let oneself be transformed by this piercing gaze of the Lord. That is why we call this action "Eucharist," which is a translation of the Hebrew word *berakah*—thanksgiving, praise, blessing, and transformation worked by the Lord. The presence of His "hour," Jesus' hour, is the hour in which love triumphs. In other words: it is God who has triumphed, because He is Love.

Eucharistic Adoration: A Gaze that Saves

During Eucharistic adoration, it is not only we who gaze at Christ, but He also gazes at us. When we adore the Blessed Sacrament, we are not just gazing at a beautiful inert object, nor are we gazing at "a very holy thing." No! We are gazing at a person, Jesus, and this presupposes that He returns our gaze. To understand what this means, we must begin with the Eucharistic sacrifice itself. At four important moments during the celebration of the Eucharist, the priest elevates the Sacred Host and the Precious Blood of Jesus.

- The first moment is the elevation during the consecration.
- The second moment occurs when, at the conclusion of the Eucharistic prayer, the priest raises the Host and the chalice together just before the recitation of the Lord's Prayer.
- Then, the third is before the distribution of Holy Communion, the priest presents the Sacred Host and the Precious Blood to the entire congregation with the words, "Behold the Lamb of God...."
- And finally, the fourth in a more personal moment, each communicant is invited to behold and adore the Sacred Host just before receiving the Bread of Life and probably also the cup of salvation.

In these four important moments, all present at Mass, the priest and people, share in the moment of the "gaze that saves," with the fruits of these "moments" applying and extending to all Christian faithful.[262] It is in these vital moments of elevation of the Blessed Sacrament that we find the roots of Eucharistic exposition and adoration, as well as the profound connection between the Eucharistic

---

[262] Bruce T. MORRILL, "Christ's Sacramental Presence in the Eucharist: A Biblical-Pneumatological Approach to the Mystery of Faith," in *American Theological Inquiry*, vol. 4, no. 2 (2011), pp. 3-26, here p. 11.

sacrifice of the Mass and Eucharistic devotion to the Blessed Sacrament.

Christ, who was raised up on the cross for our sake, is raised up again at Mass so that we may look on Him and be saved. In exposition of the Blessed Sacrament, this "being raised up for our sake" is prolonged and extended and our gazing at Him is indeed a gaze that saves. This type of "gaze" is more of a gazing with the heart, which implies gazing with love, penetrating the mystery of love which is enfleshed for us in Jesus present in the Eucharist. Jesus, who is Love, invites us to come to Him, to share our lives with Him, to love Him, to simply be present with Him in this Most Blessed Sacrament.

When one gazes at something, the "gazer" becomes affected by the object of the gaze. Adoring Jesus present in the Sacrament is a double current that flows; it flows from Jesus Himself towards the adorer and back to Him. That is, not only does one try to feel God's presence, the adorer should also let God feel his/her presence. It is in this sense that Jesus asked His disciples to keep watch with Him (cf. Mt 26:40). Though the keeping watch of the disciples would not have changed anything for Him, yet Jesus wanted to feel their presence. God also desires our presence; our feelings matter to Him. Not only does He want to know about our day, but He also wants to experience it with us. God's gaze upon us is always one of love; it is a loving gaze that reveals a lot about Him and ourselves. So it is not just we that gaze, it is also God who gazes on us.

Thus, Jesus present in the Blessed Sacrament has eyes which are not dispassionate, nor merely passive. The gaze of God in the Host is not an art gallery gaze, wandering from exhibit to exhibit and leaving what they see obviously unchanged. God's gaze engages what He sees and affects it: For God, to gaze is to love and to work favours. His eyes are effective: God's gaze works so many blessings in the soul: it cleanses, makes beautiful, enriches and enlightens. The gaze of God affects! Who can forget Jesus looking at Peter after he denied him three times?

Pope Francis in *The Church of Mercy* wrote:

> Let us also remember Peter: three times he denied Jesus, *precisely when he should have been closest to him.* And when he hits rock bottom, *he meets the gaze of Jesus* who patiently, wordlessly, says to him, "Peter, don't be afraid of your weakness, trust in me." Peter understands, *he feels the loving gaze of Jesus, and he weeps.* How beautiful is this gaze of Jesus—how much tenderness is there![263]

Think of the experience of being gazed upon by someone who loves you and whom you love. In that gaze—penetrating, knowing, benign—you find, not oppression, but joy and peace. That is how God looks upon us. This type of Gaze needs no words. We are known by Him. No need to explain, petition, or make excuses. Just *"be,"* give him your gaze and silently exchange gaze for gaze like lovers. Gazing intently and lovingly upon Him—and as we gaze—we are transformed and grow like Christ; something of the glory of His face passes into our dull faces and stays there, shining out in us! No one gazes at God or even into heaven and remains unaffected. We know what happened to Saint Stephen in Acts of the Apostles (7:55) who gazed intently into heaven and he saw the glory of God and Jesus

---

[263] Pope Francis, *The Church of Mercy* (Loyola Press, 2014). The emphases are mine.

standing at the right hand of God. So God is not hidden or eclipsed, He is present before us in the Eucharist;

> here violence is transformed into love, death into life. It is like a "nuclear fission" in the most intimate part of the being; it is the victory of love over hate and the victory of love over death. In the Eucharist there is found the secret of the renewal of the universe: it is the explosion of good which conquers evil and thus triggers the transformations which change the world.[264]

One who frequently gazes on God, falls in love with Him, and the self-focus on flaws and offenses against others dissolve because as one gazes at Him, He in turn, begins gradually to effect healing and transformation of the person into His likeness. Becoming more like Him changes the person's focus and the person becomes freer. Then the person will want to stare at Him *even more,* which changes him/her even more.

The Eucharistic adoration helps us to realign our gaze. In the front of Jesus truly present in the Eucharist, everything else returns to its proper place, and the way in which we view the world returns to an ordered perspective. This is not to say that problems, insecurities, difficulties, and sorrows will automatically disappear before the Blessed Sacrament, but in the loving gaze of Christ, we learn to see our lives differently. In Eucharistic adoration, the monstrance becomes a sort of mirror: Christ reflects back to

---

[264] Pope Benedict XVI, cited by Bishop Giovanni D' ERCOLE, "Eucharistic Adoration as a Way of Life: A Pastoral Perspective," pp. 59-66. In *From Eucharistic Adoration to Evangelisation*, ed. Alcuin REID, (Great Britain: Burns & Oates International, 2012), p. 62.

us the person that He sees—a beloved son or daughter of His heavenly Father, for whom He died and rose, and for whom He remains, under the form of a simple host, so that we might draw near to Him. In this Presence, we are able to perceive the truth more clearly. Indeed, if we spend enough time gazing at Him who shows us most fully unto ourselves, if we truly enter into the Presence of Jesus in the Blessed Sacrament, we will also learn to see beyond even ourselves and see Him who gazes back at us in complete and utter love. It is at this point, when we can finally see beyond the self and gaze upon the *Other*, that we become capable of receiving the wealth of grace offered to us in the Blessed Sacrament. This grace that Jesus offers is the grace to carry His Presence out into the world. He invites us to become an icon of Himself—a manifestation of love that is humble so that it might lift others up, love that is made perfect in weakness, love that lays life down willingly for the sake of friends and enemies alike (2 Cor 12:9; Jn 15:13; Rom 5:7-8).

In the face of the loving Presence of Jesus in the Blessed Sacrament we learn anew to say *thank you*: for the love of Father in which He sent His only Son, that we might be saved (cf. Jn 3:17); for the love of the Son in which He emptied himself unto death on a cross for our sake (cf. Phil 2:8); for the love of the Spirit who pours into our hearts a spirit of adoption through which we became sons and daughters of God (Rom 8:15); for the immeasurable graces of God that continue to be "packed down, shaken together, running over...poured into our laps" (Lk 6:38). As we gaze upon Jesus in the Blessed Sacrament, the grace of *eucharistia*—thanksgiving—is poured into our hearts, and we learn once again that all is *gift*. So let us not relent in going to the ready-made Source of love and grace, for

He waits for us. In his apostolic letter *Dominicae Cenae* (3) of Saint John Paul II, he wrote, "Jesus waits for us in this sacrament of love. Let us be generous with our time in going to meet Him in adoration." Hence, Jesus waits. He waits with patience; He waits with inexhaustible love. Will we keep Him waiting?

Chapter Seven: The Unity of These Four Forms of Prayer

Prayer, which essentially is a personal relationship with God, nourishes itself daily in intimate, dialogical sharing between the soul and God. To this fact, Hans Urs von Balthasar says: "Prayer is communication, in which God's word has the initiative, and we, at first, are simply listeners. Consequently, what we have to do is, first, listen to God's word and then, through that word, learn how to answer."[265] Although God continues daily to speak to us in different ways, we have His words par excellence in the Scriptures. The Holy Bible is the Christian compass pointing the road to follow. But sadly, this source of divine wisdom seems to have little effect in the life of most Catholics, and worst, in the lives of religious men and women. Why is this so, when the Word of God should shape our lives?

There has never been any *lectio divina*, contemplative prayer, Liturgy of the Hours, and Mass without the Bible. It is from the Bible that the unity of all four forms of prayer are derived. Thus there is unity between them because:

- They all depend on the same Book, the Bible.
- They all consist in reading it, pronouncing it, and bringing the human mind into accord with the divine words.
- They all celebrate Christ who is the Book, the Bible personified, in whom all the treasures of the divinity

---

[265] Hans Urs von BALTHASAR, *Prayer* (New York: Paulist Press, 1976), p. 12.

are contained, and who through His incarnation becomes readable, capable of being prayed and celebrated.

God has spoken to us, and His words have been written for us in a book, the Book, the Bible. The Bible has to be and is the normal food of prayer. The Bible furnishes prayer with all the words it needs to be a prayer, to be accepted by God. Thanks to the Bible, prayer can be eucharist: *eucharistia,* or *gratiarum actio.* We give back to God what we have received from Him. We say to God the words He has spoken to us.[266]

So conceived, in the four forms of prayer we are only returning thanks. We are returning to God, word for word, the joy of His message, so as to make of our whole being, in the divine reading and celebration, through our meekness and our reverence, that perfect sacrifice which God wishes, the only one He awaits and wants from us. Each time we pray, we are entering ever more and more into the mystery of Christ, to which we were first introduced by the sacraments. The essential is not so much the words, as the consenting: the presence to God of him who prays. It is to accept with our whole being the mystery of salvation of which the Eucharist is, in our human condition, the most adequate expression. More than form and sign, it is the perfect realization.

The liturgy is an ensemble of actions and texts, the union of which constitutes the rites. They are mostly biblical: inspired by the Bible, or reproduced from the Bible, or taken directly from the Bible.[267] As regards the words,

---

[266] Read Jean LECLERCQ, "Meditation as a Biblical Reading," in *Worship* 33 (1959), pp. 562-569.

[267] Examples of direct copying are the Psalms which are the book par excellence of our Liturgy of the Hours and they are

the liturgy is a succession of lessons and canticles mostly taken from the Bible. Both, but chiefly the lessons, instruct us on the content of the mystery. The canticles primarily express our thanksgiving, our enthusiasm, and our love. What is the Mass if not the drama of Christ's birth, life, death, and resurrection as narrated in the Gospels. So in prayer, our mind should accord with the mind of God, with the words of God as given to us in the Bible. That is the reason why it is indispensable to pray the Bible in order to have a direct, personal contact with this Book who is Christ.

Christtheook

Christ as the Book is a very ancient theme because the Christian tradition holds that the only book worth reading is our Lord Jesus Christ. The word "bible" means book, and all the texts of that book speak of Him and are meant to lead to Him. The entire Bible expressing God's design and purpose in salvation history is entitled "Jesus." Jesus himself is the Book. He is the one in whom we read what God wanted to do from all eternity, what now, in time, He has done in Jesus and what He continues to do daily in our lives. When Jesus' arms were stretched out on the cross, the Book was open. When Jesus poured forth His Spirit after His resurrection "that they might understand the Scriptures," the Book was interpreted. Thus, in the heart of human beings, an encounter took place between God's saving Word and the innermost human spirit hearkening

---

just taken as a whole from one book of the Bible. Another very important place where we copied is the words of the consecration.

to this Word through God's own Spirit. This is the origin of the traditional theme "the book of conscience."[268]

For the Book, Jesus Christ, was and is not some volume or scroll inscribed once for all. The Scripture as Saint Augustine said, is so ancient and ever new. Therefore, each one of us through our own personal experience must come to find what this Book means. The meaning of the phrase, "the book of experience," is that all must read in themselves, in their own heart (the book of the heart), what God wants to tell them personally through Christ in the Spirit, so as to share this message with others and help them come to understand what God wants to tell them. Religious apostolate, mission, counselling, and all forms of pastoral activities first consist in helping each other to read and live that one Book, and this is the main, indeed the only, worthy religious apostolate and commendable priestly ministry. Contrary to this, the person has missed the way.

This book, the Book, sheds light on our understanding of other books: the book of nature, the book of history, the book of the signs of the times, and the book of our individual lives. An encounter must come about between Christ and the human person, between the Book which Christ is and the human heart in which Christ is written—not with ink but by the Holy Spirit—through the books of the Bible written by the prophets and apostles. It is vital that this encounter be continuous and cover every phase of human history and of each person's history—a condition widely evident in Christian tradition and particularly in monastic

---

[268] Read Jean LECLERCQ, *Lectio Divina*, pp. 239-248.

tradition. This basic reality is reminiscent of the biblical phrase "book of life."[269]

The immeasurable value of this Book was brought out in a short, unprinted notice found in a Stuttgart manuscript: "Christ is a Book and also a Sign. The Son of God is a Book written in a colourful hand. The precious Book is never closed, its pages never discoloured with age. It is more readable by night than by day. A Book of great value, a Book of great purity. A Book for all time, to be read and committed to heart."[270]

The Book as a Sacrament of Divine Presence in the Early Sources

Some of these earliest sources emphasized the place of distinction and devotion the divine Word holds for the faithful. The Fathers of the Church also compared the Word of God and the Eucharist and they affirmed that nourishment comes from both tables—table of the Word and the table of the Eucharist—bringing divine life in a dynamic and graced way. In his "Homilies on the Book of Exodus," Origen challenges us:

> I want to urge you to this by examples drawn from your religious practices. If you are habitually present at the divine mysteries, you know how carefully and respectfully you protect the Lord's body when it is given to you, lest a fragment of it

---

[269] Here again Fr. LECLERCQ quoting from Rabanus Maurus, on Christ the Book at judgment: "The Book is Christ, for it is said in the Book of Revelation: 'another book was opened, which is the Book of Life, because Christ who is our life will appear to all in judgment.'" (PL 112:987). See Jean LECLERCQ, *Lectio Divina*, p. 240.

[270] Jean LECLERCQ, *Lectio Divina*, pp. 124-125.

> fall and a bit of the consecrated treasure be lost.
> You would think yourself guilty, and with good
> reason, if some of it were lost through your neg-
> ligence. Now if you rightly take such precaution
> when it is a question of the Lord's body, how can
> you think that neglect of God's word will be less
> severely punished than neglect of his body?[271]

Origen brings the "two tables" of the Word and the Eucharist into a formative unity, both as essential sources of nourishment for the believer. Coupled with the fundamental idea of nourishment is a sense of devotion, honour, reverence, and respect that is due to the Word of God, in which Christ is present. Origen had a strong influence on Saint Jerome, both theologically and rhetorically. We find a corresponding theological development in Jerome's *Tractate* on Psalms 145 and 147. Commenting on Psalm 145:7, "It is he who gives bread to the hungry," Jerome said, "...the bread of Christ and his flesh is the divine word and the heavenly teaching."[272]

Then, commenting on Psalm 147:14, "he feeds you with finest wheat," Jerome speaks in a similar manner and says:

> When the Lord says, "He who eats my flesh
> and drinks my blood," and although this can

---

[271] This text comes from Origen's "Homilies on the Book of Exodus" (Homily 13, par. 3). This translation of Origen's text is found in Linus Bopp's, "The Salvific Power of the Word According to the Church Fathers," in *The Word: Readings in Theology,* eds. The Canisianum (Innsbruck, New York: P. J. KENEDY & Sons, 1964), p. 151.

[272] *Tractatus de Psalmo 145, Corpus Christianorum Latina,* LXXVIII, 325-26. Quoted in Gregory J. POLAN, "*Lectio Divina*: Reading and Praying the Word of God," in *Liturgical Ministry* 12, 2003, pp. 198-206, here p. 200.

be understood in reference to the sacrament, nevertheless the word of the Scriptures is truly the body of Christ, and his blood, it is the divine teaching. If when we go to the sacred mysteries, the one who is faithful understands, if only a small particle (of the word) has fallen (into our hearing), we are in jeopardy. If when we hear the word of God, and the word of God, and the flesh of Christ and his blood, is poured into our hearing, and we are thinking about something else, into how great a danger are we running? "He feeds you with finest wheat." The divine word is most delicious, having in itself every delight. Whatever you have desired is born from the divine word.[273]

In this passage, Jerome draws a line connecting the motif of the manna in the desert with the passage in Wisdom 16:20-21, 26, which describes the manna as God's "word which preserves those who believe" in it. Similarly, Caesarius of Arles addressed the same topic in one of his sermons, in a manner similar to that of Origen and Jerome. He says:

I have an important question for you, brothers and sisters. Which do you think more important—the word of God or the body of Christ? If you want to answer correctly, you must tell me that the word of God is no less important than the body of Christ! How careful we are, when the body of Christ is distributed to us, not to let any

---

[273] *Tractatus de Psalmo* 147, *Corpus Christianorum Latina,* LXXVIII, 337-38. Quoted in Gregory J. POLAN, "*Lectio Divina:* Reading and Praying the Word of God," p. 200.

bit of it fall to the ground from our hand! But we should be just as careful not to let slip from our hearts the word of God that is addressed to us, by thinking or speaking of something else when we should be listening to it with devotion. He will be no less guilty, who listens negligently to the word of God than he who by his negligence allows the Lord's body to fall to the ground.[274]

These early sources emphasize an attitude and belief towards the Word of God.[275] It possesses a divine presence just as truly as the consecrated bread and wine. It calls for our attention and devotion. Saint Augustine's comment on the Word of God as being "ever ancient and ever new" is apt here.

The divine Word was once spoken to a community in a particular place and time, addressing its needs, hopes,

---

[274] This citation is found in *The Sunday Sermons of the Great Fathers*, vol. 2, ed. and trans. M. F. TOAL (Chicago: Henry Regnery Co, 1958), p. 458.

[275] It is worth noting that not only are there early Christian sources that develop this idea, but also other sources such as, *The Imitation of Christ*, by Thomas à Kempis, who includes a spirituality of the word in his writings. In Chapter 11 of Book 4, he talks of the importance of the Word of God in the spiritual journey. Hence the title of this section runs thus: "That the Body of Christ and Holy Scripture are most necessary for the health of a person's soul." He writes, "I perceive well that there are two things most necessary for me in this world, without which this miserable life would be insupportable. As long as I am in this body, I confess myself to have need of two things that is to say, food and light, and these two you have given me. You have given the Blessed Sacrament for the refreshment of my soul and body, and you have set your word as a lantern before my feet to show me the way I shall go. Without these two, I cannot live well." Cf. Thomas à Kempis, *The Imitation of Christ*, ed. with an Introduction by Harold C. GARDINER, S.J. (Garden City, NY: Doubleday Books, 1955), p. 224.

and desires. Today that same Word speaks to another community of faith in a vibrant and living way addressing its present situation of needs, desires, and hopes. We only have to read it with faith. Moreover, this kind of reading is rather slow and repetitive, focused on absorbing the Word itself in a reflective manner. Saint Anselm of Canterbury in the prologue to his *Orationes sive meditationes* writes: "we should read them (the words) not in agitation, but in calm; not hurriedly, but slowly, a few words at a time, pausing in attentive reflection... Then the reader will experience their ability to enkindle the ardor of prayer."[276]

It is clear from what Saint Anselm writes that this kind of reading is directed towards communion with God in dialogue, which is exactly the purpose of *lectio divina*, wherein God begins this dialogue. Our first task is to listen intently so that we might respond to whatever it is God is saying. The Prologue to the Rule of Saint Benedict speaks about the manner in which one should listen to the precepts of the Lord. In this, Saint Benedict talks about listening "with the ear of the heart" (*RB* Prol 1). That is the kind of reverence with which we should read Sacred Scripture. From time to time, we receive an important letter from someone special. We read and reread the letter with care and intensity so that we might take its message "to heart." This is the kind of reading we are talking about here— attentive reading of the Word of God in order to take the message of the Scripture to heart (cf. *RB* 73:3).

Saint Augustine provides an image where, in speaking about the reading of sacred texts, he says that one should

---

[276] Cited by Mariano MAGRASSI, *Praying the Bible: An Introduction to Lectio Divina*, trans. Edward Hagman (Collegeville: The Liturgical Press, 1998), pp. 105-106.

look to a cow for an example of how to approach this task. As the cow chews her cud over and over again, so should we read the Word of God, saying the words over and over again to digest them and to allow them to become part of us. Numerous commentators took up this image of Saint Augustine into the Middle Ages as the practice of *lectio divina* became more and more widespread.[277] The Jewish theologian and philosopher, Abraham Joshua Heschel, said, "to meditate is to know how to stand still and to dwell upon a word."[278] In reading the Word of God, there can be one word or a phrase that somehow plucks the strings of our heart and evokes a resonance within us.[279] For example, Smaragdus,[280] commenting on Saint Benedict's approach to *lectio divina*, teaches:

> The knowledge of sacred reading provides those who cultivate it with keenness of perception, increases their understanding, shakes off sluggishness, does away with idleness, shapes their life, corrects their behavior, causes wholesome groaning and produces tears from a heart pierced by compunction; it bestows eloquence in speaking and promises eternal rewards to those

---

[277] Mariano MAGRASSI, *Praying the Bible*, pp. 109-10. Saint Bernard spoke of monks as "pure ruminators," having taken the Word of God into themselves and allowed it to resonate off the walls of the human heart time and again.

[278] Cited by Gregory J. POLAN, "*Lectio Divina*: Reading and Praying the Word of God," in *Liturgical Ministry* 12, 2003, pp. 198-206, here p. 204.

[279] Gregory J. POLAN, "*Lectio Divina*: Reading and Praying the Word of God, p. 204.

[280] Smaragdus of Saint-Mihiel (c. 760–c. 840) was a Benedictine monk of Saint Mihiel Abbey, near Verdun. He was a significant writer of homilies, and he wrote the first commentary on the Rule of Saint Benedict.

who toil; it increases spiritual riches, curbs vain speech and vanities, and enkindles the desire for the Christ and our heavenly homeland. It is always associated with prayer, and must always be joined to prayer.

For prayer cleanses us, while reading instructs us. And therefore he who wishes to be always with God must frequently pray and frequently read. For when we pray, we speak with God; but when we read, God speaks with us. All progress, then, proceeds from reading, prayer and meditation. What we do not know we learn by reading; what we have learned we retain by meditations; and by prayer we reach the fulfillment of what we have retained. Therefore the reading of the Sacred Scriptures confers a twofold gift: it instructs the mind's understanding, and it brings the one who is withdrawn from the world's vanities to the love of God.[281]

As disciples of the Word, we have no reason to doubt the divine directives offered to us in Holy Scripture and the Christian classics, such as in the commentary of Smaragdus cited above. As long as we focus our attention on the text at hand, we may find more often than not that it speaks to our here-and-now situation. To abide with the text and apply its meaning to our lives, we must become accustomed to setting aside time to slow down and read

---

[281] *Smaragdi Abbatis Expositio in Regulam S. Benedicti*, eds. A. SPANNAGEL/P. ENGELBERT, CCM VIII, (Siegburg, 1974). Smaragdus of Saint-Mihiel, "Commentary on the Rule of Saint Benedict," in Cistercian Studies Series, 212, trans. by David Barry, (Kalamazoo, Michigan, 2007), p. 227.

reflectively. We may mark in the text whatever evokes in us either a spontaneous resonance or a point of resistance and ask ourselves why we feel this way. Of equal value are "aha" moments when the word on the page expresses exactly where we are, and "oh, no" moments when reading challenges us to change our lives. In both cases, new ranges of significance light up.

Conclusion

It is vital to conclude by pointing out that when we take up permanent residence in a life of love, we live in God and God lives in us—this is prayer and union with God—which is the kernel and the purpose of Christian life. Thus, this work up until now has been trying to verify this fact. The Christian's love for God, as has been shown, originates as a direct response to God's own prior overture of love, to God's own confession of love for us. God has confessed this love decisively in His living Word: Jesus of Nazareth. As the First Letter of Saint John attests, "In this is love, not that we loved God, but that God loved us…we love, because God first loved us" (4:10). Thus, in the most basic sense whatsoever, the primary desire for a relationship with God occurs as a response to the divine overture, which itself took the form of self-emptying love. Besides, the goal of this self-emptying love is love. But the term the First Letter of Saint John (1:9) uses to express this goal is "communion"—communion of human beings with God—mutual indwelling of God and human beings, and communion of human beings with one another.

Admittedly, the infinite effects of the Christian's experience of divine love awaken the trust at the heart of love and stimulate the Christian's most fundamental confession to God: hence the passionate and ardent desire for adoration and love of the divine lover.[282] As a consequence, in the Christian's most basic confession of love is condensed the entire experience of communion: the divine offer of a graceful self-emptying love and the human's reception of that love—which entails also not mere passivity, but active loving response to God, the corresponding human offer of grace-filled, grateful, and self-emptying love to God. This active, loving response to God necessitates so many modalities, all of which are reducible to what Jeff Poor called *caritas quaerens intellectum*, (love seeking understanding).[283] This is not intended in the Scholastic sense of *fides quaerens intellectum*.[284] Here love does not primarily seek self-understanding. Rather, the Christian love longs to understand the divine love *experientially*, and also desires to give expression or give an active love response. Seeking ways of giving expression to this love

---

[282] TEILHARD de Chardin expressed this passionate desire of the soul for a God to adore. See Pierre TEILHARD de Chardin, *The Divine Milieu* (New York: Harper and Row, 1960), pp. 127-128.

[283] Jeff B. POOR, "No Entrance into Truth Except through Love: Contributions from Augustine of Hippo to a Contemporary Christian Hermeneutic of Love," in *Review and Expositor*, 101 (2004), pp. 629-666, here p. 633.

[284] In the Scholastic sense of *fides quaerens intellectum*, the Christian experience of faith in divine salvation seeks to understand that experience primarily, if not only, in a cognitive sense. That is to say that when faith seeks understanding, it yearns for precision of linguistic expression and clear unambiguous conceptual definitions. In the Scholastic notion, faith seeks to understand itself. But when love seeks understanding, however, understanding differs dramatically and radically from the Scholastic interpretation of faith seeking understanding. Love seeks an experiential understanding of itself and not a rational understanding. See Jeff B. POOR, "No Entrance into Truth Except through Love," p. 633.

could be called *caritas quaerens expressum* (love seeking expression).

This has been the ground on which this work has tried to delineate these modalities of expression, these *caritas quaerens expressum,* which was called the Four Forms of Prayer: *lectio divina*—a dialogue with Jesus Christ; contemplation—self abandonment to Jesus Christ; Liturgy of the Hours—a duet with Jesus Christ; and the Holy Mass—a sealing of the covenant in the Blood of Jesus Christ. These four forms of prayer form the modalities of love expression or means of giving active, loving response.

The primary procedure used in elaborating these four forms of prayer was by establishing how Jesus displayed and lived this love-relationship with His Father. This was considered a very important step because Jesus' life was the base for the Christian's life of prayer. The Christian ought to learn to express this love-relationship in Christ-like manner. This was necessary because the Bible says if one abides in Jesus, if one loves Jesus, the person has to imitate Him (1 Jn 2:6). Therefore, the chapter attempted to show how Jesus consistently spoke of His intimate relationship with the Father. Still, it was clear that this relationship of love did not protect Him from the misunderstanding of others, their hatred of Him, and His eventual suffering and death at their hands. This does not mean that the Father did not love Him. Instead, it proves the fact that self-emptying is an indispensable condition in this love relationship, both for Jesus towards the Father and for us all. Jesus was able to give divine love to others because of this intimate union He has with the Father. So Jesus' self-emptying love points back to the self-emptying love of God and forward to the kind of self-emptying love expected of us. Following this back and forward process, the Christian life was also shown to be a self-emptying life through the baptismal promises and the religious vows. Having been made empty, the consecrated person needs to be filled with Christ in prayer. Once full, there will be need for self out-pouring in service towards neighbours, both near (immediate community) and far (in mission or apostolate). This is a continuous process of filling and out-pouring, and is learnt only from Christ Himself.

The four forms of prayer are therefore developed by the Church in imitation of Christ who prayed both aloud and in silent tears. In this way, prayer becomes growth in relationship. This growth comes about only if the "self" dies. One must break so as to grow—the necessity for self-emptying love exemplified in the life of Jesus.

The first among these four forms of prayer, *lectio divina,* a prayerful dialogue with God's Word, was basically presented as an activity of love, an exchange of love, or a dialogue that is rather a simple consent to the words read, savoured, and to God who speaks in them. Then, the well-known ancient traditional progressive stages of *lectio, meditatio, oratio, contemplatio,* was used as a paradigm. The work went further to prove that *lectio divina* is a way of praying the Scripture, different from studying the Scripture. Thus a sharp contrast was made between studying the Scriptures and praying the Scriptures. Studying the Scripture is like "going through the Scripture," while praying the Scripture is allowing the Scripture to "go through you" to take possession of your hearts and minds.

The next form of prayer, contemplative prayer, emphasized the fact that the false understanding of the Church's contemplative dimension has distorted the universal call to sanctity. Because of this bias, this chapter was an attempt to offer a new understanding that the call to contemplation is a universal call. Our authority as Christians is our closeness to the Author. One cannot say that the contemplative function of the Church is limited exclusively to some members of Christ's Body; it is for all the disciples that Jesus prays to the Father "that they may contemplate my glory" (Jn 17:24). The privileges are granted to those who live and serve the Lord in spirit and in truth, who do not fear the hour of the manifestation of glory which is the hour of the manifestation of the cross (Jn 17:1). The one word that could possibly identify the contemplative life is congruence: congruence between one's *being* and *expression*. In other words, contemplation is "a way" of being a complete "yes" to God, it is a way of being "entire" in imitation of Christ who is whole and entire.

This same Scripture, which is privately prayed in *lectio divina* and savored contemplatively in one's life, is liturgically celebrated in the community and with other members of Christ's Body, sharing in the prayer of Christ. Thus the third form, the Liturgy of the Hours, was presented as an endeavour to bring our voices into accord with the voice of God. What prevails in the Liturgy of the Hours is harmony of voices and therefore harmony of mind, heart, and of life. Attempt was made to present this harmony in two different theological dimensions: Christological and Soteriological. It was thus demonstrated that there is a unity between them. The Liturgy of the Hours is truly and fundamentally the celebration of the Paschal Mystery of Christ—of His dying and rising (Christology)— spread in the different moments of the day. This is not simply a celebration of an action which inaugurates salvation, but celebration of a salvific event actualized here and now (Soteriology). This fact is visibly accentuated in the celebration of feasts, where the mysteries celebrated are brought to the present: the *hodie* (today) of salvation.

This celebration of the mystery of salvation, which in the Liturgy of the Hours is spread in different Hours of the day so as to sanctify time, is re-enacted in one single Eucharistic celebration. Hence, it stretches in every direction: past, present, and future. Thus, Jesus Christ is actively and dynamically present in every progressive stage of the Eucharistic celebration. The Mass becomes a "looking back" with gratitude and a "looking forward" in hope. This unfolds in a threefold manner:

- in *present* blessedness—the presence of the saints and the angelic hosts of heaven, binds earth and heaven together,
- in the *hope* of eternal life with God—the communion is a foretaste of the heavenly banquet, and
- in the *passion* of Christ—the Sacrifice of the Mass is the sacrifice of the cross in an unbloody manner.

The unbloody sacrifice of Christ at Mass motivates the Christian to emulation, for we should identify ourselves with Christ by sacrificing ourselves daily for others. Subsequently, this led to the comparison between the religious consecration and the Eucharistic sacrifice of Mass as a *kenotic* self-offering. What we celebrate at Mass is basically the self-emptying love of Christ, and it is this same self-emptying love that the religious consecration is meant to represent. Because of this, using the chalice as an example, we dove into the theology of self-emptying love. As the most important part of the chalice is the part that is not there—the emptiness of the chalice—so do the religious empty themselves through their vows so as to be able to enfold Jesus, the Victim of Calvary. However, there is danger of "emptiness of self-emptying." The self-emptying, the turning away from pleasures and vanities of the conse-crated religious is meaningless if it is not geared towards a loving relationship with Jesus in prayer. This relationship could be further sustained in a prolonged, loving union with Jesus present in the Eucharist, hence the Church's encouragement of Adoration of the Blessed Sacrament as one of the means for growth in this loving union.

The core and the common source of this loving union is to be found in the Bible. These four forms of prayer, *lectio divina*, contemplative prayer, Liturgy of the Hours, and the Mass, find their conjoint foundation in the Bible, which is the Book par excellence—Christ Himself in whom all the treasures of the divinity are contained, and who through His incarnation becomes readable, capable of being prayed and celebrated.

As an ultimate point, to say that the key to journey into prayer is love and the underlying theme is relation-ship with God, is to say that, the entirety of our Christian life is prayer: thereby asserting that everything we do is implicitly prayer. For everything we do to be prayer, there must be times when we do nothing but pray. When we try to live our lives as a response to God's love and grace, we are praying implicitly. On the other hand, when, in prayer, we deliberately and consciously respond to God's words, we are praying explicitly. Our times of explicit prayer—nothing but prayer—are essential for sustaining a life of implicit prayer—everything is prayer. In that way we are returning love for love, because the divine purpose is an outgrowth of God's heart of love, which is Jesus Christ (Eph 1:9-10). Jesus Christ is the reality of God's love for us and we will never be true Christians unless we let our-selves fall in love with Love. Prayer is this attempt to seek communion with the Trinity of love. It is a relationship of love in response to this love of God—Jesus Christ. Normally one who loves gives his/her heart to the one loved. Jesus is God's heart; He gave Him to us so that we see Him more real than any other reality in the world. Thus Pierre Teilhard de Chardin remarked that:

> He to whom it is given to see Christ more real than any other reality in the world, Christ everywhere present and everywhere growing more great, Christ the final determination and plasmatic principle of the Universe, that man indeed lives in a zone where no multiplicity can distress him and which is nevertheless the most active workshop of universal fulfilment. Show him the inexactness or the error in the terms in which he tries to express his "experience" and, patiently, he will seek another formula. But his vision remains with him.[285]

Gratias tibi, Domine Jesu Christe, amor amorum. Amen!

---

[285] Pierre TEILHARD de Chardin, "Note on 'L' Ĕlĕment universel,'" in appendix to Forma Christi, cited in Henri de Lubac, *Teilhard de Chardin: The Man and His Meaning* (New York, 1965), p. v.

Bibliography

AVERBECK, Richard E. "Spirit, Community, and Mission: A Biblical Theology for Spiritual Formation." *Journal of Spiritual Formation & Soul Care*, 1, 2008.

AYTO, John. *Word Origins: The Hidden Histories of English Words from A to Z.* London: A & C Black, 2005.

BALDOVIN, John, S.J. "Eucharist: The Many-Faceted Jewel." C21 Resources. The Church in the 21st Century Center, Boston College, 2011.

BALTHASAR, Hans Urs von. *Prayer.* New York: Paulist Press, 1976.

————. *The Glory of the Lord.* San Francisco: Ignatius Press, 1982.

————. *The Truth is Symphonic: Aspects of Christian Pluralism.* San Francisco, 1987.

————. *The Grain of Wheat.* San Francisco: Ignatius Press, 1995.

BEILER, Irwin Ross. *Studies in the Life of Jesus.* New York: Abingdon-Cokesbury Press, 1936.

BLOOM, Anthony. "The Life of Prayer." *Theology Today* 61, 2004.

BORNE, E. and F. HENRY. *A Philosophy of Work.* Translated by F. Jackson. London, 1938.

BOROS, Ladislaus. *Pain and Providence.* Baltimore: Helicon, 1966.

BOULDING, Maria. "Prayer and the Paschal Mystery According to Saint Benedict." *The Downside Review* 94, 1976.

BRAXTON, Edward K. *The Wisdom Community*. New York: Paulist, 1980.

BRUTEAU, Beatrice. "From *Dominus to Amicus:* Contemplative Insight and a New Social Order," in *Cross Currents* 31, no. 3, 1981.

CAMPBELL, Stanislaus. *From Breviary to Liturgy of the Hours: The Structural Reform of the Roman Office, 1964-1971*. Collegeville, 1995.

CARRETTO, Carlo. *Was Franziskus uns heute sagt.* Freiburg i.Br., 1981.

CASEL, Odo. "Le sacrifice mystique du Christianisme." In *Revue Liturgique et Monastique*, 12, 1, 1926.

_____. *The Mystery of Christian Worship.* Burkhard Neunheuser, ed. Introduction written by Aidan Kavanagh. New York, 1999.

CASEY, Michael. "Strangers to Worldly Ways: RB 4.20." In *Tjurunga: An Australasian Benedictine Review*, 29, 1985.

CHAMBERS, Oswald. *My Utmost for His Highest: Selections for the Year.* Uhrichsville, OH: Barbour Publishing, Inc., 1963, August 30.

CONIARIS, Anthony. *God and You: Person to Person. Developing a Daily Personal Relationship with Jesus.* Edina, Minnesota: Light and Life Publishing Company, 1995.

COTTON, J. Harry. "The Corruption of the Highest." *Theology Today* 1, 1944.

CURRAN, Tom. *The Mass: Four Encounters with Jesus that will Change Your Life.* America: MCF Press, 2008.

DARRELL, Johnson. *Experiencing the Trinity.* Canada: Regent College Publishing, 2002.

DAVIES, G. *Temples, Churches, and Mosques.* New York: Pilgrim Press, 1982.

D' ERCOLE, Giovanni. "Eucharistic Adoration as a Way of Life: A Pastoral Perspective." In *From Eucharistic Adoration to Evangelisation*, ed. Alcuin Reid. Great Britai: Burns & Oates International, 2012.

DIMOCK, Giles, O.P. *The Eucharist: Sacrament and Sacrifice.* New York, 2009.

DI SANTE, Carmine. *Jewish Prayer: The Origins of Christian Liturgy.* Paulist Press, 1985.

DYSINGER, Luke, O.S.B. "Accepting the Embrace of God: The Ancient Art of *Lectio Divina*." In *Valyermo Benedictine,* Spring, 1990.

ELIAS, John L. "Reflections on the Vocation of a Religious Educator." In *Religious Education* 98, no. 3, 2003.

GAROFALO, B. S. "La Preghiera Solitaria di Gesu." In *Euntes Docete,* 1955.

GAUME, Jean Joseph. *The Sign of the Cross in the Nineteenth Century.* Aeterna Press, 2015.

GRAEF, Hilda C. *The Scholar and the Cross.* London, 1955.

GUILLET, Jacques. Cited by Brother Álvaro Rodríguez Echeverría, Superior General of the Lasallians. In *Reading reality in the light of the Word:* Lectio Divina *for Lasallians.* Secretariat "Being Brothers Today," La Salle Generalate. Rome, Italy, 2009.

HANSLIK, Rudolphus, ed. *Benedicti Regula,* CSEL LXXV. Wien, 1977.

HASTINGS, A. *Prophet and Witness in Jerusalem.* New York, 1958.

HAUGHTON, Rosemary. *The Passionate God.* London: Darton, Longman & Todd, 1981.

HAYDEN, Christopher. *Praying the Scriptures: A Practical Introduction to* Lectio Divina. London: St Pauls, 2001.

HOLLINGS, Michael, and Etta GULLICK. *It's Me, O Lord.* London, 1972.

HOPKINS, Gerard Manley. *Poems and Prose.* Penguin Classics, 1985.

HUNSINGER, Deborah van Deusen. *Pray without Ceasing: Revitalizing Pastoral Care.* Grand Rapids, MI: Eerdmans, 2006.

KNAPP, Andreas. *Brennender als Feuer: Geistliche Gedichte.* Mit einem Essay von Bischof Manfred Scheuer. Echter Verlag GmbH, 2004.

_____. *Lebensspuren im Sand: Spirituelles Tagebuch aus der Wüste.* Verlag Herder GmbH, Freiburg im Breisgau, 2015.

KUBICKI, Judith Marie. "Recognizing the Presence of Christ in the Liturgical Assembly." In *Theological Studies* 65, 2004.

LECLERCQ, Jean. "The Unity of Prayer." In *Worship* 33, no. 7, 1955.

_____. "Meditation as a Biblical Reading." In *Worship* 33, 1959.

_____. "Confession and Praise of God." In *Worship* 42, 1968.

_____. *Lectio Divina.* In *Worship* 58, 1984.

LIENHARD, Marc. *Luther: Witness to Jesus Christ.* Minneapolis: Augsburg, 1982.

LITTLE, Vilma G. *The Sacrifice of Praise: An Introduction to the Meaning and Use of The Divine Office.* London, 1957.

MACQUARRIE, John. *Paths in Spirituality.* New York: Harper and Row, 1972.

MAGRASSI, Mariano. *Praying the Bible: An Introduction to Lectio Divina,* trans. Edward Hagman. Collegeville: The Liturgical Press, 1998.

MAIN, John. *Word into Silence.* London, 1989.

MARSILI, S. "Liturgia." In *Nuovo Dizionario di Liturgia,* eds. Domenico Sartore and Achille M. Triacca. Paoline, 1988.

MERTON, Thomas. *New Seeds of Contemplation.* London–New York, 2003.

MITCHELL, Nathan. "Who is at the Table? Reclaiming Real Presence." In *Commonweal* 122, no. 2, January 27, 1995.

MORRILL, Bruce T. "Christ's Sacramental Presence in the Eucharist: A Biblical-Pneumatological Approach to the Mystery of Faith." In *American Theological Inquiry*, vol. 4, no. 2, 2011.

MOSSO, D. "Liturgia." In *Dizionario Teologico Interdisciplinare*, Torino, vol. 1, 1977.

MOULE, C. F. D. "The Manhood of Jesus in the New Testament." In *Christ, Faith and History*, eds. Sykes and Clayton. Cambridge: Cambridge University Press, 1972.

MULLAHY, Bernard I. "The Religious Life and the Mass." In *Orate Fratres*, XXIII, 1949.

MUTO, Susan. "Living Contemplatively and Serving God in the World: Two Sides of the Coin of Christian Ministry." In *Journal of Spiritual Formation and Soul Care,* vol. 6, no. 1. Biola University, 2013.

NEUFVILLE, Jean, ed. *La Règle de Saint Benoît.* (Sources Chrétiennes, 181-182), Paris, 1972.

NJOKU, Mary Bride. *Consecrated Life: A Renewed Insight.* London, 2016.

O'BRIEN, Scott. "Partakers of the Divine Sacrifice: Liturgy and the Deification of the Christian Assembly." In *Liturgical Ministry* 18, 2009.

O'DONOHUE, John. *Eternal Echoes: Exploring our Hunger to Belong.* London, 1998.

O'LOUGHLIN, Frank. *Christ Present in the Eucharist.* Strathfield, NSW: St. Paul's Publications, 2000.

_____. "Celebration." In *New Liturgy of Summer,* 1976.

PASINI, Stefano. *Il metodo nel diritto: Il rapporto tra teologia, filosofia e diritto nella riflessione canonistica contemporanea.* Rome, 2002.

PENNINGTON, Basil. *Centering Prayer: Renewing an Ancient Christian Prayer Form.* Doubleday, 1980.

PIDEL, Aaron. "An Experience of Adoration." In *The Church in the 21st Century*, C 21 Resources, Boston College, Fall, 2011.

PIEPER, Joseph. *Otium e Culto.* Brescia, 1956.

POLAN, Gregory J. "*Lectio Divina*: Reading and Praying the Word of God." In *Liturgical Ministry* 12, 2003.

Pope Benedict XVI. *Jesus of Nazareth: From the Baptism in the Jordan to the Transfiguration.* New York, 2007.

Pope Francis. *The Church of Mercy*, ed. Giuliano Vigini. London: Darton, Longman and Todd, 2014.

POWERS, Joseph M. *Eucharistic Theology.* New York: Seabury Press, 1967.

PURVES, Andrew. *The Search for Compassion: Spirituality and Ministry.* Louisville, KY: Westminster/John Knox, 1989.

RAHNER, Karl. "Reflections on a Theology of Renunciation." In *Theological Investigations* 3. Baltimore: Helicon, 1967

_____. "Christian Living Formerly and Today." In *Theological Investigations Volume 7: Further Theology of the Spiritual Life.* New York: The Seabury Press, 1977.

RENGSTORF, Karl–Heinz. "ἀποστέλλω, et al." In *Theological Dictionary of the New Testament* (TDNT), vol. 1.

RORDORF, W., and A. TUILIER. "Didache: La Doctrine des Douze Apôtres." In *Sources Chrétiennes* 248, Paris, 1998.

ROTH, S. John. "Jesus the Prayer." In *Currents in Theology and Mission* 33 (2006):488-500.

SCHERER, Paul. "The Love that God Defines." In *Theology Today*, vol. 21. 1964.

SCHILLEBEECKX, Edward. *The Eucharist.* London: Sheed and Ward, 1968.

SCHMIDT, Andreas. "We Have Come to Adore Him." Homily at World Youth Day, Cologne, 2005, in *We Have Come to Adore Him: An Introduction to Prayer at the School of Benedict XVI*, #5. The New Evangelization Series. Washington: Knights of Columbus, 2013.

SEASOLTZ, R. Kevin. "Christian Prayer: Experience of the Experience of Jesus' Dying and Rising."

SHIPLEY, Joseph T. *The Origins of English Words: A Discursive Dictionary of Indo-European Roots.* Baltimore: Johns Hopkins University Press, 1984.

SMARAGDI, Abbatis. *Expositio in Regulam S. Benedicti*, eds. A. Spannagel and P. Engelbert, CCM VIII. Siegbury 1974. Trans. David Barry. "Smaragdus of Saint-Mihiel: Commentary on the Rule of Saint Benedict." In *Cistercian Studies Series*, 212. Kalamazoo, Michigan, 2007.

SMITH, Delia. *A Journey into God.* London: Hodder & Stongton, 1989.

STEERE, Douglas V. "Solitude and Prayer." In *Worship* 55, no. 2, 1981.

STORY, J. Lyle. "Christology and the Relational Jesus." In *American Theological Inquiry*, vol. 1, no. 2, 2008.

_____. "The Dynamic, Relational and Loving Purpose of God." In *American Theological Inquiry*, vol. 3, no. 1, 2010.

TAFT, Robert. *The Liturgy of the Hours in East and West: The Origins of the Divine Office and its Meaning for Today.* Collegeville: MN: The Liturgical Press, 1986.

TEILHARD de Chardin, Pierre. *The Divine Milieu.* New York: Harper and Row, 1960.

TOON, Peter. *The Art of Meditating on Scripture.* Grand Rapids, MI: Zondervan, 1993.

TRIACCA, A. "Il rinnovamento liturgico fermento della riforma liturgica." In *Ephemerides Liturgicae* 113, 1999.

UGORJI, Lucius Iwejuru. *Words from the Heart of a Shepherd.* Enugu: Snaap Press, 2015.

_____. "The Religious and the Apostolate: A Paper Delivered to the DDL Sisters Silver Jubilarians." DRAC Enugu, 2015 (unedited work).

VAGAGGINI, Cipriano. *Il senso teologico della liturgia.* Roma, 1957. Balsamo Milano 19996. (English edition: *Theological Dimension of the Liturgy: A general treatise on the Theology of the Liturgy*, trans. Leonard J. Doyle. Collegeville, Minnesota, 1976.)

VEST, Norvene. *No Moment Too Small: Rhythms of Silence Prayer & Holy Reading.* Kalamazoo, MI: Cistercian Publications, 1994.

WEDER, H. "Disciple, Discipleship." In *American Biblical Dictionary II*, 2009.

WESTERHOFF, John H., III. "Learning and Prayer." In *Religious Education,* vol LXX, no. 6, 1975.

WHITEHEAD, J. "An Asceticism of Time." In *Review for Religious* 39, 1980.

WITCZAK, Michael G. "The Manifold Presence of Christ in the Liturgy." In *Theological Studies* 59, 1998.

About Leonine Publishers

Leonine Publishers LLC makes fine Catholic literature available to Catholics throughout the English-speaking world. Leonine Publishers offers an innovative "hybrid" approach to book publication that helps authors as well as readers. Please visit our web site at www.leoninepublishers.com to learn more about us. Browse our online bookstore to find more solid Catholic titles to uplift, challenge, and inspire.

Our patron and namesake is Pope Leo XIII, a prudent, yet uncompromising pope during the stormy years at the close of the 19th century. Please join us as we ask his intercession for our family of readers and authors.

Do you have a book inside you? Visit our web site today. Leonine Publishers accepts manuscripts from Catholic authors like you. If your book is selected for publication, you will have an active part in the production process. This book is an example of our growing selection of literature for the busy Catholic reader of the 21st century.

www.leoninepublishers.com